W9-BSS-038

Comparative Higher Education: Knowledge, the University, and Development

Contemporary Studies in Social and Policy Issues in Education: The David C. Anchin Series

(formerly Social and Policy Issues in Education:
The David C. Anchin Series)

Kathryn M. Borman, Series Editor

Comparative Higher Education: Knowledge, the University, and Development

by
Philip G. Altbach
Boston College

Ablex Publishing Corporation
Greenwich, Connecticut
London, England

Printed in the United States of America

Library of Congress Cataloging-in-Publication Data

Altbach, Philip G.
   Comparative higher education : knowledge, the university, and development / by Philip G. Altbach.
      p. cm. — (Contemporary studies in social and policy issues in education)
   Includes bibliographical references (p.) and indexes.
   ISBN 1-56750-380-2 (cloth). — ISBN 1-56750-381-0 (pbk.)
   1. Education, Higher—Cross-cultural studies. 2. Education, Higher—Social aspects—Cross-cultural studies. 3. Education, Higher—Economic aspects—Cross-cultural studies. 4. Comparative education. I. Title. II. Series
LB2322.2.A48   1998
378—dc21   97–49237
                                                      CIP

Ablex Publishing Corporation   Published in the U.K. and Europe by:
55 Old Post Road #2   JAI Press Ltd.
P.O. Box 5297   38 Tavistock Street
Greenwich, CT 06830   Covent Garden
                                      London WC2E 7PB
                                      England

Contents

Acknowledgments

I am indebted to Salina Kopellas, who assisted with the preparation of the text. Editing assistance was provided by Edith Hoshino Altbach and Patricia Murphy. Patricia Murphy helped with formatting as well. I am indebted to the publishers who have permitted the use of previously published materials. This volume is part of the program of the Center for International Higher Education at Boston College. All of the chapters in this book are reprinted with the permission of the publishers involved. All have been revised and updated for this book.

Chapter 1. "Patterns of Higher Education Development: Toward the Year 2000," *Prospects* no. 78 (1991) © UNESCO.

Chapter 2. "The University as Center and Periphery," *Teachers College Record* 82 (Summer 1991) © *Teachers College Record.*

Chapter 3. "Twisted Roots: The Western Impact on Asian Higher Education," *Higher Education 18* (1989) © Kluwer Academic Publishers.

Chapter 4. "The American Academic Model in Comparative Perspective," from P. G. Altbach, ed., *An ASEAN-American Dialogue: The Relevance of American Higher Education to Southeast Asia* (Singapore: Regional Institute for Higher Education and Development, 1985) © RIHED.

Chapter 5. "An International Academic Crisis?: The American Professoriate in Comparative Perspective," *Daedalus 126* (Fall, 1997) (American Academy of Arts and Sciences.

Chapter 6. "Professors and Politics: An International Perspective," from Mark

Ginsburg, ed., *The Politics of Educators' Work and Lives* (Westport, Conn.: Greenwood, 1994) © Greenwood Publishers.

Chapter 7. "Student Political Activism," *Comparative Education 25*, no. 1 (1989) © Carfax Publishers, Ltd.

Chapter 8. "Student Politics in the Third World," *Higher Education 13* (1984) © Kluwer Academic Publishers.

Chapter 9. "Gigantic Peripheries: India and China in the World Knowledge System," *Economic and Political Weekly 28* (June 12, 1993) © Sameeksha Trust, Mumbai, India.

Chapter 10. "The New Internationalism: Foreign Students and Scholars," *Studies in Higher Education 14*, no. 2 (1989) © Carfax Publishers, Ltd.

Chapter 11. "The Foreign Student Dilemma," *Teachers College Record 87* (Summer 1986) © *Teachers College Record.*

Chapter 12. "Higher Education, Democracy and Development: Implications for Newly Industrialized Countries," *Interchange 23*, nos. 1 and 2 (1992) © Ontario Institute for Studies in Education.

Chapter 13. "Higher Education and Scientific Development: The Promise of Newly Industrializing Countries," *New Education 12*, no. 1 (1991) © New Education Trust.

Preface

Comparative Higher Education considers the contemporary university in an international framework in an effort to analyze four central themes. Among the main concerns in this book is the complex relationship between universities in the industrialized world and those in what used to be called the Third World. A subsidiary goal is to illustrate the usefulness of a comparative approach in analyzing higher education. Each of the chapters is comparative and international in focus and content. The book is organized around four broad topics. First, four chapters explore the past, present, and future of higher education, focusing especially on the interplay between the West and the rest of the world. The second broad theme deals with teachers and students in the contemporary university. The politics of students and faculty are considered in depth, along with a chapter dealing with professorial attitudes. The third main section considers the relationships among academic systems worldwide—particularly exchanges of students and faculty—and the implications of the international scientific and academic community for two large countries—China and India. We consider the flows of foreign students in the broader context of knowledge networks and the ebbs and flows of scientific power worldwide. A final section focuses on the newly industrializing countries as a special, and increasingly important, category of academic systems that are emerging as significant academic powers.

The underlying theme in this book is the complex relationships, many based on inequality, among academic systems, and also among people, in an increasingly differentiated and at the same time interrelated world knowledge system.[1] Most of the phenomena discussed here are rooted in national realities, but are also influenced by international trends. It is unusual for analysts of higher education to consider the transnational implications of national trends and issues. This is surprising in an era of the increasing globalization of trade, industry, and culture. Universities are affected by international trends in communications. They are also by their nature international institutions—the medieval European universities, from which all of the world's modern universities stem, were international institutions operating in the international language of the time, Latin.

The interplay between West and East; between the industrialized nations and the Third World; between that segment of world academe that dominates science, scholarship, and communications, and the large majority of countries that find themselves in a peripheral relationship is a constant theme here. Few have chosen to explore these relationships. The bulk of the literature on higher education deals with single nations and is focused on specific national concerns, as if academic systems are confined within national borders at the end of the twentieth century. Researchers who venture comparatively tend to focus on similar countries, mainly the industrialized nations of North America and Europe. *Comparative Higher Education* breaks with this pattern by dealing with topics on a worldwide basis, and by paying special attention to the Third World and to the newly industrialized countries.

This volume stems from my long-standing interest in the comparative analysis of higher education as well as substantive research interests. For example, my concern with student political activism goes back to my doctoral dissertation, and has resulted in several studies.[2] The analysis of the professoriate has also been a long-standing research interest, culminating recently in a major study of the international academic profession.[3] The relationship between Asian universities and the West has been explored in *From Dependence to Autonomy: The Development of Asian Universities.*[4] I have written on Indian academics in several volumes.[5] The newly industrializing countries were analyzed in one of the first studies devoted to this important group of nations.[6] Finally, student exchange has been explored in *Bridges to Knowledge.*[7]

The chapters in this book were all written since 1984. Most appeared in print in the 1990s. All have been revised and updated for this book.

Philip G. Altbach
Chestnut Hill, Massachusetts
September 1997

NOTES

[1] For essays on a related topic, see Philip G. Altbach, *The Knowledge Context: Comparative Perspectives on the Distribution of Knowledge* (Albany, N.Y.: State University of New York Press, 1987).

[2] Philip G. Altbach, *Student Politics in Bombay* (Bombay: Asia Publishing House, 1968); Philip G. Altbach, ed., *Turmoil and Transition: Higher Education and Student Politics in India* (New York: Basic Books, 1968); Seymour Martin Lipset and Philip G. Altbach, eds., *Students in Revolt* (Boston: Houghton Mifflin, 1969); Philip G. Altbach, *Student Political Activism: An International Reference Handbook* (New York: Greenwood Press, 1989); Philip G. Altbach and Norman T. Uphoff, *The Student Internationals* (Metuchen, N. J.: Scarecrow Press, 1973); and Philip G. Altbach, *Student Politics in America: A Historical Analysis* (New Brunswick, N.J.: Transaction, 1997).

[3] Philip G. Altbach, ed., *The International Academic Profession: Portraits of Fourteen Countries* (Princeton, N. J.: Carnegie Foundation for the Advancement of Teaching, 1996), and Ernest L. Boyer, Philip G. Altbach, and Mary Jean Whitelaw, *The Academic Profession: An International Perspective* (Princeton, N.J.: Carnegie Foundation for the Advancement of Teaching, 1994). See also Philip G. Altbach, ed., *Comparative Perspectives on the Academic Profession* (New York: Praeger, 1977), and Suma Chitnis and Philip G. Altbach, eds., *The Indian Academic Profession* (Delhi: Macmillan, 1979).

[4] Philip G. Altbach and Viswanathan Selvaratnam, eds., *From Dependence to Autonomy: The Development of Asian Universities* (Dordrecht, Netherlands: Kluwer, 1989).

[5] Amrik Singh and Philip G. Altbach, eds., *The Higher Learning in India* (Delhi: Vikas, 1974), and Suma Chitnis and Philip G. Altbach, eds., *Higher Education Reform India: Experience and Perspectives* (New Delhi: Sage, 1993).

[6] Philip G. Altbach, et al., *Scientific Development and Higher Education: The Case of Newly Industrializing Nations* (New York: Praeger, 1989).

[7] Elinor G. Barber, Philip G. Altbach, and Robert G. Myers, eds., *Bridges to Knowledge: Foreign Students in Comparative Perspective* (Chicago: University of Chicago Press, 1984).

Introduction:
Comparative Perspectives for
the Twenty-First Century

It is commonplace to note that we are moving toward a global economy. The world is increasingly interdependent in terms of trade, culture, and communication. There is one institution that has always been global and that continues to be a powerful force in the world after a half-millennium. This institution is the university. With its roots in medieval Europe, the modern university is at the center of an international knowledge system that encompasses technology, communications, and culture. The university remains the primary center of learning and the main repository of accumulated wisdom. While it may be the case that the university has reached the end of a period of unprecedented growth and expansion, it remains a powerful institution. In the knowledge-based society of the twenty-first century, the university will remain at the very center of economic and cultural development.

The contemporary university suffers from a lack of self-confidence and has lost some of the support from society it enjoyed in the past half-century or so. However, it is not, as many critics within and outside of the academy would have us believe, suffering from a deep malaise that will either cause collapse or necessitate major structural and intellectual renovation. The present, and very likely the near-term future, will not be a period of great expansion or of great prosperity for higher education. The coming period will also not see the demise of the university.

The university is not flourishing as it did in the "golden age" of the middle decades of the twentieth century in North America and Europe. Yet, the university is far from collapse. It continues to play a necessary role in modern society—

as an institution that educates, performs research, provides opportunities for social mobility, and certifies expertise and professional competence. Universities have been transformed in less than a century from small, elitist institutions fulfilling a limited educational mission to one of the main engines of the knowledge-based society.

ASPECTS OF INTERNATIONALISM

The university is an international institution with strong national roots. Most analysts overlook the international origins and role of the university, focusing exclusively on national realities. The university was established as an international institution in the medieval period, attracting students and faculty from across Europe and using a common language, Latin, for instruction. Student life was organized around the "nations"—organized groups on campus, based on common national origins. After a period of competition between the student-organized universities of Italy and the faculty-dominated University of Paris, the professors won, and virtually all of contemporary academic institutions in the world stem from this common Paris model.[1] The modern American university, arguably the most influential academic model today, grows out of three basic ideas—the English collegiate model, the German research university ideal of the late nineteenth century, and the American concept of service to society. Worldwide, there is still a great deal of academic borrowing and adaptation.

It is no exaggeration to point out that all of the world's universities stem from the medieval European model. Although non-Western academic models existed, only the Islamic Al-Azhar university in Egypt survives today. In India and China, which had their own powerful indigenous traditions of advanced learning, modern universities are Western in origin. Western-style universities have been adapted to meet the needs of non-Western societies. Whether imposed by a colonial master, as was the case in India, or adopted freely after careful study, as occurred in Japan, it was the Western model that was used. The patterns of academic organization, many basic assumptions about the nature of the university, the pattern of study, relations between professors and students, and other factors have a common base. There are, of course, many variations. This creates a common academic culture worldwide.

The original medieval universities were truly international institutions, with faculty members and students from different countries. During the rise of nationalism in the nineteenth century in Europe, academic institutions became more national in outlook, and teaching and learning took place in national languages rather than in an international language, Latin. But many common elements remained and there was considerable cross-border study. Foreign study was influential on many occasions. Countries such as Japan and China sent delegations of students abroad in the nineteenth century to study Western knowledge with the aim of assisting in the modernization of the mother country. American students went to Europe—especially to Germany—to pursue graduate studies and returned imbued with ideas about the importance of research, academic freedom, and new models of academic organization. These returnees started new institutions such as Johns Hopkins and Chicago, and eventually transformed American higher education. In the twentieth century, students from the colonized nations of Asia and Africa went to the metropole to study. Students from India, Nigeria, and other British colonies went to London, Oxford, or other British universities and returned home not only with academic qualifications but with ideas of nationalism as well that contributed to the overthrow of the colonial regimes. In the same way, Vietnamese and Senegalese students went to France, and students from the Dutch East Indies went to Holland.

In the postcolonial era, foreign study mushroomed, and now more than one million students study outside their home countries. Foreign study enhances the flow of ideas internationally, builds up worldwide research networks, and permits students from countries without facilities for advanced study and research to obtain needed expertise. There is also a flow of scholars across borders, helping to maintain links among scientists and researchers at senior levels.

There has always been significant migration of scholarly talent, from the medieval period. Scholars take jobs in other countries for many reasons. A lack of opportunities, poor facilities, and racial, religious, or ethnic discrimination encountered at home are all "push" factors. Higher salaries, better laboratories and libraries, more favorable teaching responsibilities, academic freedom, and a sense of being at the "center" are all "pull" factors. What used to be called the brain drain is now considered to be a much more complex phenomenon since scholars working abroad sometimes return home, or retain contact with the academic community in the home country.

Knowledge is, of course, international. It always has been. The wisdom of the Greeks and Romans was saved in the libraries of the Islamic world, used by Arab scholars during the European Dark Ages, and later returned to Europe. When Germany was the world's premier scientific power, scholars and scientists in other countries read German journals. In the post–World War II period, the balance of academic power shifted to the English-speaking countries, and especially to the United States, and now the world reads journals in English. New communications technologies—such as the Internet—have had a profound impact on scientific communication. Access to knowledge is, of course, limited by the availability of books, journals, Internet access, and the like.

These are some of the elements of the international knowledge system, as it has evolved over centuries and as it exists today. Without question, academe will become more international in the twenty-first century. The Internet and other new technologies will continue to have a profound impact on scientific communication. The increasingly widespread use of English as the main language for scientific discussion contributes to internationalism. Universities throughout the world understand the need for an international viewpoint. In Japan, it is a national goal to host 100,000 foreign students by the year 2000. The European Union has put a variety of programs into place to foster intra-EU study. Many American universities are seeking to internationalize their curricula.

International higher education has also become a significant "industry." Thousands of students worldwide learn English, and "English as a second language" programs have expanded. Universities and other institutions offer such programs, and they are a source of considerable income. Foreign students have themselves become a major source of income for universities in some countries, and are actively recruited. In the United Kingdom, Australia, and to some extent the United States and Canada, foreign students provide income, fill places in some departments or academic institutions that are short of students, and provide inexpensive labor for research and sometimes for teaching. Universities in the industrialized nations have opened branch campuses abroad as a means of earning income as well as internationalizing themselves. The United States, Australia, and the United Kingdom have been especially active in opening branches abroad and in "twinning" with institutions in other countries. In some cases, academic programs are "franchised" overseas and degrees can be earned from an American or other Western university without ever having studied on the campus of the sponsoring institution.

All of these innovations are imaginative and often profitable. In general, academic institutions in the industrialized nations sponsor them in developing countries or newly industrialized countries where the demand for postsecondary education is very high and local institutions cannot meet it. Academic degrees from the "center" are valued at the "periphery." These examples illustrate both the long tradition of internationalism in higher education worldwide and the powerful role of international initiatives at the end of the twentieth century. The global economy and a realization that ideas have as much international currency as products and services are having a tremendous impact on higher education. Market forces are also pushing academe worldwide toward greater internationalism.

THE ESTATES

Universities are not monolithic institutions but rather communities of identifiable groups that have considerable autonomy. Several decades ago, sociologist Pierre van den Berghe wrote an insightful book on African higher education in which he discussed the several "estates" of the university.[2] He wrote of senior staff (the professoriate), students, and intermediate and subordinate staff (nonacademic support personnel). We are concerned here with the first two estates, the core of any academic institution. The professoriate is at the heart of the academic enterprise. Their centrality is reinforced by the fact that the medieval University of Paris was the "university of the masters" in contrast to the student-dominated University of

Bologna. The Paris model proved most influential worldwide. In the nineteenth century, the German research university, the "Humboldtian university," was also dominated by the professoriate.

When people discuss the future of the university, it is surprising how seldom they mention the professoriate. It is assumed that governmental action and administrative power will prevail and those working within the university will follow the new edicts and directives. In fact, over the past two decades this has largely been the case. The professoriate has not exercised much leadership, nor has it resisted initiatives from other quarters. As yet the academic profession has not been drastically affected by the changes. The proportion of part-time and nonpermanent staff has increased, but few full-time academics have been fired. Salaries in many countries have been stagnant or declining, but with few exceptions (such as Russia) not dramatically so. The professoriate still controls the curriculum and the structure of degrees, and feels that it retains most of its traditional powers. However, the fact is that the powers of the professoriate *are* being significantly eroded with the rise of the administrative cadre and the increase of accountability in academe.

The professoriate's continued quiescence cannot be guaranteed. Professors can unionize. They can seek to use the academic governance system for their own purposes. The current poor market for academic labor may change and increase the bargaining power of the professoriate. Efforts can be made to convince the public—and students—that current policies are not in the best interests of students. It seems unlikely that the professoriate will become a militant force, but professorial activism is not unprecedented.

The continued deterioration of campus working conditions, a further and more serious decline in faculty morale, erosion of the full-time faculty, and a continued downward salary trend will more than likely lead to an academic profession that is less committed to its job and in the long run less productive.[3] The professoriate has been more than a job—many see it as a "calling" and feel a deep commitment to teaching, research, and what has been quaintly called "the life of the mind." Academics traditionally have been paid less than the salaries they could command elsewhere.

The very nature of the academic profession is being altered in many countries. With the exception of some Latin American countries, the traditional core of the professoriate has been full-time faculty with permanent appointments. This core is rapidly changing—full-time faculty are being replaced by part-time and nonpermanent staff. The implications of these changes are profound and are not yet fully apparent. It is not clear how academic institutions will be governed once full-time faculty are a minority of the total. No doubt, power will further devolve on administrators. Full-time faculty—especially those in senior ranks—have conducted much of the research done in universities and have obtained most of the external funding. Indeed, most American universities only permit full-time faculty to receive grants. The academic profession is being transformed largely to save money and to permit staffing flexibility in a period of unanticipated demand for access and for specific programs of study. Those responsible for the change have yet to face the consequences of their actions.

The future professoriate will be different in a number of ways from the traditional academic model.

- Fewer faculty will hold full-time permanent positions.
- More faculty will be part-time, responsible for teaching a limited number of courses, with little or no participation in the academic community and little contact with students.
- More faculty will hold full-time, nonpermanent teaching positions. These faculty members will constitute a kind of academic lumpen proletariat, going from one job to another with little prospect of a regular appointment.
- The academic profession will be more diverse in terms of gender, race, and ethnicity.[4] In the United States and some other countries, it is already the case that faculty at the lower ranks and in nonpermanent positions are more diverse in terms of background.
- The faculty will be less research-oriented. Fewer will have positions where research is possible.
- The faculty will, on the whole, be less able academically—as the "best and brightest" are less frequently attracted to academic careers.

Students are the other major "estate" in the university. Students, after all, are the raison d'être of the academic enterprise. The expansion in student numbers in the period since World War II has been the dominant force in higher education. A slowing of expansion in the 1970s and 1980s in the industrialized nations created difficulties for many universities as they struggled to adjust to an end to expansion. In the 1990s, student demand is again increasing at the same time when financial resources for higher education are limited because of changing governmental priorities. While the academic profession and the universities have to cope with the combined pressures of increased demand for access and diminished resources, it is in the end students who face crowded classrooms and deteriorating academic facilities.

Conditions of study vary substantially around the world, as do the expectations students have of their universities. Even within countries, these may vary substantially. In the United States, the differences in campus facilities, student expectations, and institutional prestige between an Ivy League private university and a poorly supported public college are dramatic. American colleges and universities have traditionally provided more services to their students than is common elsewhere in the world—and students (and their families) have paid much more to study. The curriculum is more controlled than is the case in Europe, and American-style continuous assessment imposes a certain style of learning. At the other end of the spectrum is the European ideal of, as the Germans put it, "lernfreiheit," the freedom to learn that gives the student wide latitude concerning what to study, considerable control over the pattern of learning, and relatively few constraints concerning the time to completion of studies. Other countries fall between these two poles. The trend, however, is toward the American pattern of regulated study in order to ensure timely completion of degrees as a means of saving money and permitting better academic planning. Even in Western Europe, universities are considering restrictions on the laissez faire traditions.

Students worldwide have become more concerned with the usefulness of higher education in the employment market, and they have demanded more vocationally useful courses of study. Cost of study is a worry—especially as tuition and fees are increased in many parts of the world and new loan programs and other means of cost recovery are put into place in order to reduce public funding for higher education. At one time, students would have reacted with protests and demonstrations against tuition increases and more restrictions on freedom to study. With a few exceptions, such as in France, students have not engaged in activism or political protest. The mass protest movements of the 1960s are not, in general, part of the academic environment at the end of the twentieth century. Student protest is more an isolated and short-lived phenomenon than a significant force in higher education.

The lack of activism does not mean that students are quiet and unassertive. On the contrary, students often demand changes in the curriculum and in the pattern of studies that will meet their needs for employment and relevance. They express their preferences by enrolling in institutions and programs that offer them what they want. The "student consumerism" that has been so much discussed in the United States is becoming a worldwide phenomenon.

The nature of the student population is also changing. Students come from much more diverse social class backgrounds than was the case even a few decades ago. The proportion of women in the student population has dramatically increased, and in some countries—including the United States and a number of Latin American nations—women are now a majority. There is a massive demand by older people to attend the university, or to return to complete degrees started years earlier. Access worldwide has been expanded, with one-third of the relevant age cohort attending postsecondary institutions in many industrialized nations and a few developing countries. Even where the proportions of the age group studying in higher education institutions are much lower—as in India and China—numbers have increased. The university has been transformed into a mass institution throughout the world, and is no longer a preserve of the elite anywhere. This demographic change has had profound implications for the student population and for the ethos of higher education.

Van den Berghe wrote about nonacademic staff as one of the "estates." In the past two decades, the nonacademic side of the university has grown in both size and importance. The power of academic administrators has dramatically increased, and in many countries, senior administrators now wield considerable power in academic affairs. Expansion has made universities much more complex and more bureaucratic institutions, and administrators have become more powerful. Further, as demands for accountability have increased, administrators have been empowered to provide the information needed to measure performance. The traditional decentralized, unwieldy, and often quite slow patterns of faculty governance are no longer trusted to provide the efficient management that is demanded of modern higher education.

Administrative authority has traditionally been strongest in the United States, where college and university presidents are not elected by the faculty nor directly accountable to the faculty, but rather are appointed by boards of trustees or regents. Similarly, senior administrators are appointed by trustees and presidents, and they are basically accountable to them. Administrators increasingly see their careers in academic administration, and even though most have been professors, they seldom return to teaching. In recent years, a cadre of mid-level professional academic managers has emerged who are trained in the management of higher education and do not necessarily emerge from the academic profession. This is in sharp contrast to the traditional European pattern of governance, in which academic authorities are elected by the senior academic staff and are responsible to them, returning after fixed terms to teaching and research. Even in Europe, however, there is a trend toward professional managers for universities, and faculty power is being eroded. In Germany, for example, the power of the chief administrator, the chancellor, who is appointed by the state authorities and not by the faculty, is growing. Recent reforms in the Netherlands have greatly enhanced the power of administrators. Worldwide, traditional faculty power and the established models of governance are being weakened.

These three estates often live in tension with each other. A recent study, for example, has noted that the faculty does not trust the administration and feels a great deal of alienation.[5] The sense of community that characterized universities in an earlier period—especially when they were small and relatively uncomplicated—has dissipated in the contemporary university. Students are generally ignored by the academic hierarchy, and even where they once had power in academic governance, this power has been diminished. In Latin America, student participation in governance was enshrined by the reform movement of 1918, and although it remains in the public institutions in many countries, it has been weakened.[6] In Germany, where "participation" was one of the slogans of the student movements of the 1960s, the reforms in governance that were instituted then have largely been abolished. Administrators often feel under siege by faculty and students. The university, as a result, is often divided into a series of factions and contending interest groups. This, of course, weakens the institution when it seeks to influence policy and to make its voice heard.

ROOTS AND IMPLICATIONS OF CRISIS

The university faces unprecedented challenges. The patterns of difficulties vary from country to country, but there are few parts of the world where academe faces the future with confidence. There are, nonetheless, some patterns that persist worldwide.

- Diminished state funding. Everywhere, questions are asked about public spending for higher education. Government is reluctant—and often unwilling—to pay for escalating university budgets. Higher costs stem from higher enrollments as well as increasing costs for new technologies, higher faculty and administrative salaries, and the like. As funding is cut, or simply does not grow sufficiently to pay for new students, universities face serious problems of how to cope financially.
- Who should pay? Related to diminished funding is the question of who should be responsible for paying for higher education. Traditionally, in most countries, the taxpayer has paid most of the cost of higher education. Tuition was very low or even nonexistent. This has been called into question, and there is an increasing shift to the individual as the source of funds to pay the bills. There are many ramifications of this debate for equity, financial stability, and access.
- Privatization. In most countries, the majority of students study in public higher education institutions, where tax revenues pay for the bulk of the cost of education. There is a trend to privatize public universities—to devolve a significant part of the cost of instruction to the student and to ask the institution to develop other revenue-producing strategies. Universities have, as a response, raised tuition, started businesses, charged for the use of campus facilities, built linkages with industry, and opened branches overseas, among other efforts. Private academic institutions have also grown in importance worldwide. Even in countries which have mainly depended on public funds, private institutions have been expanding.
- Technology. The impact of technology on higher education is immense and as yet little understood.[7] Technology has implications for libraries and the retrieval and storage of research and other information, for the management of the institutions, for research programs, for on-campus instruction through computer-assisted teaching, for off-campus instruction through distance learning programs, for intra- and intercampus communication among faculty and students, and others. Technology is expensive to install and maintain, is quickly outdated, and has proved difficult to integrate into existing academic programs. It is also time-consuming and expensive to train staff to use technology effectively.
- Basic research and graduate study. Since the nineteenth century, basic research has been a central responsibility of universities, especially those at the top of most academic systems. The bulk of the world's basic research is done in universities. Linked to research is graduate study—educating advanced students at the doctoral level for research and professional positions. In the current fiscal climate, it is not clear if the universities will be able to sustain this role. If they do

not, how will research be carried out and who will train the next generations of scholars and scientists?

- Internationalization. Knowledge is increasingly international, and links among academic institutions worldwide continue to expand. Technology aids this process. The number of foreign students and scholars continues to grow, although at a slower rate than in the recent past. Internationalism is a positive aspect of contemporary higher education—although mechanisms for financing and administering it need to be developed further.
- The academic profession. As noted earlier, the traditional full-time professoriate is under pressure. The professoriate is the core of the university. If this cadre of scholars and scientists is significantly altered, it will mean profound changes in how universities are governed, and how teaching and research are carried out.

THE FUTURE

This is not an especially happy time for higher education worldwide. Academe is everywhere under attack. University leaders have been unable to defend the institution successfully from its critics and from governments committed to cutting budgets and shifting governmental priorities. The academic community does not speak with a united voice. Indeed, in general it does not speak at all. The contemporary university must present a vision of its role in the future, and defend its past contributions to knowledge and to society.

Despite its problems, the university is not about to disappear. It is likely to survive into the twenty-first century without revolutionary transformation. Students will continue to demand academic degrees and credentials, and the role of the university in providing training for most professional fields will continue. Research will continue to be produced as part of the role of the academic profession and of the university. The university will continue to be one of society's most valued institutions. The coming decade will, nonetheless, be one of considerable tension and challenge. For those who value the role that the university has played during the twentieth century, the direction of contemporary change does not generate much optimism.

NOTES

[1] A. B. Cobban, *The Medieval Universities: Their Development and Organization* (London: Metheun, 1975).

[2] Pierre van den Berghe, *Power and Privilege at an African University* (London: Routlege and Kegan Paul, 1973).

[3] For an analysis of contemporary faculty attitudes, see Philip G. Altbach, ed., *The International Academic Profession: Portraits of 14 Countries* (Princeton, N.J.: Carnegie Foundation for the Advancement of Teaching, 1996).

4 See Ann Brooks, *Academic Women* (Buckingham, England: Open University Press, 1997).

5 Lionel S. Lewis and Philip G. Altbach, "Faculty Versus Administration: A Universal Problem," *Higher Education Policy 9*, no. 3 (1996): 255–58.

6 See Richard J. Walter, *Student Politics in Argentina: The University Reform and Its Effects, 1918–1964* (New York: Basic Books, 1968).

7 Patricia J. Gumport and Marc Chun, "Technology and Higher Education: Opportunities and Challenges for the New Era," in *American Higher Education in the 21st Century: Social, Political and Economic Challenges*, ed. Philip G. Altbach, Robert O. Berdahl, and Patricia J. Gumport (Baltimore, Md.: Johns Hopkins University Press, in press).

1

Perspectives

1

Patterns in Higher Education Development

Universities are singular institutions. They have common historical roots, yet are deeply embedded in their societies. Established in the medieval period to transmit knowledge and provide training for a few key professions, in the nineteenth century universities became creators of new knowledge through basic research.[1] The contemporary university stands at the center of society. The most important institution in the complex process of knowledge creation and distribution, it not only serves as home to most of the basic sciences but also to the complex system of journals, books, and databases that communicate knowledge worldwide.[2] Universities are key providers of training in an evergrowing number of specializations. Universities have also taken on a political function in society: they often serve as centers of political thought, and sometimes of action, and they train those who become members of the political elite. At the same time, academe is faced with unprecedented challenges, stemming in large part from a decline in resources made available to higher education. After almost a half century of dramatic expansion worldwide, universities in many countries are forced to cut back on expenditures, and in some cases to downsize. The unwritten pact between society and higher education that provided expanding resources in return for greater access for students as well as research and service to society has broken down, with significant implications for both higher education and society.

This chapter is concerned with the patterns of higher education development evident in the post–World War II period throughout the world—analyzing some of the reasons for these trends and pointing to likely directions for universities in the coming decades. Issues such as autonomy and accountability, the role of research and teaching, reform and the curriculum, and the implications of the massive expansion that has characterized universities in most countries are of primary concern here. Universities are simultaneously international institutions, with common historical roots and also embedded in national cultures and circumstances. It is worthwhile to examine the contemporary challenges to higher education in both a historical and comparative perspective.

A COMMON HERITAGE

There is only one common academic model worldwide. The basic European university model, which was established first in France in the thirteenth century, has been significantly modified but remains the universal pattern of higher education. The Paris model placed the professor at the center of the institution and enshrined autonomy as an important part of the academic ethos. It is significant that the major competing idea of the period, the student-dominated University of Bologna, in Italy, did not gain a major foothold in Europe, although it had some impact in Spain and later in Latin America.[3] The university rapidly expanded to other parts of Europe—Oxford and Cambridge in England, Salamanca in Spain, Prague and Krakow in central Europe, and a variety of institutions in the German states were established in the following century.

Later, the European imperialist nations brought universities to their colonies, along with the other accoutrements of colonialism. The British, for example, exported academic models—first to the American colonies and later to India, Africa, and Southeast Asia.[4] The French in Vietnam and West Africa, the Spanish and Portuguese throughout Latin America, the Dutch in Indonesia, the Americans in the Philippines, and other colonial powers also exported academic institutions.[5] Colonial universities were patterned directly on institutions in the metropole, but often without the traditions of autonomy and academic freedom in the mother country.[6]

The university was by no means a static institution. It changed and adapted to new circumstances. With the rise of nationalism and the Protestant Reformation in Europe, the universal language of higher education, Latin, was replaced by national languages. Academic institutions became less international and more local in their student bodies and orientations. Universities were affected by their national circumstances. Protestant Amsterdam differed from Catholic Salamanca. Fledgling Harvard, although patterned on British models, slowly developed its own traditions and orientations, reflecting the realities of colonial North America. Academic institutions have not always flourished. Oxford and Cambridge, strongly linked to the Church of England and the aristocracy, played only a minor role in the development of the industrial revolution and the tremendous scientific expansion of the late eighteenth and nineteenth centuries.[7] In

France, universities were abolished after the revolution in 1793. They were gradually reestablished and the Napoleonic model became a powerful force not only in France but also in Spain and Latin America.[8] The German universities were severely damaged during the Nazi period by the destruction of autonomy and the departure of many professors, permanently losing their scientific preeminence.[9]

For the purposes of this chapter, two more recent modifications of the Western academic model are relevant. In the mid-nineteenth century, a newly united Germany harnessed the university for nation building. Under the leadership of Wilhelm von Humboldt, German higher education was given significant resources by the state, took on the responsibility for research aimed at national development and industrialization, and played a key role in defining the ideology of the new German nation.[10] The reformed German universities also established graduate education and the doctoral degree as a major focus of the institution. For the first time, research became an integral function of the university. The university was reorganized as a hierarchy based on the newly emerging scientific disciplines. American reformers took these German innovations and further transformed higher education by stressing the relationship between the university and society through the concept of service and direct links with industry and agriculture. They also democratized the German chair system[11] through the establishment of academic departments and the development of the "land-grant" concept for both high-level research and expanded access to higher education.[12] Institutions that seem deeply embedded in national soil have in fact been influenced by international ideas and models.

The world's universities follow institutional patterns that are basically derivative of these Western models, with virtually no exceptions. One of the few remaining fully non-Western institutions, the Al-Azhar University in Cairo, focuses mainly on traditional Islamic law and theology. Significantly, its science faculties are now organized along European lines.[13] There are many variations—including open universities in Britain, Thailand, India, and elsewhere, two-year vocationally oriented institutions in the United States and many other countries, teacher-training colleges, polytechnics and many others.[14] While the functions of these institutions may differ from those of traditional universities, their basic organization, patterns of governance, and ethos remain remarkably close to the basic Western academic ideal.

NETWORKS OF KNOWLEDGE AND HIGHER EDUCATION

There are many explanations for the dominance of the Western academic model and the lack of alternatives in the modern world. The fact that the Western university institutionalized the study of science and later its production is a central element. The link between universities and the dominant world economic systems no doubt is a particularly important reason for Western hegemony. In many parts of the world, academic institutions were imposed by colonizers. There were few possibilities to develop independent alternatives. Traditional indigenous institutional forms were destroyed by the colonizers, as in India when the British imposed European patterns in the nineteenth century and no longer recognized existing traditional institutions.[15]

None of the formerly colonized nations have shifted from their basically European academic models. The contemporary Indian university resembles its pre-Independence predecessor. Japan, never colonized, recognized after 1868 that it had to develop scientific and industrial capacity and jettisoned its traditional academic institutions in favor of Western university traditions. Japan imported ideas and models from Germany, the United States, and other countries in the development of its universities.[16] Other noncolonized nations, such as China and Thailand, also imported Western models and adapted them to local needs and conditions.[17]

Western universities were seen to be successful in providing advanced education, fostering research and scientific development, and assisting their societies in the increasingly complex task of development. Universities in both the United States and Germany were active in fostering industrial and agricultural development in the nineteenth century. The harnessing of higher education to the broader needs of national economic and social development was perhaps the most important innovation of this era. The idea that higher education should be generously supported from public funds, that the university should participate in the creation as well as the transmission of knowledge, and that academic institutions should at the same time be permitted a degree of autonomy was behind much of the growth of universities in this century.

Further, Western universities were at the center of a knowledge network that included research institutions, the means of knowledge dissemination such as journals and scientific publishers, and an "invisible college" of scientists. It is worth noting that the bulk of the world's scientific literature now appears in the English language. Even scholars in such industrialized nations as Sweden and the Netherlands often find it necessary to communicate their research findings in English. The large Dutch multinational publishers, Elsevier and Kluwer, publish virtually all of their scholarly and scientific books and journals in English.

The circulation of scholars and students worldwide—and in a sense even the "brain drain"—is an element of the international knowledge system, helping to circulate ideas and also maintaining the impact of the major "host" countries and their research hegemony. More than one million students study outside their home countries. The large majority of these students are from Third World nations and the newly industrialized countries of the Pacific Rim. They are studying in the industrialized nations, with the United States, Britain, France, and Germany among the major host countries. Japan is both a major sending and receiving country.[18]

Students learn many things as a result of their sojourns abroad. They gain expertise in their studies. They also learn the norms and values of the academic system in which they are located, often returning home with a zeal to reform their universities in a Western direction. Frequently, foreign graduates have difficulty readjusting to their home countries, in part because the advanced training they acquired abroad may not be easily assimilated into less well-developed economies. Such frustrations, along with the blandishments of significantly better remuneration, lead to the brain drain.

However, in the contemporary world, brain drain is often not permanent. For one thing, members of the Third World scientific diaspora often maintain contact with their colleagues at home, contributing advanced knowledge and ideas.[19] They frequently return home for periods of time and work with local academics. And increasingly, they return home permanently when academic—and sometimes political—conditions are favorable, bringing with them considerable expertise, often assuming leadership positions in the local scientific and academic communities. Without question, the massive circulation of highly educated personnel has a great influence on the transfer of knowledge. With few exceptions, the knowledge and institutional patterns transferred are from the major industrialized nations to the Third World—or even to other more peripheral industrial countries—with very little traffic in the other direction.[20]

The knowledge network is complex and multifaceted; while its centers remain extraordinarily powerful, there is a movement toward greater equalization of research production and use. Japan, for example, already has a powerful and increasingly research-oriented university system, and some of the newly industrializing countries of East and Southeast Asia are building up research capacity in their universities.[21] While hegemony may be slowly dissipating, inequality will remain endemic to the world knowledge system.

EXPANSION: HALLMARK OF THE POSTWAR ERA

Postsecondary education has expanded since World War II. Expansion has taken place in virtually every country in the world to differing extents. The growth of postsecondary education has, in proportional terms, been more dramatic than that of primary and secondary education. Writing in 1975, Martin Trow spoke of the transition from *elite* to *mass* and then to *universal* higher education in the context of the industrialized nations.[22] While the United States enrolled some 30 percent of the relevant age cohort in higher education in the immediate postwar period, European nations generally maintained an elite higher education system with fewer than 5 percent attending postsecondary institutions. By the 1960s, many European nations educated 15 percent or more of the age group—Sweden for example, enrolled 24 percent in 1970, with France at 17 percent. At the same time, the United States increased its proportion to around 50 percent, approaching universal access. By the 1990s, most European countries enrolled more than 30 percent of the relevant age group, and the United States increased by a few percentage points. While American patterns of access have stabilized, Europe continues to expand, as do many new industrialized countries.

In the Third World, expansion has been similarly dramatic. Building on tiny and extraordinarily elitist universities, Third World higher education expanded rapidly in the immediate postindependence period. In India, enrollments grew from approximately 100,000 at the time of Independence in 1947 to over 4 million in the 1990s. Expansion in Africa has also been rapid, with the postsecondary student population growing from 21,000 in 1960 to 437,000 in 1983, but with growth stagnating in the

1990s as a result of the economic and political difficulties experienced by many sub-Saharan African countries.[23] Recent economic difficulties in much of sub-Saharan Africa have meant that per student expenditure has dropped, contributing to a marked deterioration in academic standards. Enrollment growth has also slowed.

Similar trends can be seen elsewhere in the non-Western countries. In a few instances, such as the Philippines, where more than one-third of the age cohort enters postsecondary education. Third World enrollment ratios have reached the levels of many of the industrialized nations, although in general the Third World lags far behind in terms of proportions of the population attending higher education institutions. For example, despite China's student population of more than 2 million, only about 1 percent of the age cohort attends postsecondary institutions—about 4 percent of those graduating from secondary school. Expansion in the Third World has, in general, exceeded that in the industrialized nations at least in proportional terms. It should be noted that there are significant variations among Third World nations—some countries maintain small and relatively elitist university systems while others have expanded more rapidly. Among those with the highest rates of expansion, and now of participation, are the Asian newly industrialized countries such as South Korea and Taiwan.

Regardless of political system, level of economic development, or educational ideology, the expansion of higher education has been the single, most important trend. Worldwide, about 7 percent of the relevant age cohort (20 to 24 years) attend postsecondary educational institutions—a statistic that has shown an increase each decade since World War II. Higher education expanded dramatically—first in the United States, then in Europe. Currently, the main focus of expansion is in the Third World and the newly industrialized countries. There are, of course, significant variations in enrollment statistics and ratios. Women, in general, attend less frequently than men, although the former now constitute approximately 40 percent of university enrollments—with considerable variation by country. The industrialized nations, with a few exceptions, have a higher proportion of the age cohort in postsecondary education than Third World countries. Generalized statistics concerning enrollments in postsecondary education mask many key differences. For example, many industrialized nations have a higher proportion of students in technological and scientific fields as opposed to the traditional liberal arts, which tend to predominate in the developing nations, although even here there are some exceptions, such as China.

There are many reasons for the expansion of higher education. A central cause has been the increasing complexity of modern societies and economies, which have demanded a more highly trained work force. Almost without exception, postsecondary institutions have been called on to provide the required training. Indeed, training in many fields that had once been imparted on the job has become formalized in institutions of higher education. Whole new fields, such as computer science, have come into existence and rely on universities as a key source of research and training. Nations now developing scientific and industrial capacity, such as Korea and Taiwan, have depended on academic institutions to provide high-level training as well as research expertise to a greater extent than was the case during the first industrial revolution in Europe.[24]

Not only do academic institutions provide training, they also test and provide certification for many roles and occupations in contemporary society. These roles have been central to universities from their origins in the medieval period but have been vastly expanded in recent years. A university degree is a prerequisite for an increasing number of occupations in most societies. Indeed, it is fair to say that academic certification is necessary for most positions of power, authority, and prestige in modern societies. This places immense power in the hands of universities. Tests to gain admission to higher education are rites of passage in many societies and are important determinants of future success.[25] Competition within academe varies from country to country, but in most cases much stress is also placed on high academic performance and tests in the universities. There are often further examinations to permit entry into specific professions.

The role of the university as an examining body has grown for a number of reasons. As expansion has taken place, it has been necessary to provide ever more competitive sorting mechanisms to control access to high-prestige occupations. The universities are also seen as meritocratic institutions that can be trusted to provide fair and impartial tests to measure accomplishment honestly and, therefore, determine access. When such mechanisms break down—as they did in China during the Cultural Revolution—or where they are perceived to be subject to corrupt influences—as in India—the universities are significantly weakened. The older, more informal, and often more ascriptive means of controlling access to prestigious occupations are no longer able to provide the controls needed nor are they perceived as fair. Entirely new fields have developed where no sorting mechanisms existed, and academic institutions have frequently been called upon to provide not only training but also examination and certification.

Expansion has also occurred because the growing segments of the population of modern societies demand it. The middle classes, seeing that academic qualifications are necessary for success, demand access to higher education. Governments generally respond by increasing enrollment.[26] When governments do not move quickly enough, private initiatives frequently establish academic institutions in order to meet this demand. In countries like India, the Philippines, and Bangladesh, a majority of the students are educated in private colleges and universities.[27] At present, there are powerful worldwide trends toward imposing user fees in the form of higher tuition charges, increasing the stress on private higher education, and in general considering higher education as a "private good" in economic terms. These changes are intended to reduce the cost of postsecondary education for governments while maintaining access—although the long-term implications for the quality of, access to, and control over higher education remain unclear.

In most societies, higher education is heavily subsidized by the government, and most, if not all, academic institutions are in the public sector. While there is a growing trend toward private initiative and management sharing responsibility with public institutions, governments will likely continue to be the main source of funding for postsecondary education.[28] The dramatic expansion of academic institutions in the postwar period has proved very expensive for governments.[29] Nonetheless, the demand for access has been an extraordinarily powerful one.[30]

There have been significant variations in higher education expansion. For example, many analysts writing in the 1960s assumed that the world, and particularly the Western industrialized nations, would move from elite to mass and finally to universal access to higher education, generally following the American pattern.[31] The path to universal access has proved to be circuitous. For a period in the 1970s, expansion slowed, only picking up again in the late 1980s. The nations of the European Union are in general moving toward U.S. levels of access. The causes for the slowdowns were in part economic, with problems in the Western economies following the "oil shocks" of the 1970s; in part demographic, resulting from a significant drop in the birth rate and a smaller cohort of young people; and in part philosophical, as countries were less sympathetic to further growth of public institutions, including universities. Generally, the proportion of the age cohort going on to higher education in Western Europe stabilized at under 20 percent in the 1970s, and began to increase again in the late 1980s, with continuing expansion.[32] This expansion has taken place in a context of steady population trends and has been impelled by changes in the European economies, which have moved to the postindustrial stage.

In sharp contrast to Western industrialized countries, Third World universities have, in general, continued to expand without interruption. The exception is Africa, where enrollment and access have slowed recently. While with only a very few exceptions, such as the Philippines, Third World enrollment ratios remain significantly lower than those in the industrialized nations, there continues to be a strong commitment to continued expansion and access. This is the case even in countries like India, which has experienced severe unemployment of graduates and a brain drain of university graduates abroad. In sub-Saharan Africa, there has been a slowing of expansion, not so much because demand for higher education has decreased, but because of severe economic problems that have limited the ability of governments to pay the costs of continued growth. In many Third World countries, it remains impossible for local universities to absorb all of those qualified to attend, thus creating an exodus of students abroad. This is the case in Malaysia, where about half of the country's enrollments are abroad.[33] As in the industrialized nations, there is a notable trend toward shifting the burden of funding for higher education from the state to the individual.

It is necessary to analyze the prospects for continued expansion of higher education from several perspectives. While common worldwide trends exist, such as the increasingly important role of technology, there are also important differences among countries and parts of the world. The Third World presents a specific set of circumstances. While it is likely that the pace in some Third World countries will slow in the coming decade, expansion will continue to be a key factor in higher education. Regional variations will be important, with economic factors dominating. Universities will very likely grow more slowly in less successful economies. Rapidly expanding economies, such as those of the newly industrializing countries in East Asia, will have the resources to expand higher education and at the same time maintain a demand for graduates.

Taiwan and South Korea, for example, can generally absorb university graduates as well as the expenditures needed for large and better-equipped universities, especially since a majority of students study in private universities. Yet, even where evidence exists that higher educational growth should slow or even stop, it is unlikely that this will take place since popular demand for postsecondary education remains high, and political authorities will find it easier to provide access than to limit it. What has happened is that the cost of postsecondary education has increasingly been shifted to individuals and families.

The situation in Western industrialized nations is more difficult to predict. A variety of factors argue for a resumption of growth, although probably not at the levels of the 1960s. Modest upturns in population in some age categories are in evidence in some Western nations, although demographers predict that this will be relatively short lived. The large numbers of graduates trained in the 1960s and now occupying positions in schools and universities as well as in government and industrial enterprises will soon be retiring, triggering a significant demand for university-trained personnel. It is also recognized that university-based research is an important ingredient for scientific and technological strength in an increasingly competitive world economy. Much, however, will depend on broader economic trends. It is also difficult to predict whether resistance to governmental spending in general and for education in particular will continue to be an important political factor in many Western countries. The 1990s have brought a renewed growth in access to postsecondary education, although this has been combined with significant financial problems.[34]

CHANGE AND REFORM: THE LEGACY OF THE SIXTIES

The demands placed on institutions of higher education to accommodate larger numbers of students and to serve expanding functions resulted in reforms in higher education in many countries. Much debate has taken place concerning higher education reform in the 1960s—and a significant amount of change did take place.[35] It is possible to identify several important factors that contributed both to the debate and to the changes. Without question, the unprecedented student unrest of the period contributed to a sense of disarray in higher education. The unrest was in part precipitated by deteriorating academic conditions that were the result of the rapid expansion. In a few instances, students demanded far-reaching reforms in higher education, although they did not propose specific changes.[36] Students frequently demanded an end to the rigidly hierarchical organization of the traditional European university, and major reforms were made in this respect. The "chair" system was modified or eliminated and the responsibility for academic decision making, formerly a monopoly of full professors, was expanded—in some countries to include students. At the same time, the walls of the traditional academic disciplines were broken down by various plans for interdisciplinary teaching and research.

Reform was greatest in several very traditional Western European academic systems. Sweden's universities were completely transformed in the most far-reaching of the reform movements. Among changes in Sweden were a democratizing of decision making, decentralizing the universities, expanding higher education to previously underserved parts of the country, providing for interdisciplinary teaching and research, and vocationalizing the curriculum.[37] Reforms also took place in France and in the Netherlands. Reformers in both countries stressed interdisciplinary studies and democratizing academic decision making. In Germany, the universities in the states dominated by the Social Democratic Party were also reformed, with the traditional structures of the university giving way to more democratic governance patterns.

In the 1990s, the major trend in restructuring European universities has been improving the administrative efficiency and accountability of the universities. Many of the reforms of the 1960s were modified or even eliminated. Students, for example, have less power now. In the Netherlands, a national restructuring has increased the power of administrators. Students have little authority in the new arrangements. Similar tends can be seen in Germany, Sweden, and other countries.

In many industrialized nations, structural change was modest. In the United States, for example, despite considerable debate during the 1960s, there was very limited change in the structure or governance of higher education.[38] Japan, which saw unrest that disrupted higher education and spawned a large number of reports on university reform, experienced virtually no basic change in its higher education system, although several "new model" interdisciplinary institutions were established—such as the science-oriented Tsukuba University near Tokyo. Britain, less affected by student protest and with an established plan for expansion in operation, also experienced few reforms during the 1960s.[39] Some of the changes implemented in the 1960s were criticized or abandoned. In Germany, reforms in governance that gave students and junior staff a dominant position in some university functions were ruled unconstitutional by the German courts.[40]

Many of the structural reforms of the 1960s were abandoned after a decade of experimentation, or were replaced by administrative arrangements that emphasized accountability and efficiency. Outside authorities, including government but also in some cases business, industry or labor organizations, have come to play a more important role in academic governance. The curricular innovations of the 1960s, as well as later decades, have proved more durable. Interdisciplinary programs and initiatives and the introduction of new fields such as gender studies have characterized changes in many countries.

Vocationalization has been an important trend in higher education change in the past two decades. Throughout the world, there is a conviction that the university curriculum must provide relevant training for a variety of increasingly complex jobs. The traditional notion that higher education should consist of liberal nonvocational studies for elites or provide a broad but unfocused curriculum has been widely criticized for lacking "relevance" to the needs of contemporary students. Students, worried about obtaining remunerative employment, have pressed the universities to be more focused. Employers have also demanded that the curriculum become more directly relevant to their needs. Enrollments in the social sciences and humanities, at least in the industrialized nations, have declined because these fields are not considered vocationally relevant.

Curricular vocationalism is linked to another key worldwide trend in higher education: the increasingly close relationship between universities and industry.[41] Industrial firms have sought to ensure that the skills they need are incorporated into the curriculum. This trend also has implications for academic research, since many university-industry relationships are focused largely on research. Industries have established formal linkages and research partnerships with universities in order to obtain help with research in which they are interested. In some countries, such as Sweden, representatives of industry have been added to the governing councils of higher education institutions. In the United States, formal contractual arrangements have been made between universities and major corporations to share research results. In many industrialized nations, corporations are providing focused educational programs for their employees, sometimes with the assistance of universities.

University-industry relations have become crucial for higher education in many countries. Technical arrangements with regard to patents, confidentiality of research findings, and other fiscal matters have assumed importance. Critics also have pointed out that the nature of research in higher education may be altered by these new relationships as industrial firms are not generally interested in basic research. University-based research, which has traditionally been oriented toward basic research, may be increasingly skewed to applied and profit-making topics. There has also been some discussion of the orientation of research—for example, in fields like biotechnology, where broader public policy matters may conflict with the needs of corporations. Specific funding arrangements have also been questioned. Pressure to serve the immediate needs of society and particularly the training and research requirements of industry is currently a key concern for universities, one that has implications for the organization of the curriculum, the nature and scope of research, and the traditional relationship between the university and society.[42] Debates concerning the appropriate relationship between higher education and industry are likely to continue, as universities come under even stronger pressure to provide direct service to the economy.

Universities have traditionally claimed significant autonomy for themselves. The traditional idea of academic governance stresses autonomy, and universities have tried to insulate themselves from direct control by external agencies. However, as universities expanded and become more expensive, there has been immense pressure by those providing funds for higher education—mainly governments—to expect accountability from universities. The conflict between autonomy and accountability has been one of the flashpoints of controversy in recent years. Without exception autonomy has been limited, and new administrative structures have been put into place in such countries as Britain and the Netherlands, to ensure greater accountability.[43] The issue takes on different implications in different parts of the world. In the Third World, traditions of autonomy have not been strong and demands for accountability, which include both political and economic elements, are especially troublesome.[44] In the industrialized nations, accountability pressures are more fiscal in nature.

Despite the varied pressures on higher educational institutions for change and the significant reforms that have taken place in the past two decades, there have been few structural alterations in universities. One of the few places where this has occurred is in Sweden, as part of the dramatic reforms that have been undertaken there. Elsewhere, curricula have been altered, expansion has taken place, and there have been continuing debates concerning accountability and autonomy, but universities as institutions have not changed significantly. As Edward Shils has argued, the "academic ethos" has been under strain, and while in some ways it has been weakened, it has survived.[45]

THE MILLENNIUM

The university in modern society is a durable institution. It has maintained key elements of the historical models from which it evolved over many centuries. At the same time, it has successfully evolved to serve the needs of societies during a period of tremendous social change.[46] There has been a convergence of both ideas and institutional patterns and practices in world higher education. This has been due in part to the implantation of European-style universities in the developing areas both during and after the colonial era—and in part to—the fact universities have been crucial in the development and internationalization of science and scholarship.

Despite remarkable institutional stability over time, universities have changed and have been subjected to immense pressures in the post–World War II period. Many of the changes chronicled here are the result of great external pressure and were instituted despite opposition from within the institution. Some have argued that the university has lost its soul.[47] Others have claimed that the university is irresponsible because it uses public funds and does not always conform to the direct needs of industry and government. Pressure from governmental authorities, militant students, or external constituencies have all placed great strains on academic institutions.

The period since World War II has been one of unprecedented growth—in which higher education has assumed an increasingly central role in virtually all modern societies. While growth may continue, the dramatic expansion of recent decades is at an end. It is unlikely that the position of the university as the most important institution for training in virtually all of the top-level occupations in modern society will be weakened, although other institutions have become involved in training in some fields. The university's research role is more problematical because of the fiscal pressures of recent years. There is no other institution that can undertake basic research, but at the same time the consensus that has supported university-based basic research has weakened.[48]

The challenges facing universities are, nonetheless, significant. The following issues are among those that will be of concern in the coming decade and beyond.

Acess and Adaptation

Although in a few countries, access to postsecondary education has been provided to virtually all segments of the population, in most countries a continuing unmet demand exists for higher education. Progress toward broadening the social class base of higher education has slowed and, in many industrialized countries, stopped in the 1970s. With the arrival of democratic governments in Eastern Europe, the reemergence of demand in Western Europe, and continuing pressure for expansion in the Third World, demand for access and the consequent expansion of enrollments continue in many countries. Limited funds and a desire for "efficient" allocation of scarce postsecondary resources will come into direct conflict with demands for access. Demands for access by previously disenfranchised groups will continue to place great pressure on higher education. In many countries, racial, ethnic, or religious minorities play a role in shaping higher education policy. Issues of access will be among the most controversial in debates concerning higher education.

Administration, Accountability, and Governance

As academic institutions become larger and more complex, there is increasing pressure for a greater degree of professional administration. At the same time, the traditional forms of academic governance are increasingly criticized—not only because they are unwieldy but also because, in large and bureaucratic institutions, they are inefficient. The administration of higher education will increasingly become a profession, much as it is in the United States. This means that an "administrative estate" will be established in many countries where it does not now exist. Demands for accountability are growing and will cause academic institutions considerable difficulty. As academic budgets expand, there are inevitable demands to monitor and control expenditures. At present, no general agreement exists concerning the appropriate level of governmental involvement in higher education. The challenge will be to ensure that the traditional—and valuable—patterns of faculty control over governance and the basic academic decisions in universities are maintained in a complex and bureaucratic environment.

Knowledge Creation and Dissemination

Research is a central part of the mission of many universities and of the academic system generally. Key decisions concerning the control and funding of research, the relationship of research to the broader curriculum and teaching, the uses made of university-based research, and related issues will be in contention. Further, the system of knowledge dissemination, including journals and books and the new computer-based data systems, is rapidly changing. Who should control the new data networks? How will traditional means of communication, such as journals, survive in this new climate? How will the scientific system avoid being overwhelmed by the proliferation of data?[49] Who will pay for the costs of knowledge dissemination? The needs of peripheral scientific systems, including both the Third World and smaller academic systems in the industrialized world, have been largely ignored, but are nonetheless important.[50]

While the technological means for rapid knowledge dissemination are available, issues of control and ownership, the appropriate use of databases, problems of maintaining quality standards in databases, and related questions are very important. It is possible that the new technologies will lead to increased centralization rather than wider access. It is also possible that libraries and other users of knowledge will be overwhelmed both by the cost of obtaining new material and by the flow of knowledge. At present, academic institutions in the United States and other English-speaking nations, along with publishers and the owners of the communications networks, stand to gain. The major Western knowledge producers currently constitute a kind of cartel of information, dominating not only the creation of knowledge but also most of the major channels of distribution. Simply increasing the amount of research and creating new databases will not ensure a more equal and accessible knowledge system. Academic institutions are at the center, but publishers, copyright authorities, funders of research, and others are also necessarily involved.

The Academic Profession

In most countries, the professoriate has found itself under great pressure in recent years. Demands for accountability, increased bureaucratization of institutions, fiscal constraints in many countries, and an increasingly diverse student body have all challenged the professoriate. In most industrialized nations, a combination of fiscal problems and demographic factors led to a stagnating profession. Now, demographic factors and a modest upturn in enrollments are beginning to turn surpluses into shortages.[51] In the newly industrializing countries (NICs), the professoriate has significantly improved its status, remuneration, and working conditions in recent years. In the poorer nations, however, the situation has, if anything, become more difficult with decreasing resources and ever-increasing enrollments. Overall, the professoriate will face severe problems as academic institutions change in the coming period. Maintaining autonomy, academic freedom, and a commitment to the traditional goals of the university will be difficult.

In the West, it will be hard to lure the "best and brightest" into academe in a period when positions are again relatively plentiful, for in many fields, academic salaries have not kept pace with the private sector and the traditional academic lifestyle has deteriorated. The pressure on the professoriate not only to teach and do research but also to attract external grants, do consulting, and the like is great. In Britain and Australia, for example, universities have become "cost centers," and accountability has been pushed to its logical extreme. British academics who entered the profession after 1989 no longer have tenure, and will be periodically evaluated. In the NICs, the challenge will be to create a fully autonomous academic profession in a context in which traditions of research and academic freedom are only now developing. The difficulties faced by the poorer Third World countries are perhaps the greatest—to maintain a viable academic culture under deteriorating conditions.

Private Resources and Public Responsibility

In almost every country, there has been a growing emphasis on increasing the role of the private sector in higher education. One of the most direct manifestations of this trend is the role of the private sector in funding and directing university research. In many countries, private academic institutions have expanded, or new ones have been established. Students are paying an increasing share of the cost of their education as a result of tuition and fee increases and through loan programs. Governments try to limit their expenditures on postsecondary education while at the same time recognizing that the functions of universities are important. Privatization has been the means of achieving this broad policy goal.[52] Inevitably, decisions concerning academic developments will move increasingly to the private sector, with the possibility that broader public goals may be ignored. Whether private interests will support the traditional functions of universities, including academic freedom, basic research, and a pattern of governance that leaves the professoriate in control, is unclear. Some of the most interesting developments in private higher education can be found in such countries as Vietnam, China, and Hungary, where private institutions have recently been established. Private initiatives in higher education will bring a change in values and orientations. It is not clear that these values will be in the long-term best interests of the university.

Diversification and Stratification

While diversification—the establishing of new postsecondary institutions to meet diverse needs—is by no means an entirely unprecedented phenomenon, it is a trend that has been of primary importance and will continue to reshape the academic system. In recent years, the establishment of research institutions, community colleges, polytechnics, and other academic institutions designed to meet specialized needs and serve specific populations has been a primary characteristic of growth. At the same time, the academic system has become more stratified—individuals within one sector of the system, find it difficult to move to a different sector. There is often a high correlation between social class (and other variables) and selection to a particular sector of the system. To some extent, the reluctance of the traditional universities to change is responsible for some of the diversification. Perhaps more important has been the belief that it is efficient and probably less expensive to establish new limited-function institutions. An element of diversification is the inclusion of larger numbers of women and other previously disenfranchised segments of the population. Women now constitute 40 percent of the student population worldwide and more than 50 percent in 15 countries.[53] In many countries, students from lower socioeconomic groups, and racial and ethnic minorities are entering postsecondary institutions in significant numbers. This diversification will also be a challenge for the coming decades.

Economic Disparities

There are substantial inequalities among the world's universities—and these inequalities will likely grow. The major universities in the industrialized nations generally have the resources to play a leading role in scientific research—in a context in which it is increasingly expensive to keep up with the expansion of knowledge.[54] At the same time, universities in much of the Third World simply cannot cope with the continuing pressure for increased enrollments, combined with budgetary constraints and, in some cases, fiscal disasters. For example, universities in much of sub-Saharan Africa have experienced dramatic budget cuts and find it difficult to function, not to mention to improve quality and compete in the international knowledge system.[55] In the middle are academic institutions in the Asian NICs, where significant academic progress has taken place and where universities will continue to improve. Thus, the economic prospects for postsecondary education worldwide are mixed.

CONCLUSION

Universities share a common culture and reality. In many basic ways, there is a convergence of institutional models and norms. At the same time, there are significant national differences that will continue to affect the development of academic systems and institutions. It is unlikely that the basic structures of academic institutions will change dramatically. The "Humboldtian" academic model will survive, although administrative structures grow stronger, and the traditional power of the faculty has diminished. Open universities and other distance education institutions have emerged, and may provide new institutional arrangements. Efforts to save money may yield further organizational changes as well. Unanticipated change is also possible. For example, while conditions for the emergence of significant student movements, at least in the industrialized nations, do not seem likely at the present time, circumstances may change.[56] The circumstances facing universities in the first part of twenty-first century are not, in general, favorable. The realities of higher education as a "mature industry" with stable rather than growing resources in the industrialized countries will affect not only the funds available for postsecondary education but also practices within academic institutions. Accountability, the impact of technologies, and the other forces discussed in this chapter will all affect colleges and universities. Patterns will, of course, vary worldwide. Some academic systems, especially those in the newly industrializing countries, will continue to grow. In parts of the world affected by significant political and economic change, the coming decades will be ones of reconstruction. Worldwide, the coming period is one of major challenge for higher education.

2

The University as Center and Periphery

This chapter concerns complexities and dilemmas in higher education.[57] It examines the relationship between universities in the industrialized countries and those in the Third World. An effort is made to understand how universities located in countries at very different levels of economic and technological development relate to one another in an international knowledge system. Universities function in several different contexts at the same time. They are rooted in their own cultures and affected by national realities. They are also parts of an international knowledge system. They are producers and disseminators of knowledge in their own nations, playing increasingly important roles in technologically developing societies. They also interact with institutions and ideas from abroad, because knowledge has no national boundaries.

The basic point of this discussion is that universities in the Third World find themselves at a disadvantage in the international knowledge network even as they play a key role in their own societies. The problems of looking outward and inward at the same time are substantial, particularly when combined with immense pressures to contribute directly to national development and to participate in the international system. This chapter discusses the nature of that disadvantage, its implications for the international knowledge system, and the manifold roles of Third World universities, and then suggests some steps that might ameliorate the situation.

It is widely assumed that a "new international order" predicated on a more equitable international system should include a greater degree of autonomy and equality for educational institutions in "have-not" parts of the world. The inequalities of the international knowledge system run very deep, have strong institutional support and significant historical roots, and are often in the interests of those who wield power, whether that power is military, economic, intellectual, or technological. It is unlikely that even the best intentions, buttressed by resolutions of the United Nations or the programs of UNESCO, can dislodge the basic power relationships among nations, especially when those in the industrialized nations hold the power and have shown so little inclination to yield it in the past. Yet there are some signs of change, particularly in the development of regional centers of research and higher education in the Third World and especially in the newly industrialized countries.

At the heart of this discussion is the idea of center and periphery.[58] A subsidiary theme is that of neocolonialism.[59] The center-periphery concept has been applied to various societal relations but only recently to education, and it is important to understand the nuances of the idea as it is applied to the national and international roles of universities. The present international educational equation has certain institutional and intellectual "centers" that give direction, provide models, produce research, and in general function as the pinnacles of the academic system. At the opposite end of the spectrum are universities that are "peripheral" in the sense that they copy developments from abroad, produce little that is original, and are generally not at the frontiers of knowledge.

The central institutions are research-oriented, prestigious, and part of an international knowledge system. Their libraries are large and their laboratories well equipped. The central institutions have access to the bulk of research funds, produce a high proportion of the doctoral-level research degrees, and are recognized as leaders. In a sense, the central universities are the producers, although they also have a teaching function. The apparatus of knowledge access and distribution is concentrated at the center and is communicated through such world languages as English and French. Major publishers of scientific materials, the prestigious academic journals, and the like are predominantly located at the centers. Scholars tend to gravitate to the centers for advanced research and "refresher" training. Central universities are, almost without exception, located in the central nations—those countries with high per capita incomes, a high level of technological development, substantial academic traditions, those that use a major world language and possess all the infrastructures of intellectual life.

Peripheral universities, which are in the large majority, are basically distributors of knowledge, mainly through the training of students and to some extent through the replication of research developed at the centers. They are dependent on the central institutions for innovation and for direction. Their facilities are, in general, less adequate, the professors are compensated less and less prestigious. Peripheral universities suffer a variety of disabilities. They have less distinguished and supportive traditions, tend to be located in poorer nations, have less well trained staff, and in general have not reached the "takeoff" point for academic excellence. Peripheral institutions are often, but not always, located in peripheral countries.

The concept of center and periphery (or, as some call it, metropolis-province) was developed in a number of academic fields to deal with the realities of inequality in the international setting. Johann Galtung articulated the concept as part of a structural theory of imperialism.[60] He based some of his work on Lenin's notion of imperialism and also relied on contemporary dependency theorists such as James Cockcroft and Andre Gunder Frank.[61] Edward Shils first applied center-periphery theory to the role of intellectuals in the Third World.[62] While Shils has tended to see the relationship as a "natural" result of inequality, Galtung and others have stressed the responsibility of the industrialized nations for the maintenance of the peripheral status of the Third World. It is at this point that the concept of neocolonialism enters the equation.[63] Neocolonialism, in this context, consists of the policies of the industrialized nations that attempt to maintain their domination over the Third World. These frameworks, borrowed as they are from a variety of disciplines and ideologies, continue to be controversial, but are nonetheless useful in helping us to understand a complex phenomenon.

Centers and peripheries exist not only among nations but within national university systems, and the concept has relevance beyond international comparisons. As David Riesman has pointed out, a handful of universities in the United States set the academic tone for the rest.[64] His concept of the meandering academic procession has relevance to this discussion. A small number of recognized central universities in the United States dominate the large majority of universities. Relatively few institutions present alternative models or go in radically different directions. Debates concerning the undergraduate curriculum are typically led by Harvard University or other top institutions. When the elite sector gives its approval to a new trend, as it has done in the past with regard to legal and business education, other institutions generally follow. Further, the central universities receive an overwhelming proportion of research funds, have research-oriented faculty, and the like. In the United States, 80 percent of federal government research funds go to the top one hundred universities. The peripheral institutions not only are followers, but they also seldom blaze new trails in education even in the United States, where fiscal and other constraints are not as serious as in most Third World countries. In Britain, the impact of Oxford and Cambridge on postsecondary education is immense, and in France, Paris has dominated the entire system. Thus, the center-periphery concept functions in national settings and is related to many elements, not only the economic inequalities that pervade the international scene.

Third World universities are without exception peripheral institutions in an international context. They look to universities in the industrialized world and particularly to the United States, Britain, and France for models, for research, and for direction. Relatively few Third World universities produce top-level scholars and researchers as they usually lack the infrastructures—such as libraries and laboratories—to aid in the production of advanced scholarship. Further, they often lack an orientation toward scholarly production. Third World institutions usually do not often "feel" themselves to be central institutions. Thus, there is a combination of psychological dependence and the lack of necessary facilities and traditions.

Yet, Third World universities are, in many cases, key institutions in their own societies, and in this sense are probably more important to their societies than the major international universities like Harvard or Oxford are to theirs. Third World universities are among the few fully modern institutions in their societies. They produce the highly trained elites necessary for the operation of the modern state, are very often at the political vortex of their societies, produce cultural commentary and criticism, and, in some nations, make important contributions to defining newly established political entities. Professors are often called on for advice and frequently serve in high government positions.[65] Students often play a central political role through their activism, and in a number of instances have toppled governments. The "moral authority" of the academic community is a force in societies without a large number of politically articulate individuals. In this sense, Third World universities face a curious paradox: peripheral in the international sense and dependent on foreign institutions in many respects, at the same time they are quite central to the local society.

Can a peripheral university become central in the international context? This is a question often raised, and it is a complicated one. The question assumes that universities throughout the world should aspire to centrality as defined by the prestigious research-oriented universities in the industrialized nations. Theorists from Gandhi to Nyerere and Illich have argued that education, including higher education, should strike out on different paths.[66] But the recognized standard of excellence in higher education remains the major metropolitan research institution, and many institutions aspire to this kind of centrality. There are examples of individual institutions and of major parts of academic systems moving to a central position in the international academic hierarchy. The German universities did this in the twentieth century, and the American universities, influenced by Germany, followed early in the twentieth century.[67] More recently, universities in Japan, also influenced by the German academic model, have moved in this direction. Other institutions have dropped in international prestige and are no longer as important as research producers and as arbiters of academic excellence. Since the Nazi period, for example, German universities have lost some of their international role, and German is no longer a key scientific language.

It is nonetheless quite difficult to move to a position of centrality in the modern world. Given the complexity of science and scholarship, it is probably more difficult now than it was in earlier times. As will be indicated later, the problem is not simply one of money. Kuwait, for example, has been unable to develop a fully functional research university despite major efforts. Without question, lack of resources is a major factor in the Third World, since the infrastructures of academic development are relatively costly. The detailed factors of academic dependence will be discussed later in this chapter. It is clear, however, that while examples exist of universities, academic systems, and even of individual departments or institutions moving from a peripheral to a central status, they are relatively rare, and very few are in the nations that constitute the Third World.

Third World institutions not only confront the reality of the historically and eco-nomically based power of the industrialized nations but must also deal with the wide-spread desire by industrial nations to maintain their dominant positions. This desire, and the specific policies that are used to continue that dominance, have been called neocolonialism.

Foreign aid programs, technical assistance, and other aspects of aid to the Third World have complex motivations and varying, often unanticipated, outcomes. The donor nations often have several goals in mind for providing assistance, one of them being the perpetuation of educational and political structures that will ensure sta-bility and a generally pro-Western orientation.[68] While this chapter is not primarily concerned with neocolonialism and foreign assistance, these phenomena are ingre-dients in the relationship between the Third World and industrialized nations on which we focus.

THIRD WORLD REALITIES

The role of universities in the Third World is complicated and diverse. It is difficult to generalize because of variations in colonial development, economic and political real-ities, and divergent conceptions about the role of higher education in modernizing societies. Colonial traditions have had a varying and a continuing impact on the nature of higher education. The most obvious area is that of language—countries formerly under British control generally continue to use English, at least at the upper reaches of the educational system, while former French colonies remain linguistically linked to France. Further, the colonial powers had quite different education policies. In India, the British were relatively permissive in the establishment of educational institutions, while in Africa they were more reluctant to invest funds or permit local initiative, fear-ing that universities might breed discontent.

The French had even more restrictive policies with regard to the establishment of higher education in their colonies, although a larger number of students were educat-ed in the metropole.[69] Further, French policy was different in Vietnam and in West Africa. The Dutch and the Portuguese paid less attention to education in their colonies, and were mostly opposed to the establishment of universities. The Belgians had the most drastic policy of all—they forbade the development of postsecondary schools in their colonial areas. Even the Americans, in their relatively short colonial encounter in the Philippines, had a distinctive educational approach. They stressed education more than the other colonial powers and made some effort to build an edu-cational system in their image. A partial result of American policy is the fact that the contemporary Philippines has one of the highest proportions of young people enrolled in postsecondary education in the Third World.[70]

The educational policies of the colonial powers generally reflected metropolitan ideas about education, but usually in a watered-down form. The colonial powers did not invest much in education and were relatively reluctant to permit the rapid growth of university-level institutions, for fear of engendering political opposition and producing an unemployed urban intelligentsia, as well as an unwillingness to spend for expanded academic institutions. Higher education, where it was provided, was generally intended to produce loyal civil servants able to operate a bureaucracy. It was not intended to develop scientific research or to stimulate modernization. The colonial educational heritage remains powerful in continuing a liberal arts orientation of many universities, in the use of European languages in education and intellectual discourse, and in the metropolitan pattern of organization of the educational system.

Contemporary differences among Third World nations are also substantial. A few countries—such as India, the Philippines, Egypt, and Mexico—have large and diverse university systems producing some research and scholarship as well as educating a significant segment of the urban sector of the population. Other systems remain highly elitist, with access limited to a tiny proportion of the urban upper classes. The proportion of young people going on to higher education—even in India, which has a student population of more than 5 million—remains smaller than in any of the industrialized nations. Typically, the student population constitutes under 5 percent of the relevant age cohort. Almost regardless of political ideology, universities remain elitist institutions in the Third World, and they are seen as a key means of social mobility. Universities also tend to be mainly urban institutions, and it is commonly pointed out that they are separated physically as well as intellectually from the large rural majorities. The colonial powers established universities in capitals, and these institutions have remained strongly linked to the metropolitan centers of their countries.

The language of instruction is often one of the European languages, but a few countries (Indonesia and Malaysia among the most notable) use indigenous languages. Some universities remain closely tied to institutions in the industrialized nations, while others are more independent. The academic profession is in some cases well remunerated and prestigious, while in others it has fared less well. Indigenous elites are trained within the country in some areas, while in others students are sent overseas. The autonomy of institutions also varies, with a substantial amount of freedom being permitted in some nations even where parliamentary systems do not operate. In others, universities are subjected to rigid control and sometimes to repression. It is very difficult to generalize about the causes for these differences, since political orientation and economic system do not account for all of them.

THE ANATOMY OF INEQUALITY

The anatomy of international inequality is complicated, but some of the key factors are worth describing as they are crucial to understanding the status of universities in the Third World. The following elements contribute, in varying degrees, to this situation.

1. The historical tradition of universities is a Western tradition, and has little if anything to do with the intellectual or educational traditions of the Third World.[71]

Although many Asian and African countries had highly developed indigenous educational ideas and systems, the institutional models followed in the creation of modern schools were uniformly Western in nature. The impact of adapting a basically foreign education model has been considerable. The institutional models, the curriculum, the pedagogical techniques, and basic ideas concerning the role of higher education in society were all Western. The particular Western institutional model followed had to do with the accident of colonial domination, although even those Third World nations—such as Thailand, China, and Ethiopia—that were never formally under colonial control used Western models. In these latter cases, however, the choice was at least up to the countries involved. It is significant that no Third World nation, regardless of political ideology or orientation, has altered, in a basic way, a Western university model. Substantial efforts have been made to adapt the curriculum to suit perceived national needs, but even these have been only partly successful. The lack of textbooks and scientific background, and the fact that most Third World academics have been trained according to Western models have made adaptation difficult.

2. The language of higher education in many Third World nations is a Western language. Colonial authorities, without exception, established higher education in their colonies through the use of European languages. This educational policy was linked to the use of Western languages for administrative, commercial, and legal purposes as well. The impact of the use of Western languages was—and remains—immense. These languages became the languages of power and of wealth, and they were the languages of prestige. European languages were also quite limited in the extent of their use. Only a tiny minority was able to use the colonizer's language—in India perhaps 1 percent of the population was literate in English at the end of the colonial period. The proportion is significantly higher now but is still a small part of the population. Much of higher education is still conducted in English. Similar proportions were probably common in other colonies. The impact of the colonial language has remained strong throughout the Third World. Even Third World nations not under colonial domination were influenced by European languages—there was a debate in Japan in the nineteenth century concerning the possible use of English in some parts of the educational system. While some Third World nations have attempted to substitute indigenous languages for Western media—and in a few cases these efforts have met with considerable success—the impact of Western languages in the Third World remains very great.

The importance of language cannot be overemphasized when discussing the development of Third World education—and even of the growth of the nation state. Where European languages continue to hold sway in higher education, as they do in many Third World countries, universities are automatically cut off from the majority of the population, and they are inevitably oriented even more than would normally be the case toward the European or North American center. Despite considerable efforts in Indonesia and some attempts in India, Pakistan, and a few other nations, European languages continue to occupy a key place in higher education, especially in the elite sector.[72] Language has sociological and psychological implications as a status-maintenance device and as a means of conferring elite membership. It should be added that the means of effectively using indigenous languages for all purposes, particularly in multilingual societies, are complicated and often politically volatile.[73]

3. Third World nations are basically "consumers" of knowledge, dependent on industrialized nations for research, interpretations of scientific advances, and, in general, information. The vast bulk of the world's scientific research is done in the industrialized nations, since funds and facilities for research exist there. If anything, the research gap is increasing, as knowledge grows rapidly and research in many fields requires more sophisticated and expensive equipment. There is a danger that the Third World will be priced out of the research market. It is perhaps significant that one of the key demands of a United Nations conference on science and technology was that more funds be spent on research and development in the Third World. Even though the amounts mentioned were quite small by world research standards, the industrialized nations were not favorably inclined toward the proposals.

There are special problems with developing research capabilities in the Third World, although most agree that such capabilities are important since much of the research done in industrialized nations is of limited relevance in the Third World. Academic institutions, for example, generally place only limited stress on research and publication as criteria for advancement, and a number of Third World nations have chosen to build separate research laboratories, thus depriving the universities of important infusions of funds and talent. Scientists in the Third World are often reluctant to engage in "applied" work, feeling that the international community rewards "basic research."[74] Further, the limited scientific development in the Third World has in many cases been encouraged and funded by Western sources, perhaps skewing its orientation. Thus, the development of research capability is a manifold problem related to indigenous Third World personnel and financial resources, the rapid growth and increased cost of research in the industrialized countries, and the difficulty of developing indigenous models in a world dominated by Western scientific thought and orientation.

4. The means of communication of knowledge are in the hands of the industrialized nations. The major scholarly journals, publishers, bibliographies, and libraries are in Europe and North America. This simple fact determines the flow of knowledge and means that in many ways the needs of the Third World are not met. Journals focus on their own national audiences for the most part, and pay little attention to developments in the Third World. Publishers are largely uninterested in Third World authors. And, perhaps most serious, there are relatively few outlets for scholarship, creative writing, and research reports by Third World intellectuals.[75] The implications of the control of communications networks are considerable and tend to orient the academic systems of the Third World toward the industrialized nations.

Recent innovations such as the Internet present a complex picture. Some have argued that this technology will free the "have nots" from dependence on the industrialized world. To some extent, there is some potential in this direction. But many in the Third World, even in academic institutions, do not have access to the Internet.

Further, the Internet, databases, and other products that have emerged from the use of computer networks are owned by the industrialized nations, and the networks and products that have emerged reflect their needs.

5. Large numbers of students from the Third World study in the industrialized nations.[76] More than 450,000 students from foreign countries study in the United States, the majority from Third World nations. Many thousands more study in Britain, France, and Germany, and other European nations. Perhaps one million students study outside their home countries. While assessing the impact of foreign study is difficult, training in the industrialized nations clearly orients students to the educational system, intellectual directions, methodological focuses, work habits, and professional expectations of the "host" country. While many students do not return home, resulting in the much discussed brain drain, large numbers do return, and many tend to orient themselves to the educational experiences they underwent in the industrialized world. While the skills obtained in the West are of importance to the Third World, the "unanticipated" results of foreign training often have an impact as well.

DEPENDENCY AND NEOCOLONIALISM

All the above factors are perhaps inevitable results of an international system based on deep historical and contemporary inequalities. These, and other, elements reinforce the peripheral status of universities in the Third World. They also make these universities dependent, in varying degrees, on educational and intellectual structures in the industrialized nations. There is little that can be done about these realities. In addition to these inevitable results of an international system, the policies of both industrialized and Third World nations reinforce and sometimes deepen the inequalities. Foreign aid projects, cultural exchange programs, and similar policies often serve to continue relationships of dependency. The use of Western "experts" often reinforces Western models of academic research, the curriculum, and other aspects of higher education. The provision of Western textbooks may have the same result.[77] The industrialized nations supply expertise in part to maintain their influence over Third World universities, in part for altruistic motives, and perhaps also out of a sense of intellectual superiority. In some cases, foreign assistance is "tied" to products and services produced in the donor country, further linking the recipient to the donor. While educational aid is but a small part of broader political struggles, there is no question but that it is linked to these struggles.

Governments are not alone in pursuing policies that maintain their advantageous role in the Third World.[78] Corporations like International Telephone and Telegraph, McGraw-Hill Publishers, Longmans Publishers, and many others are important forces in the communications fields in the Third World. Governments of industrialized nations often work closely with multinational firms. The now defunct Informational Media Guaranty Program of the United States government, which underwrote the export of American books by private publishers, is an example of this cooperation.

As Philip Coombs has pointed out, education is a "fourth dimension" of foreign policy because it is seen to fit integrally into the national objectives of industrialized nations.[79] Third World nations accept foreign educational assistance for a variety of reasons. To some degree, it is felt that any help is a useful increment to very perplexing problems of development. In addition, it is not unnatural for academics who were trained in Western universities to feel that the continued use of Western models and equipment is natural, even if in some cases this impedes indigenous development. The whole question of foreign assistance in education is a complicated one. For the purposes of this chapter, it is only necessary to point out that such assistance is a double-edged sword, maintaining patterns of dependence, while at the same time often providing needed technical help.

PERIPHERAL CENTERS AND CENTRAL PERIPHERIES

This discussion has argued that Third World universities are peripheral in an international academic system and that this situation is the result of a combination of factors, most of which reflect international inequalities in wealth, power, and resources. The policies of the industrialized nations have also reinforced established relationships, thus helping to maintain the peripheral status of the Third World. It is not necessary to analyze the current status of universities in the Third World fully, as the situation is fairly evident to most observers. It is, however, useful to discuss several key issues in order to indicate both the nature and the complexity of the peripheral status of these institutions.

Books and journals are an important element of the knowledge communication process. The world's book production is concentrated in the industrialized nations. This is especially true for scholarly books, research reports, and other publications that are crucial for universities. It has been estimated that 62 percent of the world's periodicals in the social sciences are published in the United States, Britain, and France.[80] The prestigious scientific journals are virtually all published in the West and largely in the United States, Britain, France, and to a lesser extent Germany. Scholars orient themselves to these journals, write in the languages in which the journals publish—largely English, at present—and to some extent address the research issues that are important to the major journals. There is a similar phenomenon in the world of books. The major publishers are located in the industrialized nations, and scholars in the Third World often prefer to have their books published by metropolitan publishers since these firms offer greater remuneration and exposure to an international audience. Books are not readily accessible in the Third World, and the location of publishing firms, patterns of international trade, and the language of publishing in the sciences all reinforce the peripheral status of Third World universities.

There are relatively few universities in the world that produce major research discoveries and have the laboratories and other facilities to support high-level research. These universities are located in the industrialized nations, and constitute a small elite among universities. Even in the United States, there are major differences among universities. Of the more than 3,000 American campuses, only about 100 were selected to receive federal government science grants of more than $50 million per year. The top 10 universities received more than $300 million annually in research support from all sources. Third World universities simply do not have the resources for advanced scientific research in most fields, and they are, in this sense, at a considerable disadvantage. Funds are lacking, the infrastructures do not exist, and the nucleus of creative researchers is often too small to permit research work to take place.

Yet, as was indicated earlier, universities play local and regional as well as cosmopolitan roles.[81] In the Third World, universities that are clearly peripheral in an international context are central nationally in terms of training and sometimes in terms of applied research and knowledge dissemination. A number of Third World universities also play an important regional role as well. These institutions act as "mediators" between the central institutions in the industrialized nations and the bulk of institutions in the peripheral nations. These regional institutions often serve as focal points for research and publishing in their areas and attract students and staff from other countries. There is often a good deal of tension, and considerable confusion, between the various roles of these Third World institutions. Government authorities are rarely concerned with the cosmopolitan or international elements of the university but rather demand the production of trained personnel and useful research. The public sees higher education as a means of social mobility in societies with severe economic problems. Faculty members often see themselves as part of an international academic community, and look abroad for models and norms.

A number of universities have emerged as regional centers. Several African institutions, most notably the University of Nairobi, were identified by international organizations and American foundations, and funds provided to assist these institutions achieve international standards of quality.[82] This infusion of funds, visiting staff, and the like has helped these institutions become linked to the international knowledge system and has raised standards of instruction and research. The University of Cairo became a regional center for the Arab world because it is one of the oldest and largest modern universities in the region and is located in the traditional center of Arab culture and publishing—Egypt. The University of Cairo, as other "regional center" institutions, educates large numbers of students from other countries, in this case from the Arab world. The National University of Mexico (UNAM) is a regional center for Latin America for similar reasons. Mexico is a large country and has become the most important publishing nation in Latin America. The university's proximity to the United States, the presence of a large number of foreign staff members, and its large size have made it a leading institution in Latin America. In India, the University of Delhi, one of the country's oldest institutions, has built up impressive strength in a number of fields and for a long period was recognized as the best university in South Asia. Large numbers of students from other countries in the region study there. The University of Delhi has received substantial foreign aid and is located in India's capital. The Indian Institutes of Technology, located in several major cities, have also achieved international status through a combination of significant support from the Indian government, foreign assistance, and the maintenance of high academic standards. One of the newer universities, the Jawharlal Nehru University, located in New Delhi, has also made significant progress.[83]

The regional centers are usually located in the capital cities of important countries, have fairly long traditions of modern higher education, are large institutions by local standards, and in many cases have received substantial foreign assistance. Their status has not only given them added prestige but has promoted them as centers for research, publishing, and scholarship. Their faculty tend to study abroad and to obtain postdoctoral fellowships, they attract visiting scholars, and their libraries tend to be relatively well stocked.

Maintaining the quality and visibility of these universities is sometimes difficult. For example, political and economic problems facing Kenya have had severely negative consequences for the University of Nairobi. After a promising start and considerable foreign assistance, the 1990s brought crisis and deterioration to the university, and it has lost much of its status as a regional center. In the case of the University of Delhi, the relentless pressures of enrollment combined with financial cutbacks have brought progress toward international status to a halt. Nonetheless, these institutions play an important regional role.

In some cases, it has been possible for specific departments or disciplines in Third World institutions to develop a strong research record, thereby becoming part of the international academic community. Some academic departments have specialized in tropical topics with impressive results and become centers of research in these areas. By providing substantial funding in limited areas, Third World universities can build up limited expertise in areas of special relevance to their nations. Such centers are still rare, however, despite the relatively limited resources needed to establish and sustain them.

There is often an implicit conflict between centrality and localism, with pressures on universities from both sides. In some ways, a peripheral, locally oriented institution is better able to serve immediate national needs than a university with strong ties to the international academic system. Such an institution can better train personnel needed for specific national tasks, respond quickly to development needs, and is inclined to be more involved with the immediate problems of the society. On the other hand, its expertise will be limited, it may not be linked to the major trends in research and scholarship, and the technology it provides may be obsolete. A primarily local institution will also be somewhat cut off from new ideas—not only in scholarship but also in broader fields of intellectual life.

EXAMPLES

Several different nations will illustrate some of the problems of the Third World. India is a very large nation with a well-developed university system, a large number of trained scholars, and considerable infrastructure.[84] Kuwait, on the other hand, is a small nation that began to develop higher educational institutions in the 1960s. It has the considerable advantage of virtually unlimited wealth to help in the establishment of new universities but has been hindered by the war with Iraq, which destroyed its existing academic infrastructure. Academic institutions in both nations continue to be peripheral and are likely to remain so.[85]

India now has the third largest university system in the world, but the standards of quality in much of the system are fairly low. In addition, even in the small sector of the system that is concerned with research, graduate training, and participating in the international scholarly world, India faces serious problems. The academic system is in general poorly funded and top-quality laboratories are rare. Libraries tend to be small and often out of date. There is very limited access to Internet-based databases. While there are many Indians who are well trained and quite able, they tend to be geographically dispersed (with many of the best working abroad). Very few Indian universities have the "critical mass" of research personnel, facilities, and the will to produce top-quality research to contribute in the international knowledge system. Perhaps most important, the pressure of numbers of students combined with inadequate financial resources cannot sustain high quality research programs.

Several specialized institutes, such as the Indian Institutes of Technology and the Tata Institute for Fundamental Research, have made solid contributions. But most of the academic system, including the graduate university departments, remains limited in the quality of work. Because the upper levels of the Indian academic system continue to function in English, there is no problem with communicating with scholars in the industrialized world—in many fields there is as much contact between Indian scholars and their colleagues in other countries as there is within the country. While the publishing industry is fairly well developed and a number of specialized scholarly journals exist, there is nevertheless a reliance on books and journals published abroad, since most advanced work is done in the industrialized nations.

India's peripheral status is based on a number of factors. In a few fields, it has come close to a takeoff point in terms of scientific development, but its resources are stretched to the breaking point. Science and research must fight for meager funding with the demands of industry, agriculture, and the other levels of the educational system. India has, in a sense, "overtrained" its personnel, and many qualified Indians leave the country to work elsewhere. The cost to the Indian economy of this brain drain is immense, yet the country cannot offer suitable employment in many fields. While Indian scientists have provided technological expertise for local agriculture and other fields, it is fair to say that much of Indian science is oriented toward metropolitan models, because of the use of English, because of the prestige of Western science, and because of the foreign training of many key Indian researchers. Despite significant investment in science, in relative terms, India remains isolated scientifically in international terms. There is just too little money, too many demands on top-quality personnel, and too much temptation to follow exogenous models. It is significant that the two South Asian scientists to have won Nobel prizes in recent years have both worked abroad—one in the United States and one in England.

Kuwait's problems are, in many respects, the reverse of those in India. Funds for the development of higher education are virtually unlimited, and the problem is one of lack of infrastructure, trained personnel, and clear direction for academic and scientific development. In addition, Kuwait has only a small population and area with which to work. Kuwait University was established in 1966 and has grown to an enrollment of 20,000 students, 6,000 of whom are from other countries.[86] The university began with graduate programs in several fields, but had to abandon the enterprise because of the low quality of the programs. Many have been reestablished. Despite impressive plans, large fiscal allocations, and a committed top leadership, the university has been slow to develop a consolidated campus, and still relies on foreigners (mostly Egyptians) for a significant part of its academic staff. It remains short of middle-level personnel of all kinds. Courses in the science and medical faculties are conducted in English, since textbooks are unavailable in Arabic. This creates problems for many students whose knowledge of English is not adequate. In the arts, social sciences, and education, which use Arabic as the medium of instruction, there are insufficient books in Arabic, and students must use English-language texts, particularly for upper-division courses.

While it is possible that Kuwait's higher education system may be able to develop top-level research and training facilities in a few areas such as petroleum technology, it is unlikely that even with massive expenditures Kuwait University will emerge as a world-class university. The problems of building the infrastructure are too great. The disadvantage of functioning in a language that has yet to develop a significant scientific literature, the continuing shortage of highly trained personnel (particularly for graduate-level research and training), the lack of a clearly understood local "academic ethos," and the small population of the country are all formidable. Expatriate staff—Egyptians, other Arabs, and some Europeans and Americans—have not, generally, participated in institution building. In the Kuwait example, money just cannot buy quick academic development. The problems of a traditional society, lack of infrastructure, small size, and an undeveloped academic culture all hinder Kuwait's emergence as a major university center.

Both of these examples illustrate some of the problems of building universities that can function at the international center of knowledge. Even with the advantage of a long historical development—India's first universities were established in 1857—and a large academic community, India has not been able to develop world—class universities. If Indian policymakers had been able to sacrifice rapid expansion for quality, India might have been able to establish and support such universities, but this was not possible given the political realities. Kuwait's impressive financial resources have not been able to develop a top-quality university, although impressive strides have been made. Massive foreign assistance, such as that provided to the University of Nairobi, has not fully moved that institution to the center. It helped to build the university's infrastructures, and at the same time provided links to metropolitan institutions, which may make independence more difficult in the long run.

Academic peripheries are by no means limited to the Third World. The smaller European nations have recognized their peripheral status, and have in some cases tried to adjust to it. Language is an example of an issue that must be addressed. Increasingly, international scholarship is communicated in English. Universities in Scandinavia and the Netherlands, as well as in the other smaller European nations, have increasingly relied on English as a key language of scholarly interaction, and academics in these countries often communicate in English. A number of academic journals published in Scandinavia and the Netherlands now appear in English in order to be integrated into the international scholarly community.[87] Scholars in the smaller Western European nations regularly study abroad and maintain contacts with academics in the United States or Britain. Australian and Israeli academics feel sufficiently isolated that their universities provide support for them to travel abroad regularly to keep up with current scholarly developments. The academic profession worldwide, with the partial exception of the United States, feels that international links are important and that knowledge of the international research literature is necessary for keeping up with new knowledge.[88]

These universities in the industrialized world are peripheral because they use a peripheral language or are located at great distances from the major academic centers. It is rare that universities in the smaller industrialized nations are considered among the central institutions despite often long academic traditions (Charles University in Prague, for example, is one of the world's oldest universities, dating from 1347). Yet, these institutions are often able to maintain a high level of research productivity, and their facilities are linked to the international academic system. Their problems are of a different magnitude than those of Third World institutions. The existence of long academic traditions, generally adequate financial resources, and the support of public authorities for traditional university norms permit such institutions to function as part of the international academic system, even if not exactly at the center of this system.

REMOVAL OF INEQUALITY

Given the complicated—and perhaps inevitable—nature of centers and peripheries in the international academic world, how is it possible to move from the periphery to the center? A few nations have been successful in transforming their universities and as a result moving to an academic center. The United States is the most successful example. Less than a century ago, American colleges and universities were unquestionably intellectual colonies of Europe—and especially of Britain. Little original research was conducted, and it was not possible to reach the pinnacle of research and scholarship by studying only in the United States. By adapting the emerging German academic pattern—which stressed research and graduate training—by investing large sums in education, by developing an academic system that served national and local needs through applied research and development (and could thereby call on increased financial support), and by slowly building up the infrastructures of scholarship, the United States was able, over a period of a half-century, to build an academic system of great influence.[89] A considerable factor was also the growth in wealth and power of the United States and its industrial development. Similarly, German universities went from a peripheral status in the late eighteenth century to the center of international scholarship by the mid-nineteenth century. Again, a strong commitment to higher education by the state, an increasingly powerful national state, industrialization and a "new idea"—that of research and graduate education—all contributed to the growth of the German university.[90]

More recently, Japanese universities have attempted to improve and to become first-class institutions. Clearly, the University of Tokyo is an internationally recognized institution of excellence, but the Japanese academic system has not developed the eminence and research productivity that the country's present status as a world power might indicate. Insufficient funds have been devoted to higher education, and Japan's industrial and technological development has been in part based on the use of foreign models.[91] The fact that Japanese is not a world language has also hindered the development of world-class universities. The key universities in Taiwan, Singapore, and Hong Kong, among a few other countries, have improved dramatically in the past several decades, yet are not comparable to many top universities in the United States or Western Europe. Sustained economic growth combined with national policies that have supported higher education have fostered this development.

Thus, moving from the periphery to the center is not impossible, but it is very difficult. Most national university systems, especially in the Third World, will simply be unable to make the transition. This does not mean that academic systems should not strive for excellence or that some of the inequalities on the international scene cannot be ameliorated to some extent. It has been the purpose of this discussion to point out, through the use of the center-periphery model, that a seemingly simple goal of removing inequalities as part of a commitment to a new international order is extraordinarily difficult to achieve.

CONCLUSION

This discussion has focused largely on higher education and on the factors that relate to the role of universities in the Third World. But universities and educational policy are linked to larger political, social, and economic factors in society and in an international context. For higher education, there is no dramatic new international order, and none is emerging. The basic world economic and social system remains intact—despite oil crises, worldwide inflation, the emergence of the Third World as a vocal and sometimes effective force on the world scene, and the success of several of the Pacific Rim countries. Neither the wealth transfer brought by the oil crisis of the 1970s nor even the collapse of Communism in the 1990s has significantly changed the basic configuration of the world system of higher education. By and large, the Western industrialized nations have sought, with considerable success, to maintain their power and influence. Foreign aid has not substantially altered the equation of academic inequality, and some have argued that such aid is intended, in considerable part, to maintain the status quo.[92]

The prognosis for major change in the international academic status quo is mixed. The poor will, in general, remain poor. They will not have the resources to develop advanced research capability. Those few Third World nations, such as India and China, that have a large number of skilled individuals and a fairly broad industrial and technological base can develop some advanced capability, as the manufacture of nuclear weapons by those two countries testifies. The majority, however, will remain peripheral in most every sense. A few nations, such as rapidly industrializing countries like Singapore, Taiwan, and Malaysia, have built up impressive academic infrastructures. While it is unlikely that they can catch up fully with the industrialized nations of Europe and North America, some universities in these countries are close to or at top levels of international excellence. Virtually all Third World nations will remain linked to the technological networks dominated by the industrialized West—even those nations, such as Tanzania and China that have tried consciously to alter their development models remain dependent to a considerable degree. Both experiments failed and China and Tanzania have rejoined the international academic system.

If understanding is a prerequisite to change, it may be helpful for the international community to understand the nature of the "old international order" in general terms and the very complex ways in which this order relates to higher education. This chapter has focused on the nature of the international knowledge network in an effort to provide such an analysis. Such a discussion can at least permit those in a peripheral position to understand the nature of their plight and perhaps to ameliorate it to some extent. There are some things that can be done to maximize independence and freedom of choice. The following is a partial discussion of changes that can be implemented without major costs and that can help to ensure a degree of intellectual independence.

A clear and realistic appraisal of the position of a national academic system in its international and regional context can help with planning. The status of a particular system and of institutions within a system is complicated. Some universities can successfully try to build up excellence in some areas, while others may be best suited for knowledge transmission. Most academic systems are to some extent peripheral to the major universities in the industrialized nations, but the nature of that peripherality varies. Those in authority, at both government and in the universities, should also have a consciousness of the nature of the center-periphery relationship.

The building of academic and intellectual infrastructures—such as libraries, journals, publishing houses, laboratories, and the like—will stimulate self-reliance and aid in the establishment of an independent academic culture. The development of such accoutrements of modern intellectual life is not expensive when compared with military equipment or industrialization, but the funds needed are still considerable. It may be possible, in some places, to develop these infrastructures on a regional basis, particularly when a number of small countries are involved. Experiments with regionalization, however, such as the University of East Africa and in the Arabian Gulf region, have not been successful although regionalism remains a promising ideal.

The research function of universities is very important. Even if it is possible to sponsor research in only a few areas—perhaps related to local economic or agricultural conditions and in fields that will foster a national culture—such initiatives will be useful. In many fields requiring expensive laboratories and equipment and a tradition of scientific research, Third World nations will continue to be dependent on industrialized countries, but an independent research base can be established. Such a base will provide an example of a successful research enterprise, has the potential of building up journals and related activities, and may bring the university international and regional recognition. Some Third World nations have been successful in developing a limited research capability.

The question of language, as indicated earlier, is one of the most serious for Third World universities. Attention needs to be paid to national and regional languages as media for intellectual communication, political life, and scholarship. In some countries, reliance on European languages is probably inevitable, but there is no question that much more can be done in the Third World to foster indigenous languages. It may be difficult to shift to an indigenous language for higher education, and there would clearly be some loss of contact with the international scholarly community, which functions in the world languages.

Foreign assistance must be examined carefully for its intended and unintended consequences. Third World nations have, in many instances, been too willing to accept aid without considering the long-term consequences. Even assuming the best intentions on all sides, the implications of assistance projects may be sufficiently detrimental as to make them questionable. Foreign aid programs may in many instances be justified, but careful consideration needs to be given to all such efforts.

The impact of advanced training abroad needs to be examined more carefully from the viewpoint of the Third World. What does the brain drain cost Third World nations? Are the research skills learned by the foreign-educated relevant to local needs?[93] What are the psychological and political impacts of foreign study? What are the direct costs to governments? The answers to such questions, which will differ from nation to nation, should determine the kinds and amount of foreign study encouraged by Third World governments and universities.

Without question, the issues raised in this chapter are multifaceted and complicated. The concept of center and periphery, as applied to the world of universities and particularly to the problems of higher education in the Third World, is a way of thinking about inequalities, institutional and academic hierarchies, and differing roles of academic institutions. While Third World universities function as peripheries in an international system, they are clearly central to their own societies. The problems of adjustment to this dual role are difficult.

3

Twisted Roots: The Western Impact on Asian Higher Education

Two realities shape Asian higher education systems—the foreign origin of the academic model and the challenges of indigenization of the universities as part of the development process. The foreign models differ considerably, as do the indigenization responses of individual countries. Countries that experienced colonialism faced a different reality than nations that were able to use some independent judgment in the adoption of foreign influences. In Asia, as in other parts of the Third World, the impact of Western academic models and institutions has been significant from the beginning, and it remains important even in the contemporary period.[94] This chapter discusses the various aspects of the Western influence on Asian higher education—the initial encounters with colonialism or Western ideas, the period of borrowing, and the continuing Western influence in the context of independence and autonomy.

Western influence is complex and diverse. The colonial powers that influenced Asian higher education include virtually all of the major European nations involved in the colonial enterprise: the Dutch in Indonesia; the British in India, Malaysia, Singapore, and elsewhere; the Spanish—and later the Americans—in the Philippines; and the French in Vietnam. Japan made a late entry into the world of Western institutions and though it chose a variety of foreign influences after the Meiji Restoration in

1868, the German impact was probably the greatest until the United States tried to reshape Japanese institutions after World War II.[95] Japan, in its turn, colonized Korea and Taiwan, where it left its imprint on higher education. China, never formally colonized, was nonetheless subject to significant foreign influences from Germany, France, Britain, Japan, the United States, and, after 1950, the Soviet Union.[96] The direct impact of these Western influences and the interplay between these and indigenous ideas upon education, both during the colonial era and more recently, form an extraordinarily complex story.

There are two basic periods of links between Western and Asian academic systems. The first encompassed the colonial period and ended with the advent of independence in the years following World War II. Even for nations not formally under colonial domination such as China, Japan, and Thailand, the relationship with the West was different prior to 1945. In the postwar era, Western influences have continued, but the relationship altered. Asian nations were able to choose, with increasing self-confidence, from among various Western models and academic practices, and there has been more adaptation than imposition, more selection than wholesale use. Our concern in this chapter is with the postcolonial period, where it is possible to see a fascinating interplay between Western influences and Asian needs.

Overall, the relationship between the West and the Third World has been one of inequality with considerable adaptation by the Third World of Western higher education patterns, especially during the period of colonialism. The Western powers have until quite recently been dominant in political, military, economic, technological, and intellectual terms. With all Asian nations now fully independent, Japan an economic superpower, and the "little dragons" of Singapore, South Korea, Malaysia, Taiwan, and Hong Kong having achieved significant economic prosperity and growth, the situation has dramatically changed; yet Western influences continue to be quite important in an independent and increasingly prosperous Asia. The English language, for example, is the main means of scientific communication throughout the world.[97] The Western academic model continues to be dominant worldwide, and remains powerful in Asia.[98] When one measures intellectual interactions—whether the number of books translated into Third World languages from the major Western languages, or the flow of foreign students across international borders—the balance is clearly in favor of the West.[99] There is little sign of change in this respect.

Despite this broader context of inequality, the end of the colonial era has seen an impressive development of Third World academic and scientific systems and a considerable degree of independence. Nowhere has this been more impressive than in Asia—especially in the newly industrialized countries of the Pacific Rim. Many countries that formerly used Western languages for higher education have shifted to indigenous languages. A majority of India's universities, for example, function in one or more of India's languages, although English remains the main language of research and postbaccalaureate study. Indonesia quickly shifted from Dutch to Bahasa Indonesia after independence. Malaysian universities function in Bahasa Malaysia. Korea and Taiwan dropped Japanese as the language of the university in favor of

Korean and Chinese, respectively. On the other hand, universities in the Philippines and Singapore continue to function mainly in English.[100] Academic models have also been adapted to meet local needs. In some instances, the old colonial models were completely jettisoned. Indonesia, South Korea, and Taiwan are examples of this development. China has experimented with several models, including a purely indigenous approach during the Cultural Revolution that proved disastrously unsuccessful.[101] There has been an impressive development in Asia of an independent scientific establishment: Japan has joined the ranks of the major scientific powers, with world-class academic and research facilities. India, among Third World nations, is the science and technology leader, and has built up pockets of high-tech industry.[102]

Each Asian country has its own pattern of historical and contemporary interaction with the West. In some countries, very close links with the West are strengthened by economic and linguistic factors. Singapore is an example of this phenomenon.[103] Japan has become a full member of the Organization for Economic Cooperation and Development (OECD), the club of the major industrialized nations. While it is in some ways influenced by Western scientific developments, Japan has developed a fully independent economy and academic system.[104] China has exhibited a changing relationship with foreign academic models, first adopting the Soviet model, then rejecting it; in the past two decades, attempting an independent development; and presently looking toward the West, particularly the United States. Thailand has a long history of interaction with different Western academic models in the context of independent development. Each Asian nation has had major encounters with Western academic and intellectual currents and has been influenced by them, but each has reacted in distinct ways and has—with varying degrees of success—developed a functioning and independent academic system of its own. This chapter focuses on some of the common elements of these encounters and also on some of the Asian responses.

THE WESTERN MODEL

Throughout the world—regardless of ideology, economic system, or historical circumstances—a variation of the Western university model predominates. The faculty-based medieval University of Paris is the basic academic framework. Variations on this original academic theme are numerous. Some of the more important later influences came from the Spanish tradition, especially in the case of Latin America and the Philippines. In the former French colonies, mainly in Africa—as well as in many Latin American countries—French orientations toward higher education and the French intellectual tradition continue to be influential.

The British university has been another central model, and is especially important in Asia. The English tradition of collegiate education for an elite, as well as the more egalitarian Scottish model were influential mainly in the large number of countries formerly under British colonial control.[105] British ideas—powerful in the American colonies in the eighteenth century—were combined with other Western European ideas and indigenous patterns to form the American academic model—which itself has been an extraordinarily powerful force, particularly in the post-World War II period. British ideas concerning the role of the university in society, the pattern of governance, the curriculum, and academic culture all had a profound impact. The English language as the foremost language of instruction and scholarship is one of the most important legacies of the British academic and intellectual tradition.

The other major Western academic model to have worldwide implications is that of the nineteenth century German university. The idea that research is a key element in higher education was stressed by Wilhelm von Humboldt, the most important German thinker on higher education and the founder of the University of Berlin. The concept of academic freedom—or, more precisely, freedom of research and of teaching within the academic environment—was also enshrined in the German university. The German academic idea was influential first in Eastern Europe, where German political and cultural influence was strong.[106] It came to dominate higher education in Russia, and it is strong there even now. Perhaps most important from the perspective of the growth of Asian higher education, the German academic idea was one of the three main ideas that shaped the emergence of the university in the United States after 1865 and, shortly thereafter, in Japan. The Americans married the British collegiate idea to the German research emphasis and the concept of advanced postgraduate training to American populist ideals and thus created the contemporary American university, which is now the main academic model throughout the world.[107] The Japanese—after experimenting with several academic models in the late nineteenth century—eventually borrowed most heavily from Germany. While Germany never established universities outside Europe—with the partial exception of an institution in China—the German idea of higher education proved to be extraordinarily powerful.

Every academic institution in contemporary Asia has at its root one or more of the Western academic models. Patterns of institutional governance, the ethos of the academic profession, the rhythm of academic life, ideas about science, procedures for examination and assessment, in some cases the language of instruction, and a myriad of other elements are Western in origin. It can be said that the Western idea of the university is perhaps the most successful of all Western concepts in terms of overseas influence—certainly much more than the "Westminster" parliamentary pattern.

In parts of Asia, the Western model has been transmitted by Asians. Japan, for example, imposed its academic system in Korea and Taiwan, which were under its colonial control during the first part of the twentieth century. It also influenced some Chinese universities.[108] The British-style Indian university was also an example for other South Asian nations and to some extent in the Middle East.

Virtually all of the major Asian civilizations have impressive intellectual traditions; a "high culture" of literature, history, and the arts; and well-developed written languages. Asian civilizations and ideas have also been important influences on other Asian cultures over the centuries, as evidenced by their educational, linguistic, and religious impact prior to the arrival of the West. Buddhism spread from India to virtually all of East Asia where it remains a central religious and intellectual theme. Islam spread from the Middle East to South and Southeast Asia and is also a highly influential religious and intellectual tradition. Chinese culture, language, and religion are found in Korea and Japan.

Asian scientific development prior to the arrival of Western culture was also impressive. Chinese inventions such as paper and gunpowder reflect a high level of scientific knowledge at a period when European science was in a comparatively backward state. It must be remembered that much of the Western intellectual tradition was preserved by Islamic scholars during the European Dark Ages. The development of mathematics and astronomy was advanced in the Islamic world and India. There were also important Asian centers of learning. The al-Azhar in Cairo is today the oldest continuously operating university in the world and remains a key center for Islamic learning.[109] University-like institutions existed in India at Taxila and Nalanda. The Chinese, of course, perfected the examination system for purposes of selection, by meritocratic means, into the civil service. There was, in sum, no shortage of scientific, intellectual, and cultural activity or institutions in Asia prior to contact with Western culture. Further, there was significant Asian influence on Western science and thought in the medieval period. The Jesuits, for example, not only brought European ideas to Asia, but returned with Asian scientific and philosophical concepts, as well as with products.

Despite this rich history, contemporary higher education in Asia continues to follow Western models. While Asian academic systems have been greatly influenced by indigenous forces and are as much an amalgam of influences as they are Western, the impact of the West is clear. While it is impossible to explain the dominance of the Western model in Asia fully in this short chapter, one can point to a number of contributing factors.

Colonialism was a powerful influence. An emerging world economy dominated by the West had inevitable scientific and educational implications. Trade increased between the Western "centers" and Asian "peripheries." The intellectual skills needed to engage in this Western-oriented commerce required knowledge of Western languages, commercial practices, and the like. Colonial powers thus dictated which academic models would be dominant in their colonies. The British exported their academic models, as did the French, Dutch, Spanish, and, later, the Americans. Some colonial rulers were willing to let their new institutions exist alongside traditional institutions, while other colonizers attempted to eliminate indigenous forms. The colonial institutions, invested with the power of the state and linked to developing economic and bureaucratic systems, naturally proved attractive and eventually displaced traditional institutions, which lost much of their purpose.[110]

As a consequence of the industrial revolution, the products and the science of Europe, and later North America, came to dominate much of Asia. The wealth accumulated by the West was, in part, put into higher education and science in order to produce ever more sophisticated products. At the same time, the economic and political fortunes of much of Asia were at a low ebb. Indeed, until quite recently, the only country fully able to adapt to Western industrialism was Japan. Now, Asian nations like South Korea, Taiwan, and Singapore have also joined the industrial club.

While science had at one time been advanced in Asia, the technological development of the nineteenth and twentieth centuries has been largely a Western phenomenon. Scientific research and industrial innovation have been a virtual Western monopoly for more than a century. It is therefore not surprising that Western academic and scientific institutional structures have achieved a great deal of power and authority. In addition, Asian scientific traditions went into decline for a series of complex reasons.

Asian nations—regardless of ideology or stage of development—are trying—sometimes with considerable success—to be involved in Western scientific and industrial developments. Despite a few disastrous efforts in Cambodia and China—during the Cultural Revolution—to develop an independent non-Western—often anti-Western—approach, there is almost universal agreement that Western science and technology are the cornerstones of development. It is not surprising that Western institutional patterns are commonly used to achieve these goals. Indeed, the prototype for successful Third World development—Japan—successfully adapted Western institutional models, including academic models, to assist in development.[111]

There is, in the twentieth century, an international knowledge network, and that network is Western in nature.[112] Most of the world's research and development is carried out in a few Western nations. Virtually all of the key scientific journals are published in the West. The new technologies, such as computer databases, are Western controlled. Most patents are Western in origin. The rest of the world must participate in this network, and consequently, Western institutional models and norms predominate.

The West tries to retain its central position. The expansion of Western cultural and intellectual influence and institutions is in part a reflection of this effort.[113] Indeed, the governments of the industrialized nations have sponsored a web of programs aimed at maintaining their influence. Some of these programs are cultural and intellectual in nature.

These are some of the factors that have contributed to the fact that Western academic models and intellectual and scientific influences have become so powerful in the past century and maintain their strong impact even now. I am not arguing that Western models have simply been imposed on Asian cultures. There has been considerable interplay between foreign institutions and influence and Asian realities. While basic institutional models may be Western, there is a great deal of local initiative as well. The development, and current realities, of higher education in such countries as Thailand, Japan, and China—which were never under direct colonial rule—are particularly interesting from this perspective.

THE HERITAGE OF COLONIALISM

The theme of colonialism is inevitably a part of this historical analysis. For much of Asia, colonialism was the initial point of contact with the West, and its heritage remains relevant. Colonial policies and practices were distinct and, moreover, changed over time. Colonialism is characterized by the domination of one country over another through direct rule. While the relationship is one of force, it is also the case that colonized populations had some degree of initiative and there is always an interaction between the colonizers and the colonized.

It is very difficult to generalize about the colonial experience or its impact on higher education. For much of Asia, the colonial experience was a long one—the Spanish came to the Philippines in the seventeenth century, as did the Dutch to what is now Indonesia.[114] Direct British rule came to India more than a century later, yet British colonial higher education was the most widespread model in Asia.[115] The French were relative latecomers to Vietnam, and the Japanese and Americans, in Taiwan, Korea, and the Philippines, respectively, had short but quite influential colonial roles.

Colonial policies varied considerably. The Dutch were uninterested in higher education and actively curtailed its development until fairly late in their rule. As a result, the number of Western-educated Indonesians was small at the time of Independence. In a sense, this relatively weak colonial higher education infrastructure made it easier for Indonesia to break with Dutch colonial patterns. The Spanish relied heavily on the Roman Catholic Church for educational ideas and practices, and this shaped higher education in the Philippines during the Spanish period. The American colonial authorities moved in a very different educational direction, rapidly expanding higher education during their period of colonial domination in the first half of the twentieth century. The British colonial legacy is quite significant because several Asian nations were ruled by Britain. India, the Jewel in the Crown, was the largest British colony and also the home of early British efforts in higher education.[116] British-oriented academic systems, however, were also established in Sri Lanka, Bangladesh, Pakistan, Malaysia, Hong Kong, and Singapore. The British never actively promoted the establishment of large academic systems, but when local people demanded the development of universities, British colonial authorities attempted to shape the institutions and to control their growth. The early—and from the British perspective, not entirely satisfactory—development of higher education in India partially shaped British policies in its other colonies. Japanese colonial educational efforts in the nineteenth century present a quite interesting case, since Japan had developed its own higher education system only a few years earlier.

It is not possible in this chapter to trace the development of colonial higher education in Asia in its entirety. However, it may be useful to draw some broad generalizations from the Asian experience:

• Colonial authorities always used the language of the mother country for higher education. While in some cases primary and, on occasion, secondary education was conducted in local languages, the universities always functioned in the metropolitan language. The British considered local languages in the early policy debates but opted for English as the medium of instruction. Other colonial powers did not seriously consider alternatives in their language policies. The ramifications of the use of European languages were profound historically and have contemporary implications. The issue of language, as will be seen later, is one of the most perplexing for many Asian nations. In this sense, the heritage of colonialism lives on. The entire academic structure was built in the metropolitan language—teaching and learning, textbooks, scientific research, and communication with colleagues overseas. The fact that several European languages were used, later hindered the integration of Asian higher education. While Indonesia used Dutch, Malaysia functioned in English, and Indochina in French. The Philippines shifted from Spanish to English after the United States took control in 1898.

- Basic academic structures were patterned after metropolitan models, although there were subtle variations. The academic models used had evolved over time in the metropole but did not necessarily have any relevance at all to Asian realities. Governance structures, the organization of the academic profession, the research system, and many other aspects were copied directly from metropolitan models. Thus, universities in Bombay or Singapore resembled their counterparts in London or Leeds. Hanoi's university was similar to a provincial French university, and institutions established in the Dutch East Indies looked like those in Amsterdam or Leiden. In many cases, the colonizers did not export their best academic models but rather attempted to build less expensive and less elite academic institutions in their colonies. Thus, it was the London model that was exported to India rather than that of Oxford or Cambridge.[117]

- The curriculum was very much like that in the metropole and in general was not especially relevant to the needs of Asian societies. It should be kept in mind that the metropolitan institutions themselves did not stress science or research at the time that the models were being exported, and thus it is not surprising that science and research played only a minor role in most Asian colonial institutions. The books used were largely those used in the metropole. In some instances, the curriculum was offered in a watered down format in the colonies, although in general there was considerable continuity with the metropole. Teaching and learning were conducted in a highly formal manner.

- Many of the academic staff, especially at the higher levels, were from the metropole. These expatriate academics reinforced metropolitan norms and values. In some Asian countries, there was little scope for local academics to rise in the hierarchy. Most universities were hierarchical in organization and many were controlled by the chairholding professor—typically an expatriate.

- The Indian colonial university has been described as characterized by a "culture of subordination," in which academic freedom was limited and strict controls were kept on staff and students alike.[118] This was also true of most other colonial universities. Colonial authorities were very much concerned about the loyalty of the universities and of their graduates and students, making a considerable effort to ensure that loyalty and to weed out "undesirable" elements.

* Despite the controls over them, the colonial universities were sources of cultural, political, and intellectual ferment. University-based indigenous intellectuals in country after country in Asia were responsible for the growth of nationalist ideas, cultural renaissance movements, and modernizing ideas. In a sense, the colonial universities became the seedbeds of the downfall of colonialism and the emergence of independent nations. University-trained intellectuals were the key nationalist leaders virtually everywhere. While religious fundamentalism may be a contemporary force in many countries, the generation that achieved independence and, in a sense, created the modern nation-state in Asia was trained in the colonial universities and espoused ideas learned there.

* The structures of communication and the academic culture of the colonial universities stressed contact with the metropole. As a result, contacts among the universities of Asia were minimal. Divided by language and by differing institutional models and orientations, the Asian institutions looked toward the colonial power and not to other countries in the region.

These elements of the heritage of colonialism shaped the nature of the Asian universities and remain a powerful influence today. The colonial heritage can be seen in the contemporary Asian university—from obvious elements such as the language of instruction to subtle factors such as senior common rooms and the nature of the academic hierarchy. No discussion of Asian higher education can be complete without careful consideration of the impact of the colonial experience.

THE NONCOLONIZED HERITAGE: JAPAN, CHINA, AND THAILAND

Three key Asian nations were never colonized, thus the impact there of Western higher education, while significant, was different from what it was in countries that were at one time colonies. Japan, China, and Thailand had varying degrees of independence to develop higher education without direct foreign domination. The fact that these three countries have university systems that are largely Western in terms of their basic organizational models is significant. The historical development of higher education in these countries is also noteworthy, not only because they are large Asian nations but because they illustrate how Western influences developed under conditions of independence.

Japan—because of its contemporary importance as a major economic power and also because of its own experience until 1945 as a colonial power—is a very important case. In all three countries, it became clear to indigenous elites that there had to be an "opening" to the West because of the demands of Western economic, military, and political interests. Thus, the decision to "modernize" along Western lines was not a truly independent one since without such development, Western and perhaps colonial penetration would have likely been inevitable. Japan reluctantly opened itself to Western commerce in the mid-nineteenth century after an American naval force entered Japanese waters. After the Meiji Restoration in 1868, Japan plunged actively into a process of Western-style modernization that transformed the nation and made Japan a major Asian power by 1905, when it defeated Russia in the Russo-Japanese War. Higher education was an important part of that modernization process. The newly established universities were among the key conduits for new knowledge and technology as well as for training the Japanese to function in an industrialized society. The universities helped to translate essential materials from European languages into Japanese. It was immediately clear to the Japanese that they had to find an appropriate model of higher education and rapidly develop a university system suitable for transmitting Western knowledge. Japanese were sent abroad to study—interestingly, students were sent to a number of Western nations in order to bring back different ideas. Foreign scholars were invited to Japan as well, and there was even some discussion of using a foreign language—English—as a medium of instruction in higher education. Several Western university models were considered, and it was decided to use elements of the German university, since nineteenth-century Germany was close to Japan in terms of its goals for development. Furthermore, the German university was seen to be one of the most lively and innovative in Europe at the time. The German model continued to dominate Japanese higher education until the end of World War II, when the American occupation authorities imposed American higher education ideas on top of the traditional academic hierarchy. The contemporary Japanese university has powerful elements of its older German origins as well as a number of elements from American higher education.

Japan was able to borrow a number of higher education ideas from other countries and adapt them to suit Japanese national needs. Books were translated from many languages, and foreign teachers were commonplace in Japan during its formative period. In a 30-year period, Japan was able to build a university system that was to be instrumental in Japan's development as a major power. The university became, in a sense, Japan's window to the world of research and technological development. The universities also trained a new generation of bureaucrats who would shape Japan's modernization.[119] The Japanese university was also looked to as a positive example elsewhere in Asia. It was imposed as the model for the growth of modern higher education in Japan's colonies—Korea and Taiwan. It also had some influence in China, where a number of foreign academic ideas were contending for supremacy.

China's higher education development was more difficult than that of Japan—in part because by the nineteenth century China had become an arena for the colonial rivalries of the European powers (and, later, Japan as well), and in part because the Chinese imperial government did not have a clear policy concerning the direction of higher education and science. As a result, no unified policy existed and development was both slow and haphazard. In those parts of China where Western nations held sway, their academic patterns were used when universities were established. German,

French, and British, as well as American and Japanese influences, could all be seen in Imperial China. It is probably fair to say that China's academic development was a mix of independent development and semicolonial influences.[120] In Hong Kong, where British rule was firmly entrenched, higher education was patterned after the British universities and the medium of instruction was exclusively English. In China itself, there was a mix of influences and languages, although for the most part instruction was in Chinese.

Postrevolutionary Chinese academic development exhibits a mix of East-West interactions. Communist authorities simply replaced various Western institutional and curricular models with Soviet ones. Chinese higher education was thus quickly transformed in the Soviet image.[121] After the Sino-Soviet dispute, efforts were made to modify this model and develop a distinctive Chinese approach to higher education. However, these experiments proved unsuccessful and were followed by the massive disruptions of the Cultural Revolution. In the most recent period, China has again looked toward the West for ideas about academic development and is currently engaged in a process of significant higher education reform. Large numbers of Chinese students are now studying in Western countries. It is clear, however, that China has been buffeted by a range of foreign influences over time and that confusion, conflict, and, at times, failure have been evident. China, a large nation with extraordinarily rich cultural traditions, has nonetheless attempted to adopt a number of different academic models from the industrialized nations. China's modern history illustrates some of the problems encountered when foreign academic models are followed. At the same time, it is clear that China's experiments with a "go it alone" educational policy failed. Most recently, China has emphasized Western academic models, and has imposed tuition payments on students for the first time.[122]

Thailand, being smaller than China or Japan, was able to move more deliberately to develop a modern university.[123] The Thai experience exhibits a good deal of independence in choosing an academic model that Thai authorities felt appropriate to Thai needs. The process of university development was much slower and it was largely controlled by the monarchy.[124] The Thai language, although it had not been used for scientific or academic purposes previously, was from the beginning the language of instruction in higher education. Experts from France, Britain, Germany, and, later the United States advised Thai authorities and worked in Thai academic institutions. With the early influence from these three European nations and significant contemporary impact from the United States, Thai universities today exhibit a variety of foreign influences.

The experiences of these three noncolonized Asian nations are significant in many respects. It is clear that in all three countries—especially in Japan and China—pressure from the West demanded an educational response as these nations carved out their place in the world, maintained their independence, and developed their scientific and administrative capability. The educational response was in all cases to adapt Western institutional and other models in the development of postsecondary education. While no model was forced on any of these countries, there was much external pressure. Each country attempted to find the best available institutional structure for its needs. Nonetheless, in the end, the institutions, curricula, and scientific culture were quite similar to Western prototypes.

THE CONTEMPORARY IMPACT OF THE WEST

Asian academic systems function in an international knowledge network. The continuing impact of the West is significant throughout Asia, although it varies and is exhibited in different ways. Even Japan—fully industrialized, wealthy, and highly educated as it is—remains affected by Western academic, scientific, and curricular developments. It is not possible to discuss all Western impacts in this chapter. We shall, instead, focus on several important factors in an effort to stress how the West continues to play a key role in Asia.[125]

The influence of the English language is both pervasive and subtle. It is not just a scientific language and the medium of instruction in a number of Asian nations, it also reflects a specific scientific culture. Every Asian nation must cope with the worldwide role of English. English holds close to a monopoly on the international distribution of scientific knowledge. At least half of the world's 100,000 scholarly journals are published in English, including most of those circulated internationally. Most databases are in English. English is the predominant language of international scientific meetings. A majority of the world's foreign students study in English-speaking nations.[126]

English has significantly influenced Asian higher education. Britain was the major colonial power not only in India, but also in Malaysia, Singapore, Hong Kong, Burma, Pakistan, Bangladesh, and Sri Lanka. The United States was the colonial power in the Philippines and played an important role in Korea, Japan, and China. Japan turned to English as its main "window to the world" early in the Meiji period. English remains a medium of instruction in higher education in a number of Asian nations—including Singapore (where it is the sole medium of instruction), Hong Kong, India, the Philippines, and several others. It is the chief second language throughout the continent. In many Asian countries knowledge of English is mandatory for advanced graduate study and for academic careers in many fields, including most of the sciences.

The use of English ties Asian academic systems to purchases of books and journals from the major Western nations. It builds up English-speaking academic networks, with Asian academics naturally gravitating toward English-speaking scholars. In countries where publication in international journals is necessary for academic advancement, that publication is predominantly in English-language journals. The increased use of English in higher education in China, for example, is particularly dramatic and will have long-term implications. While many Asian academic systems have shifted from English as the medium of instruction, English remains perhaps more important than ever at the upper reaches of the academic system, for access to research, and for scholarly communication. It is clear that the language used most often among Asian scientists is English.

A very large number of Asian academics, particularly those at the highest ranks in the universities, were educated abroad—largely in the industrialized nations of the West. The impact of foreign training is often considerable, with returnees forging continuing links with Western universities and collegial networks, and keeping an orientation toward Western scholarship.[127] The precise effects of foreign study remain to be analyzed, but in the Asian case, because of the very large numbers of students involved and the continuing ties with metropolitan academic systems, foreign training is a particularly important factor. Many Asian academics have also taught in Western countries, and this has given them a further opportunity to imbibe Western academic orientations and practices. When these professors return home, they frequently assume leadership positions in local universities. The impact of expatriate professors, largely from Western industrialized nations, in Asia is also significant. In a few countries, such as Singapore and Hong Kong, a sizable proportion of the academic staff is expatriate. In others, there are frequently foreign visiting professors and scholars as well as a large number of Western academics who do research in Asia. These individuals have an influence as well since they are representatives of the prestigious metropolitan academic systems of the West. In short, the large-scale exchange of academics and students is a source of Western impact. In general, Western academic institutions are not greatly affected by Asian scientific and cultural models, even though there are large numbers of Asians teaching in the West. The flow is usually from the center to the periphery.[128]

Western scientific products of all kinds are found in Asian universities. Textbooks are an important Western export.[129] Western academic texts are used throughout Asia, sometimes in the original English editions, sometimes in translated versions, and sometimes in adaptations written by local academics but using Western concepts, orientations, and curricular approaches. The use of Western textbooks is, of course, of particular importance because the ideas in them are transmitted to large numbers of Asian university students and the texts help to shape the curriculum in specific disciplines. Western academic journals are the standard of excellence and are the most respected sources of knowledge. Asian scholars frequently publish in these journals in order to have access to the international knowledge network. These journals help to set the agenda for research. Also, Western scientific equipment is often used—from electron microscopes to computers—and are considered to be the best available. The monopoly on scientific exports has, however, been broken, for Japan and, increasingly, Korea and Taiwan are manufacturing sophisticated scientific instrumentation and publishing their own journals and books.

As noted earlier, Asian universities are all Western in terms of their basic model and organizational structure. Except for unsuccessful attempts in China, there have been no efforts to break dramatically with Western academic structures. The pervasiveness of the Western organizational model and much of the intellectual baggage that goes along with it is notable. Academic hierarchies, the structure of the curriculum, the system of examination, and the very rhythm of academic life are Western in origin and Western in feeling. The idea of the university as a pure meritocratic organization is deeply ingrained—although compromised in Asia, as it is sometimes in the West. The concept of academic freedom is also an accepted norm, although in the Asian context it is often significantly constrained by political authorities worried about the loyalty of the academic community.[130] The point here is that a pattern of academic organization is not only a series of structures—such as the hierarchy of academic ranks and the idea of the department or the chair—but is also accompanied by ideas, norms, and values about the nature of higher education and the university. Thus, in adapting primarily Western models of organization, Asian universities may have also accepted underlying Western values that may not accurately reflect their own culture and traditions.

The impact of contemporary Western academic ideas and structures is, indeed, powerful. When considering expansion, innovation, or reform, Asian universities consider internal realities while looking to Western ideas and practices. The American academic model has, in the past several decades, been particularly attractive.[131] The United States not only has a large and successful academic system, but its universities have also been significantly involved in research and have pioneered the growth of a mass higher education system. Asian nations frequently want to move in both of these directions. Further, many Asian academics have been trained in the United States and naturally gravitate toward the American academic orbit. The American academic system is also somewhat more "democratic" than the more hierarchical chair models of Germany, or even Britain, and thus appeals to universities wishing to provide for the maximum participation of all segments of the academic staff. The American land-grant idea has been a powerful one in many developing nations.[132] This concept stresses the role of the university in directly serving the state and the community. Land-grant-style institutions have been established in a number of Third World nations—including Nigeria and India—with varying success. Elements of the idea—such as the importance of applied research and service, the role of a practical curriculum, and the direct links between the university and the surrounding community and the wider society—are appealing to Asian nations since these are key goals for emerging academic systems.

American academic concepts such as organization by departments rather than around the professorial chair, the notion of general education at the undergraduate level, the idea of continuous assessment rather than examinations at the end of degree study, and the inclusion of multidisciplinary centers to stimulate creative thinking and research have become as commonplace in Asia as they are in the United States.[133] When new institutions are established in Asia, they are often consciously patterned on a particular Western university or on a key Western academic idea.[134] Academic planning committees frequently include professors or administrators from Western nations in order to take advantage of their expertise.

These are a few examples of the contemporary importance of Western ideas and models on Asian higher education. It is by no means surprising that Asian academic institutions follow Western trends. Asian institutions are patterned on Western models and many of the innovations in the West have direct relevance to Asia. The fact that many Western nations—particularly the United States—have previously undergone the stages of higher education growth and development that Asian nations are now experiencing also makes Western models attractive.

THE INDIGENOUS RESPONSE TO WESTERN HIGHER EDUCATION

Asian universities are not simply copied from Western institutions. A great deal of adaptation occurs. The fact is that Asian institutions of higher education reflect their social, historical, cultural, and political contexts at least as much as they do the Western models on which they are based. Asian universities are hybrids, combining elements of several different cultures.[135] The Western academic culture and organization predominate but are shaped by indigenous influences.

It is clear that total rejection of Western academic ideas has not worked. There have been efforts to establish fully indigenous systems of higher education or to ignore higher education altogether. The rejection of Western higher education by the Muslim elites in India in the late eighteenth and early nineteenth centuries succeeded only in relegating Muslims to an inferior place in society as the subcontinent moved toward independence.[136] This feeling of educational disadvantage was a contributing factor in the emergence of the idea of a separate state for Muslims in South Asia—Pakistan. The Muslims tried vainly to keep their traditional power by holding to traditional values and rejecting Western higher education. The Hindus, and other groups, were happy to fill the vacuum that was created. In another case, Japan—prior to the Meiji Restoration in 1868—kept Western influences of all kinds at bay, and had Japan not moved quickly after 1868, it would have likely been unable to keep its full independence. In the more recent period, Chinese experiments with a rejection of the established academic institutional models—Western in origin but with Soviet overtones after 1950—proved disastrous.

In India, the rather cumbersome British-based academic system inherited from the colonial period remains basically intact, although it has been modified. Some of these changes are universally criticized. For example, pressures from the middle classes and others have forced a massive expansion of higher education, so that a university degree is of modest value in securing remunerative and prestigious employment in many fields.[137] Further, the concept of meritocracy has been vitiated by the growth of influence peddling in academic appointments and widespread dishonesty in the centrally evaluated university examinations. Mass higher education plays as much a political and social role as it does an educational one in India.

In Malaysia, the original elitist British university has been significantly modified to make it more relevant to local needs.[138] One of the most important decisions—a common one in many Asian nations—was to change the medium of instruction from

English to the local language, Bahasa Malaysia. The ethnic politics of the nation is played out in higher education, as it is in other spheres of life, and thus pure meritocracy has been diminished. *Bumiputra* (Malay) students are given preference over the other two major racial groups in the country, the Chinese and the Indians. The new universities that have been established are as much American as British in their organizational structure.

Academic freedom has been partially restricted in some Asian countries and this is a matter of considerable controversy. The contemporary Western concept of academic freedom includes not only the traditional German idea that the university teacher should have freedom of research and teaching in his or her field of specialization but also the notion that the academic profession should have complete freedom of expression, on and off campus, in virtually all fields, subject only to the laws of libel and related penalties. Western academic freedom also includes virtually complete freedom to publish, not only the results of research and scholarship, but other writings as well.[139] In some Asian countries, such as Japan, the Philippines, and India, virtually all of the norms of Western academic freedom are accepted. In others, however, political realities have placed restrictions on academic freedom. In China, the restrictions are severe and academic freedom, in the Western sense, is not accepted as an academic norm. In Singapore, Malaysia, and Taiwan certain topics are considered highly sensitive for research and analysis by academics. In Taiwan, some kinds of research relating to mainland China are subject to political controls and analysis of some aspects of Taiwanese society is considered sensitive. In Malaysia and Singapore, potentially volatile ethnic and religious questions must be treated with extreme care by the academic community. Both countries have governments that are quite sensitive to criticism, and academics can face problems if they are too critical of government policy—although it is very rare that professors are jailed or lose their jobs because of the publication of academic materials.[140] In Indonesia, there is an expectation that academics should belong to the ruling political party, Golkar.

In Western countries, it is expected that academics, particularly those in the senior ranks, should have permanent (tenured) appointments as one means of protecting them from violations of academic freedom and to ensure freedom of teaching and research, unfettered by fear of loss of employment. While the tenure system has come under some criticism in the West—in Britain, permanent appointment for new university staff was abolished by the Thatcher government—in general, the system is well entrenched and almost universally honored. The approach to tenure in Asia shows considerable variations on the Western theme. A few countries, such as Japan, use the basic Western tenure system and guarantee academic appointments—as Japan does for many other jobs—for life. In India, in the postgraduate university departments, there are strong guarantees of tenure and generally untrammeled academic freedom, whereas college (undergraduate) staff in India have weak job protection and firings are not infrequent. In Taiwan, however, there are no permanent appointments in higher education. All academic staff are appointed for renewable two-year terms. While renewal is virtually automatic and, in practice, most academics have de facto tenure, the lack of de jure job protection creates feelings of insecurity, especially among academics in the social sciences. In a number of countries, including China, Korea, and Indonesia, it is expected that academic staff will have job protection. However, guarantees of tenure are weak and scholars who express views at odds with government, or sometimes university policies, can easily find themselves in serious difficulties.

Asian academic systems have, in general, adopted national languages as the main medium of instruction and discourse in higher education. In some countries, such as India, more than one language is used in higher education but English remains a language of instruction, especially in the sciences and at the postbaccalaureate level. Indian universities also offer instruction in the national language, Hindi, and in a dozen regional languages. The bulk of undergraduate instruction is now in an Indian language. Textbooks have been provided in these languages for most undergraduate specialties, although English books are still widely used in the postbaccalaureate curriculum. Japan has always offered postsecondary instruction exclusively in Japanese, and pioneered the translation of textbooks and other scientific books into Japanese. Nonetheless, English is a major scientific medium in Japan, and it is a required language for virtually everyone in the universities. As noted earlier, Malaysia shifted its academic system from English to Bahasa Malaysia more than a decade ago, and while there were serious problems in adjusting to the new language and in providing books in that language, the transition was made.[141] Most other Asian nations use indigenous languages for higher education, and while most have problems in providing textbooks—particularly at the upper levels—and research materials in local languages, the system works well. The Philippines has made a few efforts to use its Tagalog-based language in higher education, but English remains entrenched, as it does in Singapore. In Hong Kong, English is the predominant language of higher education, although there is also a university that uses Chinese as the medium of instruction. Language choice was a key element of indigenization in Asian higher education, and while transitions were difficult, change has taken place.

While it is clear that Asian universities are patterned on Western models, it is also the case that every Asian nation has adapted this model to meet local needs and realities. In some cases, careful plans for indigenization of higher education have resulted in change. In others, political and other pressures have resulted in accommodation. The fact is that Asian universities are as much Asian as they are Western. The process of change, accommodation, and growth continues and the Western model continues to evolve.

CONCLUSION

Asian universities are affected by the industrialized nations of the West in important respects. The historical model of the Asian university is Western, and the basic ethos, organizational structure, and curricular development are significantly based on

Western traditions. In many cases, the original language of higher education in Asian nations was Western as well. There are also key contemporary Western influences. The overwhelming fact is that North America and Western Europe produce the bulk of the world's scientific research, publish most of the scientific and academic books and journals, and spend the major portion of the world's research and development funds. English is the main scientific language in the twentieth century. The large majority of the world's foreign students come from the developing nations to study in the industrialized nations. Contemporary scientific culture is basically Western—created in the West and communicated in Western languages. Most of the rest of the world recognizes that they must accommodate this reality.

Asian nations have made impressive strides in creating an autonomous academic and scientific culture. Academic systems, while remaining Western in organizational structure, reflect national needs and orientations. Indigenous languages are widely used. Indigenous scientific capabilities have been built up, and subjects of special importance to Asian nations are studied. In a few Asian nations, notably Japan, India, and to some extent China, a scientific publication system has been created. While Asian academic systems generally look to the West and not to other Asian nations, some efforts at regional cooperation have been made.

While no Asian academic model has emerged, Asia has produced a series of variations on Western themes, with accommodation to specific national needs and realities. Some countries have encouraged the growth of large academic systems, with considerable variation in quality; others have maintained a more elitist approach. Research has been stressed in a few countries, while most have academic systems largely oriented toward teaching. Few Asian nations look to the experience of their neighbors; most seek out ideas and models from the West.

Asia is inevitably part of an international scientific system in which the nations of the region play an increasingly important role. Japan is the most advanced scientific power—its highly developed university and research system is now one of the world's academic systems. Nonetheless, Asia, including Japan, will need to relate to scientific developments in the West and will depend on Western science to provide paradigms and models. It is also likely that most Asian countries will look to the West as the "gold standard" for higher education. However, the larger Asian nations—such as India, China, and Japan—have already become part of the academic "big leagues." Smaller countries that emphasized their universities—such as Singapore, Taiwan, and South Korea—have also made impressive strides in developing "centers of excellence" in higher education.

4

The American Academic Model in Comparative Perspective

Much has been written about the history and contemporary status of American higher education. As the world's largest education system and the most productive in terms of research, knowledge production and distribution, and training of high-level personnel, the American academic system naturally has influence worldwide. The purpose of this chapter is to discuss key elements of the development of the American academic system in the context of its relevance for other countries. Most of the discussion focuses on the American system in its national context.[142] Without question there is much that can be learned from the American experience—from both its successes and failures. The American university system was the first to confront the phenomenon of "mass" higher education and has been involved for more than a century in direct service to society and in the application of research to agriculture and industry.[143] The American academic system is also quite diverse, ranging from research universities at the top of the system, to undergraduate colleges, comprehensive universities, and community colleges.[144] Some segments of the system are highly selective and place great emphasis on research, while others provide virtually universal access. Thus, generalizations are difficult, but at the same time, there are aspects of the American academic system that may be relevant to a variety of problems and institutions in other countries.

Because the United States has a large and powerful academic system, because

English is the key language of scholarly communications, because the majority of internationally circulated journals and many of the most prominent academic publishers are in the United States, and because many scholars and policymakers overseas have studied in the United States, its universities are a powerful attraction. This attraction is not limited to Third World nations, it is also evident in the industrialized nations of Western Europe, and, since the collapse of Communism, in Central and Eastern Europe as well. In the post–World War II period, many of the changes that have taken place in higher education in Europe have been in a basically "American" direction—expansion, the addition of new fields of study, some democratization of decision making, and the like. Most recently, the pattern of academic organization has also been influenced by American thinking.[145] European academics and planners have carefully studied American higher education policies.[146] It is not surprising that, as a "central" academic system in the contemporary world, the American university should attract considerable attention.

Yet, it is clear that the "transfer" of educational policies and practices must be approached carefully. The history of educational transfer is dominated by the imposition of educational models through colonialism.[147] There are also many examples of voluntary borrowing—the experiences of Japan and Thailand are instructive in this regard.[148] The imposition of foreign education models under colonialism or even the indiscriminate borrowing that took place in the immediate postcolonial era have caused severe problems for Third World educational systems. The use of a foreign language for education has caused severe dislocations although the language situation in many nations is quite complex. The focus of educational systems on metropolitan instead of indigenous concerns has also had negative implications for academic institutions and for society. It has been a common complaint in India and other excolonial countries that the focus of higher education was on training a subservient elite for the colonial rulers rather than for building an independent nation.[149] Despite these and other complaints, the Western academic model continues to dominate worldwide. The metropolitan centers continue to have a powerful pull on the peripheries. The metropolitan languages, English and French, remain a powerful force in higher education and research, and English especially is growing in influence. Metropolitan academic models are the international standard.

Despite the heritage of colonialism and the continued impact of the international academic system, there has been significant independent academic development. In Southeast Asia, for example, the early decision in Indonesia to shift the medium of instruction to Bahasa Indonesia and the example of institutions like the Dewan Bahasa dan Pustaka (National Book Agency) in Malaysia are significant. In Thailand, the Ramkhamhaeng Open University is an interesting innovation, while the Philippines has developed a distinctive approach to higher education despite the continuing impact of the American academic model. Thus, there is a combination of influences and impacts evident in the Third World. It is in this complex context that any consideration of further borrowing must take place. It is critically important that those involved in educational reform and change be aware of these traditions and understand the international academic system and its implications.[150]

A comparative approach has significant benefits. It permits a broad perspective and an understanding of how other societies have attempted to solve their problems. Problems can be examined in a comparative context and solutions critically evaluated. This approach raises possibilities, and warns of problems. It lets policymakers look at the implications of specific solutions in a comparable society. In contrast to the situation in the sciences, it is not possible in the field of higher education policy to create an experimental situation. A comparative perspective provides an opportunity to examine alternatives. Yet, it is seldom possible to borrow an institution or even a specific policy from abroad successfully without considerable modification and adaptation. And the specific details of the necessary modification are seldom clear. Thus, a comparative approach can raise consciousness and indicate direction, but it is seldom possible simply to graft external solutions onto a domestic problem. Where this has been tried—as in the export of the American land-grant concept to Nigeria, India, and other countries—the results have been mixed and, in most instances, quite different than anticipated by the planners.

Thus, this chapter is based on several underlying assumptions. One is that a comparative perspective is useful for analysis but that it is seldom possible to borrow institutions or policies from abroad without significant modification and a careful understanding of the context in which the policy has developed as well as the situation in which it will be applied. Third World and other academic institutions are in a situation of inequality in an international academic system that is dominated by the metropolitan universities in the industrialized nations.[151] Modern universities are, after all, Western institutions everywhere, and this fact creates problems of adaptation in non-Western societies and ensures that the Western nations will have an advantage with regard to higher education. Further, it is often in the interests of the metropolitan nations to maintain their dominance in intellectual and academic spheres as well as in politics and economics. Understanding the context both of comparison and of the "world system" in which contemporary universities exist is crucial if Third World nations are to make effective decisions regarding higher education policy. And while it may be tempting to reject all international involvements and to build a truly indigenous academic system, this has not proved possible, even in a nation as large as China.[152] Thus, involvement in the international system is inevitable.

THE AMERICAN ACADEMIC SYSTEM IN HISTORICAL PERSPECTIVE

The American university developed out of specific historical realities, which have shaped the nature of the system. While it is not possible here to present a thorough history of American higher education, it is useful to examine some of the factors that have shaped the American academic system.[153] All university systems are a combination of national and international traditions. The basic university model, of course, is European and goes back to the medieval universities of Paris and Bologna.[154] This is true not only for the universities of North America and Europe, but also in Asia and Africa.[155] In the American case, the earliest models were English and copied from Oxford and Cambridge—at a time when these universities were mainly concerned with the education of Protestant clergymen. More democratic educational ideas from Scotland were also influential. The early American colleges were religiously oriented for the most part and aimed at training a small elite. With a few exceptions, such as Thomas Jefferson's University of Virginia, the curriculum was narrow and strictly followed English patterns.

At the end of the eighteenth and the beginning of the nineteenth centuries, American higher education expanded impressively, but did not change its basic curricular orientation. The colleges provided a fairly narrow curriculum steeped in classical studies and languages. Many of these new institutions were established in the newly settled parts of the nation and were symbolic of the growing egalitarianism of American society. No longer was higher education a preserve of the urban elite, but the middle classes of the new towns and of rural areas gained access to higher education. They did this largely by establishing their own colleges. The new institutions on the frontier copied the established curriculum of Harvard and Yale. Most of them were established by religious denominations concerned not only with general education but also with the inculcation of Christian values. As the number and variety of Protestant denominations grew in America, their educational institutions also expanded. Even today, the American heartland of Ohio, Indiana, Illinois, and even New York and Pennsylvania is dotted with undergraduate colleges, some of which—Oberlin, Swarthmore, Knox, among others—are of very high standard. These colleges are oriented toward liberal education, offer few graduate-level degrees, and have maintained an ethos over the years. This English academic tradition, changed and democratized by the American experience, is one of the key historical elements of the American academic system.

A second, in many ways more complicated, historical tradition involves the emergence of graduate education at the end of the nineteenth century.[156] This development was accompanied by the rise of the public universities, the ethos of public service, and the linking of research to agricultural and industrial development. Facilitated by the Morrill Act of 1862, which provided large amounts of government land to each of the states for the support of public higher education, the great land-grant universities of the Middle West grew and took a key position in the academic system. The land-grant concept, exemplified by the "Wisconsin Idea," argued that the boundaries of the universities are the boundaries of the state, and that a state university has the responsibility of serving the entire population not only with traditional education but also with applied research that would promote emerging industry and agriculture. The University of Wisconsin, along with the state universities in Michigan, Illinois, Indiana, Minnesota, and several other states exemplified this new tradition. They grew rapidly and became America's first "multiversities," offering a variety of services, including traditional undergraduate education, but also extension courses, informal advice, and other services.[157] The land-grant institutions combined several key ideas in American higher education—the concept of direct service to society, the traditional idea of liberal education as the cornerstone of undergraduate education, and the emphasis on research as part of the academic enterprise. These ideas spread from the great state universities to the established private institutions such as Harvard and Yale, and had significant impact on the smaller institutions.

The gradual implantation of research as part of the American enterprise was the other key development of the early twentieth century. In this, the American academic system looked to Germany as the model, imported the German concept of academic research and expanded the German ideal of academic freedom. The German universities did not stress "pure" research, but rather strove to make their research relevant to the emergence of Germany as a major industrial and scientific power. Americans traveled to Germany in large numbers prior to World War I to obtain their doctoral degrees, and they returned to the United States imbued with the importance of research as an integral part of the university. In this regard, Americans returned from their academic "Mecca" in Germany much as students from the Third World now return from metropolitan universities fired with enthusiasm for the academic institutions and ideas that they experienced during their formative student days.

The contemporary American university was shaped by these three influences, two of which were foreign: the English liberal arts tradition, the German research concept, and the synthesis of these elements with the idea of service to the state as embodied by the land-grant public universities. Today's leading academic institutions combine these elements effectively. The American university was shaped by foreign ideas, and a key generation of American scholars, including the leaders—such as William Rainey Harper, who transformed higher education in the early years of this century— were educated abroad at the graduate level.

The changes noted here took place over a long period of time, and they were opposed by important segments of the academic community. It is significant that Harvard became a research-oriented university rather late—only after this new model proved to be successful at institutions such as the newly established universities of Chicago, Johns Hopkins, and Stanford. In some ways, it was easier for academic innovators to establish new institutions than to attempt to reform the existing universities.[158] It was only when the power of the new academic ideas was clear that the established institutions changed.

By 1910, the basic structure of the research-oriented American university was entrenched. While it is true that the large multiversities underwent their most dramatic expansion between 1950 and 1970, their orientation and structure date from the early years of the twentieth century. With the exception of the development of the community college, there have been no major innovations in American higher education in terms of organization and function since that period.[159]

The historical development of the American academic system illustrates several important points. The American system is a combination of a number of foreign influences that melded together in the American context over a period of time. English and

German influences combined with forcefully articulated public policy and substantial financial support to produce the contemporary American university. Reform and development were, in the United States, a slow and often only partly successful process. On many occasions, reformers found it more useful to establish wholly new institutions rather than to change existing universities. As an increasing proportion of the population, particularly the articulate middle classes, became involved with colleges and universities and saw higher education as a means of social mobility, public support for higher education increased.

THE ELEMENTS OF THE AMERICAN ACADEMIC SYSTEM

The American academic system is a complex set of institutions that serve many different needs. The system is a hierarchy, with the research-oriented universities having the highest prestige and most influence.[160] But there is also considerable variety within the system. With more than 13 million students in postsecondary education and more than 3,000 colleges and universities in the United States, diversity is inevitable. It is important to understand the various elements of the academic system and how the elements are woven into a coherent nexus of institutions with different yet overlapping purposes to see the scope of American higher education.

At the pinnacle of the system stands the research university—institutions like Harvard, Berkeley, or Wisconsin. These are the "multiversities" that Clark Kerr discussed in his classic statement of contemporary higher education.[161] The top one hundred American universities dominate research funding from both government and private foundations. They produce a large part of the research output. Their professors tend to dominate the national and, to some extent, the international knowledge networks. The multiversities offer a wide range of academic specialties not only in the arts and sciences but also in applied areas such as management, medicine, and even hotel administration. These are the most prestigious institutions in the country, and they produce influential policymakers and the successive generations of the academic profession. The research function and graduate education generally are the most important missions of these institutions, although they offer a full range of undergraduate programs. Just under these top universities is a somewhat larger group of perhaps two hundred research-oriented universities that have aspirations to greatness and follow the trends set by the academic elites. Many of these institutions are excellent in their own right, but in the current increasingly competitive and fiscally constrained academic environment, it is more difficult to join the elite.

A second major category of institutions is made up of the undergraduate arts and sciences colleges. These range from a few of the most prestigious and competitive academic institutions in the nation to a large number of four-year colleges in both the public and private sectors that educate large numbers of students but have no pretensions to greatness. There is some diversity among this large number of institutions, although most are rather similar. They offer a basic education in the liberal arts with some specialization in an academic or vocationally oriented field toward the end of the four-year curriculum. Some of these colleges, particularly in the public sector, also offer limited graduate programs, especially at the master's level. The more prestigious liberal arts colleges retain many of the traditions of the English curriculum and are the inheritors of the liberal tradition in American higher education. It is somewhat difficult to generalize about this sector given the variation in institutional prestige, but in general there is some commonality in curricular orientation and direction. Many of the midlevel four-year liberal arts colleges in the private sector currently have severe enrollment problems because of demographic changes and alterations in student interest, and a few have closed their doors.[162]

The third major segment of the academic enterprise is the community college, a uniquely American institution that stems directly from the American commitment to "open access" to higher education. The community college sector enrolls close to one-third of all American students in postsecondary education, and at present is the only major segment of the system that continues to grow. Community colleges generally offer two-year degrees called "associate" degrees. Their curriculum is varied, with a stress on providing applied and vocational training in a range of fields that lead directly to employment such as data processing, restaurant management, metal working, automobile mechanics, and many other fields. In addition, most community colleges provide some liberal arts courses that are intended in part as an exposure to general education for vocational students and in part as a "transfer" curriculum for students who wish to obtain a bachelor's degree from a four-year liberal arts college or a university by transferring after two years. The community college provides virtually open access to anyone who has completed secondary education—in general no entrance examinations are given and, with the exception of some high-demand major fields, there is little competition for entry. One of the major purposes of the community college is to provide a means of social and occupational mobility for segments of the population that have been disadvantaged. Community colleges are available for individuals of varied age groups as well. As Burton Clark has indicated, the community college is intended as an "open door" institution.[163]

The American academic system is intended to provide mobility between and among its various segments, and there is indeed some mobility. In general, however, a student entering one of the segments does not transfer to another. The system is also hierarchical in nature, with the research-oriented universities at the top dominating the others and setting the pattern for curricular and other developments. Funding patterns reinforce the basic inequalities in the system. Generally, the universities are better funded than the other segments. Community colleges, with a few exceptions, are public institutions that are funded by local government agencies with little help from the larger (and usually wealthier) jurisdictions. The universities have the largest amount of research funding, and their academic staff are better paid than instructors at the other institutions. A university degree has the highest prestige and with some exceptions, their graduates have the best occupational chances.[164]

While the United States has no centralized educational policy—education is one of the functions left to the states in the American constitution—there is, broadly defined, an academic system.[165] The "system" is best articulated in California, where each of the segments of public higher education is clearly defined with regard to purpose, orientation, organizational pattern, and role.[166] The University of California (UC) stands at the pinnacle of the system, and its campuses offer doctoral and professional degrees. Its academic staff teach relatively few courses and are expected to do research and publication, and the levels of remuneration are higher. The California State University (CSU) system controls four-year institutions (most of which offer master's level work), with provision for students to transfer from the CSU to the UC system. At the bottom, the community colleges, which are controlled by local jurisdictions, offer open access to anyone wishing to obtain higher education. Research has shown that there is relatively little transfer among the segments of the system, although procedures for transfer are in place.

American higher education has some elements of a "system" while at the same time exhibiting considerable anarchy. The private sector, for example, is free to develop independently so long as funding can be obtained. There is considerable diversity among institutions and the freedom to strike out in new directions. Yet, the largest majority of colleges and universities fairly carefully follow the established patterns of curriculum, organization, and direction in higher education. Thus, there is both more than meets the eye in the American academic system—and less.

THE RELEVANCE OF THE AMERICAN MODEL

With this overview of some of the historical and contemporary aspects of American higher education, it is possible to consider some of the specific aspects of the American system that may be relevant abroad. The purpose of this discussion is to indicate some of the more creative American organizational and curricular models that have helped the American university develop and cope with rapid expansion. This is not a full discussion of all of the aspects of American higher education that may have international relevance—nor is there any focus here on those elements of the American system that have proved unsuccessful. American higher education experts, understanding the shortcomings of their own system, often wonder why others are interested in an academic model that they see as cumbersome, highly traditional, and too conservative. It should also be pointed out that there may be good arguments for a conservative approach to change in higher education—academic institutions are fragile, and too much reform and external interference may be more damaging than the conservative tendencies generally evident in universities.

The Community of Scholars and Governance

The internal governance of American colleges and universities is based on the idea of a community of scholars and shared governance. The basic building block of governance, the department, is a unique organizational model that was adapted from the European "chair" system, in which one senior professor dominated a discipline or field of study. The department assumes that all members of the academic staff within the department are equal. All votes on decisions affecting academic programs, curriculum, staffing, and other matters are open to every member of the department. In many universities, the chair of the department is elected by a vote of the academic staff and he or she serves for a limited term—usually not more than five years.[167] The department structure builds a basic level of participation into the governance structure and does not permit domination either of the curriculum or of concepts or approaches to a field by a single individual. The American departmental structure generally has not permitted the direct participation of students in governance, although student involvement through consultation is widespread. This fairly democratic decision making structure ensures that junior members of the department have a voice in departmental affairs and thus can reflect new ideas within the disciplines. There is also flexibility among the various academic ranks. The major decision that is made, usually by the department faculty and with the ratification of senior bodies, concerns the granting of tenure (permanent appointment), which is usually linked with promotion from assistant (the most junior professional rank) to associate professor. There are, generally, no quotas on the numbers of staff within a department in each rank, so the competition to be promoted to full professor is not as fierce as it sometimes is in the European academic system.[168]

While American academic departments have their share of disputes and acrimony, the departmental structure permits as wide as possible participation in academic decision making. Further, the participatory nature of the department is reflected in the other governance bodies—such as senates, faculty councils, and the like—at least in the better American universities.

There has been, of course, much criticism of the department as the key governance structure. Especially during the 1960s, many argued that the department was too rigid a structure and that it hindered interdisciplinary teaching and research. It is certainly the case that the individual member of the academic staff must look to the department for his or her promotion, and if the department does not encourage interdisciplinary work, it is sometimes risky to engage in it. It has also been argued that the department rigidifies the academic disciplines by giving them an organizational base that is hard to alter. Finally, many critics point out that the department will tend to see decisions in the context of its own narrow interests and not with the total university in mind. These criticisms all have some validity, but the structure of the department is sufficiently ingrained in the American university that it is unlikely to be dislodged.

An Administrative Cadre

In order to effectively administer very large academic institutions with a variety of functions and roles, a professional administrative cadre has developed, with responsibility for the day-to-day administration of the university. Indeed, this cadre has divided into a number of subspecialties that serve particular needs. For example, business officers, student affairs staff, international education administrators, and others have organized their own professional associations. It is possible in most American colleges and universities to have a career entirely in the administrative field, and graduate programs have been established to train academic administrators as well as to produce higher education researchers and scholars.[169] American universities were the first to recognize the profession of academic administration. While the emergence of the profession has been controversial, it is by now well established.

It is important to differentiate between two levels of administrators in American higher education. Senior administration remains dominated by professors trained in one of the academic disciplines who often take administrative posts as a temporary assignment.[170] They obtain their training "on the job." Although some senior administrators have their academic training in the field of higher education, the tradition of appointing discipline-based academics to leadership positions from the level of the department chairperson to dean to president remains strong and is unlikely to change significantly. The new career-based higher education administrators function in the middle-rank service functions of the university. For example, the dean of the graduate school is likely to be a professor from an academic discipline, while the associate dean increasingly holds a doctorate in higher education and has a career that has been completely in administrative positions. The vice president for academic affairs (responsible for faculty and curriculum) is usually a professor, but the vice president for business affairs is increasingly a career administrator.

Large universities employ as many as 4,000 or more individuals—including academic staff, support staff, and others—and have budgets of more than $100 million dollars that require a sophisticated administrative apparatus. An academic field has grown to serve this new career line—the field of higher education. It is now possible for the doctoral degree in higher education to be earned at more than 50 American universities. Those trained in the emerging field of higher education learn about the theories and practice of administration but also about the nature and traditions of the university. A considerable literature, several research journals, and a professional organization serve this field of study and research.[171]

Curricular Expansion

The traditional European university had a narrowly circumscribed curriculum and an ideology that stressed a fairly narrow role for academic institutions. Even with the expansion of higher education in Europe and the increasing involvement of the university in societal affairs, the curriculum remained fairly traditional. The American university, in contrast, has been open not only to expansion of enrollments but also expansion in curricular scope. Its curriculum has grown to include many specializations not previously appropriate for university study, and while in some cases curricular offerings have reached absurd levels, by and large, curricular expansion has served both the university and the society.[172] During the twentieth century, American colleges and universities have been attuned to changing societal needs and have often moved to serve them by adding specializations, curricular offerings, or research directions. Even such prestigious institutions as the University of Wisconsin offer academic degrees in poultry science, mass communications, and recreational education.

A willingness of academic institutions to serve quite specific employment needs, the relative flexibility of the departmental structure, an academic governance process that permits rapid changes in the curriculum, and a tradition in the academic profession itself that encourages rapid adjustments all contribute to the ability of the American university to respond to societal needs. Some have argued that higher education has prostituted itself to external demands at the cost of giving up the idea of liberal education.[173] The multifaceted functions of the university once led Clark Kerr to define the American multiversity as a series of academic buildings connected by a common heating system.[174]

Despite the dilution of the traditional concept of the university, it is clear that curricular expansion has been a key factor in permitting the American university to play the important role in society that it has in recent decades. A combination of a fairly flexible structure of governance, a tradition of adaptation by the faculty to perceived societal needs, a strong element of vocationalism in the student body, and pressures on the university by government and the public permits this curricular responsiveness.

Research

Research has been a hallmark of the American academic system for more than a century. The ways in which American universities promote research may be useful in stimulating research productivity and capability in other countries.[175] It should be noted that not all American universities and colleges are directly involved in the research enterprise, and that many individual professors do not produce much research.[176] The bulk of the research is produced in the top one hundred American universities, which also receive most of the research funds allocated by the federal government. Liberal arts colleges do not expect their academic staff to produce much research. Studies show that a small minority of the total professoriate produce the bulk of published research.[177]

Despite considerable variation in mission and in productivity, research and publication are considered to be the most prestigious functions of an academic. Research-oriented professors have the highest prestige and usually the highest salaries. They are able to obtain external funding for their work and are the most "cosmopolitan" in their careers, involving themselves in national and international meetings and more frequently changing jobs.[178] The system of earning tenure (permanent appointment) and promotion stresses, in most universities, research and publication. In other words, the prestige structure of the profession and the norms of productivity have research and publication built into them. Further, the salary structure in most universities varies and is not uniform, and individual professors may earn different amounts. Those who are productive in terms of research and publication tend to be somewhat more highly paid than nonproductive scholars although the differences are not very great. Research-oriented faculty members have greater access to external funding. In short, the ethos of the American academic system stresses research and publication.

The combination of normal expectations, the prestige structure, rewards through tenure and promotion, and access to funding all promote research and publication. The syndrome of "publish or perish," while exaggerated in the folklore of academe, nonetheless provides a set of expectations. In addition, universities that have attempted to improve their stature rapidly have often stressed research and publication and have sometimes tried to hire new staff who reflect this norm.

Autonomy and Accountability

This topic has been considered at length by Robert Berdahl, and it is one of the key issues in the current debates in the United States.[179] The appropriate mix of autonomy and accountability remains a point of contention, and at the same time is of crucial importance not only in the United States but abroad as well. On the one hand, academic institutions must have a large measure of autonomy if they are to provide creative teaching and useful research. On the other, the demands of the society, expressed through government, are legitimate, especially when the bulk of financial support for higher education comes from public funds. At issue is the proper mix. It is clear that academic institutions must have a large measure of academic freedom and internal autonomy. The academic staff, and students as well, must be free to teach, without political or ideological fetters, in their classrooms. The university community must be free to push forward the frontiers of knowledge even if this is sometimes of potential embarrassment to governments. Knowledge is not a commodity that can be controlled without hindering creativity. At the same time, universities are not ivory towers. They function as integral parts of society and have responsibilities to agencies that provide their financial sustenance. The American experience shows that the universities flourish, intellectually and financially, when they have links with society.

There is no formula that can be easily applied in order to define appropriate autonomy. The current debate in the United States is proof that even in an established academic system, this question remains very much at issue. At present, while academic institutions still have a considerable measure of autonomy, with the more prestigious research-oriented universities having more autonomy than the others, there has been a slow but steady intrusion of government authority into the affairs of higher education. This intrusion has taken place regardless of the political ideology of the states involved or of the federal administration in Washington. There is, at least, a recognition that the issues are of key importance although the outcome of the debate is as yet unclear.

Service

The role of the university in providing direct service to society—to government, industry, agriculture, and a variety of special interests including labor unions, public interest organizations, and others is an important part of the ethos of American higher education.[180] This tradition dates from the nineteenth century, when the state universities developed with a strong and direct commitment to aiding the development of their regions. The state universities in Wisconsin, California, Illinois, and other states were very important in the development of agriculture. They engaged in research with direct practical implications and then ensured that research results were disseminated widely through extension agents and other efforts such as noncredit courses. In Wisconsin, the university still employs staff in each of the state's counties who have the responsibility to bring knowledge created at the university to agriculture and industry. The university owns a radio and television network that reaches most parts of the state, again as a means of providing educational and other services.

Universities actively solicit research contracts with government agencies and the private sector, both for "pure" research and for applied topics. Increasingly, academic institutions have entered into long-term agreements with industrial firms that provide funding for university-based research and guarantee to the funding agencies initial control over any commercially useful results. Individual professors also engage in a range of service to the community—some are involved in private consulting for industry or other agencies that provide them with added income in return for their expertise. This has become a controversial issue, with some critics arguing that universities have become commercialized and have strayed too far from their mission of teaching and research.[181]

University policy encourages service activities in a number of ways. Individual academic staff are permitted to spend a portion of their time on remunerative consulting activities and are encouraged to perform unpaid service. Evaluation procedures for promotion and tenure include service as a component, although it is generally of lesser importance than the other two elements, teaching and research. University fiscal policy encourages obtaining external grants and permits individual professors as well as departments and institutes to engage in relationships with external agencies for research and service under rather broad university guidelines. In other words, institutional policies provide a considerable scope for service activities. Service has become an important part of the ethos of the American university. It is particularly important at the middle-range comprehensive universities, with the top-ranking institutions more concerned with basic research and the liberal arts colleges only peripherally involved in large-scale service work.

Stability and Change

In the twentieth century, the American academic system has evolved a fairly unique combination of considerable institutional stability, even conservatism, on the one hand, and the ability to adjust to new demands and directions, on the other. This situation is not the result of careful planning but rather of evolution. The basic organizational structure of American higher education has not changed for almost a century. When a major new requirement is at hand, the traditional institutions either incorporate it by adding functions without basically changing or entirely new institutions are created.

Established universities have been most resistant to basic change, but they have nonetheless been able to add new specializations fairly easily and accommodate to changing functions. Large-scale institutional reforms have been quite rare, but there has been a great deal of change at the periphery. The basic models have been growth by accretion—by simply adding on new functions (and added resources, in most cases) to existing institutions, departments, or programs. By this means, the institution operates without major disruption or change, and yet it has been possible to accommodate, often at relatively low cost, new demands.

Departments, for example, have seldom been abolished, but it has been possible to add new departments to an academic institution as new specializations develop. Or existing departments may bifurcate, with their professors dividing into several entities. It has also been common to establish interdisciplinary institutes or centers, using academic staff from several different departments. Such arrangements permit the departments to remain untouched while at the same time providing stimulus for innovative research and teaching. It has been noted earlier that entirely new institutions sometimes were established to meet new needs. When the German-trained scholars returned from their studies abroad and found that they could not change Harvard or Yale, they started new institutions, and eventually the old elite universities adapted to new realities.

The traditional undergraduate curriculum, with its stress on the liberal arts and general education, has been maintained for more than a century with periodic updating but with a basic adherence to the concept. During the 1960s, many universities permitted more student choice in the curriculum, responding to the student activism of the period, and later, in the 1980s, there was an increasing vocationalism in student interests. In each of these periods, there has been some accommodation, but without basic alteration.[182] The trend in the 1990s has been to reestablishing the traditional undergraduate liberal arts curriculum, ensuring that students are exposed to a range of disciplines and perspectives as part of their undergraduate education.[183]

The fact that there is no master plan for higher education and that institutions have a considerable degree of autonomy means that change has occurred in different ways and to varying extents in different institutions. This has helped to maintain some diversity in the academic system and has prevented the wholesale adoption of policies that might later be found to be erroneous. In the American pattern, academic change takes place without central planning, but not without direction.

Dealing With Adversity

American higher education has been faced with multiple problems in the decade of the 1980s and 1990s.[184] Financial problems caused first by inflation combined with economic downturn have been followed by changes in public policy concerning public expenditure as the economy revived in the 1990s. In many parts of the country, the increases in student enrollments that had characterized higher education for two decades slowed or stopped. Demographic changes mean that there will be a decline in the population of college-age young people in many areas. Further, government cutbacks and shifts in emphasis away from education have caused further problems. Fiscal difficulties have caused severe problems for many universities. In the private sector, a small number of institutions have closed and others are struggling for survival. In the public sector, few if any institutions have closed, but there has been retrenchment at various levels. In a few states, academic staff have been fired from their jobs because of fiscal problems. In a few instances, full professors have been fired. This is a shift away from the traditional concept of tenure, which assumed lifetime appointments for those who were awarded tenure. There have also been programmatic cutbacks. Colleges and universities have carefully examined their curricular offerings and have eliminated courses in some low-demand areas. Some student services have been eliminated, and budgets at all levels trimmed. This has had an adverse and in the long run dangerous impact on libraries, for example, which have been unable to maintain their collections. Further, many institutions have cut support services and activities before harming academic programs or firing professors. This has meant that buildings may not be properly maintained, a policy that has negative implications in the long run.

Surprisingly, the adversities of the past decade have not affected academic institutions more seriously. In most institutions, there has been an unwillingness to engage in comprehensive planning for fiscal austerity and problems have been dealt with in an ad hoc manner. The pressures on administrators, faculty, and support staff have been great and morale has suffered.[185] The basic stability of the institutions has meant that, as in the case of reform, retrenchment has taken place at the edges of the academic system and of individual colleges and universities. In some cases, recently established innovative programs that had not fully embedded themselves in the system have been cut.[186] In general, the major universities have suffered less than more marginal institutions. Particularly hard hit are undergraduate colleges in the private sector that rely mainly on student tuition payments for their survival.

While American higher education, as well as academic systems in Western Europe, are struggling with the problems of financial austerity, enrollment declines, and drastically changing student curricular interests, few satisfactory models have emerged to deal with austerity. In the United States, the problem of shifting from a mode of expansion to one of "steady state" or decline has been serious. The academic community has not been able to make the change. Further, while it was possible to expand by adding on new functions and programs without much alteration in existing practice, it is more difficult to follow the same model when reducing activities. European nations have generally been similarly unsuccessful in developing useful models for planning reductions. However, former Prime Minister Thatcher's comprehensive reorganization of the British higher education system and recent Dutch reforms provide quite different approaches to downsizing and reorganizing academic systems.

Student Services

Not only does the American university system have a large student enrollment, but the American academic tradition has been to provide many services to students. The European tradition, in contrast, assumes that students are adults, and academic institutions have not been involved in providing student services. In the United States, young people begin their college studies earlier than in Europe (typically at 18 years of age). The concept of in loco parentis (the university acting in place of the parent), which gave universities responsibilities for the extracurricular lives of students, contributed to a tradition of providing a range of services to undergraduate students. While the tradition of in loco parentis has been substantially weakened by the turmoil of the 1960s and by some abdication of responsibility by the professoriate, American colleges and universities provide a wide range of services to students. Most academic institutions provide recreational facilities, counseling services (for psychological problems and other matters), intramural sports and athletic facilities, career placement offices, and a wide range of extracurricular activities. Most colleges provide dormitory (hostel) facilities for their students and have not only the responsibility for the management of these buildings but also include staff to help the students who reside in the dormitories.

The student services apparatus of most American academic institutions is large and complex. Staff with special training in counseling, in extracurricular activities, and in other areas are generally employed by the institution. It is possible to obtain advanced degrees in such fields as college student counseling, which prepare individuals for careers in this area. In many institutions the cost of such services is borne by the students through their tuition fees or through specifically earmarked fees for services. Dormitories and food services are usually self-supporting and paid for by the specific student fees. The complex administrative structures that have evolved to deal with student services may be a useful model as academic institutions in other countries move to provide an increasingly wide range of services and facilities to students.

CONCLUSION

No academic system develops entirely on its own, and there are probably elements of the American experience that may be useful to planners, policymakers, and administrators in other countries. The topics discussed in this chapter have been chosen with an eye to their relevance to other countries. The United States, with a large and complex academic system, has dealt with many issues that have international relevance. Yet, as pointed out earlier, each university system has a unique combination of indigenous and international elements, and it is seldom possible to copy directly from the experience of others.

Further, the American academic system has had its problems recently, and many have criticized the universities for their handling of issues such as retrenchment. The undergraduate curriculum, discussed earlier, was allowed to fall into some disarray during the 1960s, and efforts had to be made to rescue it.[187] Thus, it would be a mistake to think that all of the challenges faced by higher education have been successfully met in the United States. While this chapter has generally focused on the positive examples, there are many negative ones as well.

The issue of the indigenization of higher education also enters into this discussion.[188] Universities are Western institutions in terms of their models and curricula. Yet, academic practices should be as relevant as possible to local needs. The battle between borrowing foreign models and technologies, on the one hand, and developing indigenous models, on the other, is a complex one. Universities are inevitably part of the international knowledge network, yet they are at the same time national institutions.

The American innovations and practices described in this chapter may be useful in thinking about solutions to problems elsewhere. Where the United States has dealt with challenges that will face others and can suggest new ideas and approaches, these insights may be relevant. But it is unlikely that their immediate problems can be solved by applying foreign models. An international perspective can suggest approaches and experiences that have been used in other contexts.

II

Teachers and Students

5

An International Academic Crisis? The American Professoriate in Comparative Perspective

The academic profession faces significant challenges everywhere. Financial pressures have contributed to ever-increasing demands for accountability. The privatization of public higher education and the expansion of private academic institutions in many countries have changed the configuration of academe. Questions about the relevance of much of academic research have been linked to demands that professors teach more. The traditional high status of the professoriate has been diminished by unrelenting criticism in the media and elsewhere. This chapter provides a discussion of the problems facing the contemporary university and the way they affect the academic profession. This discussion is presented in a comparative and international context because similar issues affect higher education worldwide and an international perspective can shed light on American realities.

The academic profession, in the United States and abroad, continues to function without basic change or even much consciousness of the external forces that buffet the universities. Yet, change is inevitable, and it is quite likely that the working conditions of the professoriate will deteriorate. The profession's "golden age"—characterized by institutional expansion, increased autonomy, availability of research funds, and growing prestige and salaries, at least in the industrialized countries—has come to an end. We are concerned here with understanding the realities that confront the professoriate in the United States and abroad at the turn of the century.

The modern American university is an international institution. It traces its origins to the medieval University of Paris, was deeply influenced by academic models from England and Scotland and from nineteenth-century Germany, and today educates students from all over the world.[189] The American university stands at the center of a world system of science and scholarship, and is the largest producer of research and scholarly publications. The English language dominates world science and is, in a sense, the Latin of the twenty-first century. The American professoriate operates in an international system at the same time that it is embedded in a national environment.

The masters of America's earliest colleges followed the English collegiate tradition, with its emphasis on the moral and religious as well as the intellectual formation of students. From this tradition came in loco parentis. Later, in the period following the Civil War, American higher education was greatly influenced by the German research university, with its emphasis on research and on the application of knowledge to the needs of society. The German ideals of *Lehrfreiheit* and *Lernfreiheit* contributed to the development of the academic profession by opening up the curriculum, entrenching the ideals of academic freedom, and ensuring the domination of the professoriate over the curriculum.

The American academic profession is today the largest in the world, with a half-million full-time scholars and scientists. It is very difficult to generalize about the professoriate—divisions by discipline, institution, rank, gender, race, and ethnicity characterize the profession. As Burton Clark points out, the professoriate is made up of "small worlds, different worlds."[190] The life of a full professor of biology at a major private research university in the East is very different from that of an assistant professor of history at a public comprehensive college in the Midwest. There are some common elements—the experience of having undergone that most arcane of rituals, study for the doctorate, the practice of teaching, and perhaps, the most elusive thing of all, a commitment to the "life of the mind." There is a vague but nonetheless real understanding that an academic career is a "calling" as well as a job.[191]

INSULARITY AND INTERNATIONALISM

The contemporary professoriate is poised between the national and the international. In terms of numbers, American universities are more international than ever, educating 450,000 students from other countries and employing staff members from around the world. Professors, mainly from research universities, are involved in research and teaching in many countries. At the same time, the recent Carnegie survey notes that the American professoriate is least committed to internationalism among scholars from 14 countries.[192] Only half of American faculty feel that connections with scholars in other countries are very important, and while more than 90 percent of faculty in 13 countries believe that a scholar must read books and journals published abroad to keep up with scholarly developments, only 62 percent of Americans are of this opinion. American faculty are similarly unenthusiastic about internationalizing the curriculum. Fewer than half agree that the curriculum should be more international.[193] Americans travel abroad for research and study less frequently than do their counterparts in other countries. The Carnegie data show that 65 percent of American academics did not go abroad for study or research in the past three years. This compares with 25 percent of Swedes, 47 percent of Britons, and just 7 percent of Israelis. The Americans rank last among the 14 countries included in the survey. At the same time, American professors have much more contact with international students than do faculty in other countries—96 percent indicate that foreign students are enrolled at their institutions. There are, of course, significant variations among the American professoriate, with faculty teaching at the prestigious research universities reporting higher levels of international involvement. Academics who are more cosmopolitan in their approach, focusing on their disciplines and on research, seem to be more international than those who are more local in their orientation, stressing the campus and teaching.[194]

These attitudes indicate a complex relationship with internationalism. American faculty seem to feel that U.S. higher education is at the center of an international academic system. The world comes to the United States and therefore international initiatives are superfluous. Of course, there is a grain of truth to this perception, and it is reinforced by the relative ignorance of foreign languages on the part of American faculty. Besides being the language of science and scholarship internationally, English is the dominant language of the new communications technologies such as the Internet. International conferences often use English as the primary language. Increasingly, journals edited and published in such countries as Sweden, Japan, Taiwan, the Netherlands, and Germany are also in English so that they can achieve an international readership and join the ranks of the top international journals. Even the large multinational academic publishers active in academic fields—such as the Dutch-owned Elsevier or Germany's Bertelsmann or Springer—publish increasingly in English.

American academics do not often cite work by scholars in other countries in their research. The American research system is remarkably insular, especially when compared to scientific communities in other countries. A few, such as Singapore and Hong Kong, make it a priority to hire scholars from abroad—frequently from the United States—precisely to ensure an international perspective. The American system accepts scholars and scientists from abroad, but only if they conform to American academic and scientific norms. To be sure, generations of foreign-born and foreign-trained scholars have been welcomed in the American academic system, and have contributed much to science and scholarship. Their role in the New School for Social Research, in influencing the social sciences following World War II, and their involvement in the research that contributed to the Manhattan Project come immediately to mind. Ultimately, however, they have been assimilated into the American system. Their research and scholarly accomplishments may have had an impact, but their ideas about higher education have had little salience.[195]

Other countries look to the United States as the academic center. In most disciplines, Americans are among the leaders, and scholars from abroad find the United States an attractive place. In 1995, more than 59,000 visiting scholars studied in the United States.[196] Americans still win a preponderance of Nobel prizes. Although its preeminence is decreasing, the United States remains by far the largest producer of basic research. American academics have an ambivalent relationship with the rest of the world. They welcome scholars from abroad as visitors or as permanent colleagues and eagerly accept students from abroad in their classes and seminars. But they pay little attention to the knowledge that the rest of the world produces.

CENTERS, PERIPHERIES, AND KNOWLEDGE NETWORKS

Being at the center of the world academic system places American professors in a powerful position and also imposes special responsibilities on them. The advent of the new technologies for knowledge distribution complicates matters, but may strengthen the position of the United States. A small segment of the American professoriate, the top 10 to 20 percent or so, centered at the major research universities, who can be characterized as the "research cadre," is the arbiter of many of the scientific disciplines for much of the world. This group includes full-time faculty who are more interested in research than in teaching, and whose positions require them to be regularly engaged in research. This research cadre is composed of fewer than 20 percent of all academics and 37 percent of those in research universities.[197] The group produces much of the research published in the mainstream academic journals, obtains a large proportion of research grants, and edits the major journals. Many are members of the various disciplinary decision making elites.

The American research cadre consists of fewer than 100,000 scientists and scholars. They are largely tenured (88 percent), male, and in the sciences. These academics teach mainly in the research universities—the 236 institutions in the Carnegie classification's doctoral and research categories. These institutions constitute 6.1 percent of all institutions with 31.4 percent of enrollments.[198] This group dominates knowledge production and its distribution. They are the primary producers and gatekeepers of science and scholarship. The research cadre, not surprisingly, publishes more than other faculty. For example, faculty at research universities published well over twice as many journal articles in a three-year period as faculty in nonresearch colleges and universities.[199] The leaders of this group occupy the commanding heights of a complex knowledge system, and hold tremendous power to determine what becomes legitimate science. There are, of course, some fields in which U. S. domination does not hold sway, such as literary theory, which is dominated by European thinkers. And there are many prominent scholars and scientists working in other countries.

The knowledge distribution system that the research cadre controls dominates science and scholarship. It is dominated by widely-cited journals in most scientific fields, for although an estimated 100,000 journals exist worldwide, only a small proportion of them are widely read and share in shaping the disciplines and reporting the key advances in science and scholarship. Most of these influential journals are edited in the United States. Americans are responsible for a significant proportion of scholarly books.

In fact, the United States is the largest market for new academic "products" of all kinds. The library market alone, although it has suffered significant cutbacks in recent years, remains the world's largest purchasers of scientific materials. The sheer size of the academic community and the number of institutions—more than 3,000 colleges and universities—give the United States advantages in size and scope. Technological innovations such as the use of the Internet for scholarly communications, online journals, bibliographical services, and document delivery through computer-based means have all been developed and are most widespread in the United States. Americans are by far the most active users of computers, e-mail, and other database services. The American professoriate remains far ahead of other academic communities in the use of these, and other, new technologies. The bulk of e-mail communication worldwide is in English, and many of the new data services operate primarily in English, giving further advantages to academic communities that use English. It is perhaps significant that only American e-mail addresses do not have to list a country identifier—an artifact, no doubt, of the American origins of the Internet, and symbolic of U.S. domination of this key communications tool. The agencies that have developed database services, bibliographical resources, and document delivery arrangements are, for the most part, American. Their origins and ownership make a difference. For example, the ERIC (Educational Resources Information Center) system, the most important source of research and bibliographical assistance in the field of education, is based in the United States and funded by the U.S. Department of Education. It is not surprising that the orientation of the material available through ERIC is American, and very little research or documentation from other countries is available.

The American professoriate—especially those academics active in research—is at the center of the international knowledge network. Their paradigms tend to be most influential simply because they are the key decision makers—as well as the major users—of the new systems. Most American scholars do not consider the international dimensions of their decisions simply because, as noted earlier, they do not have a high degree of international consciousness. In this respect, their insularity works to the detriment of academic communities in other countries, which are to some extent excluded from the mainstream.[200] Academics in other countries depend on the major international journals, publishers, and increasingly on the new technologies. In some ways, they reinforce their peripherality by emphasizing the mainstream international journals, sometimes requiring publication in them to qualify for academic promotion.

Academics even in such highly developed countries as Denmark have become in part peripheral to the American scientific center. So too are scholars and scientists in the United States, such as those at small liberal arts colleges, who are not part of the mainstream research system and are to some extent marginalized.[201] Those who wish to publish in the major internationally circulated publications often must adhere to the trends of the dominant elites in the discipline. Researchers who do not teach at research universities often find themselves at a disadvantage in terms of access to publication outlets and to research funds from major foundations and governmental agencies—it is estimated that 80 percent of federal research funds go to scholars and scientists at the top 100 universities.

Academe has always been stratified and hierarchical. These characteristics, which can be observed internationally as well as within a large university system such as that of the United States, differentiate the profession and are salient factors for academic careers. Hierarchies in the disciplines are combined with a pecking order of institutions to forge a powerful system of centers and peripheries. Although access to knowledge has been made easier by the new technologies, the ability to participate in the system remains controlled by scientific elites in the various disciplines.

THE DECLINE OF THE TRADITIONAL PROFESSORIATE

The traditional concept of the professoriate is being supplemented by new hiring and promotion arrangements across the United States, and in other countries as well. The proportion of the professoriate in tenured and tenure-track positions is steadily declining in many countries. In the United States, approximately 35 percent of all faculty are part-timers, and over one-third of the full-time faculty hold term appointments.[202] Criticism of the concept of tenure itself is heard in policy circles, and the recent unsuccessful efforts by the University of Minnesota Regents to modify the tenure system are but the first part in what is bound to be a continuing debate. These changes come at a time of significant financial pressure on higher education—universities and colleges are trying to squeeze more productivity from the one segment of the academic enterprise heretofore thought to be immune—the professoriate.

The full-time tenured and tenure-track professoriate will very likely continue to decline as a proportion of the academic workforce although it will remain the "gold standard" to which all aspire. Academic institutions gain flexibility and incur lower costs by hiring non-tenure-track teachers. Significant nonmonetary costs enter into this shift. The traditional faculty are those who perform the complex governance functions of the institution. They serve on committees, design new curricula, become department chairs, and later fill some senior administrative positions of the university. They also produce most of the research. Perhaps most importantly, they have loyalty both to the institution and to the academic profession. They are, in short, the traditional core of the university. Indeed, the statutes of most colleges and universities reserve full participation in governance, including voting on important academic decisions, the full-time faculty, and usually to those with "regular" appointments.

The American university is becoming a kind of caste system, with the tenured

Brahmins at the top, and the lower castes occupying subservient positions. The part-timers are equivalent to the Untouchables in the Indian caste system—relegated to do the work that others do not wish to do and denied the possibility of joining the privileged.

In this hierarchical order, the traditional faculty ranks may constitute half (or even less) of the profession. The new and growing middle category of full-time but non-tenure-track faculty is growing rapidly. Hired mainly to teach, these new ranks teach more, are not expected to engage in research, and have only a limited role in institutional governance. They receive the standard benefits from the institution, but their terms of appointment are limited by contract to five years or some other finite period. Paid somewhat less than tenure-track faculty, these staff members are part of the academic community, but not fully involved in the affairs of the university. They provide a reliable teaching force. They also permit the institution flexibility in staffing, since there is considerable turnover in positions in response to the demands of enrollment changes or institutional priorities. This institutional category is new at most institutions, but we can expect it to expand.

Part-time faculty have been part of the academic landscape for a long time, and they are a rapidly growing part of the academic labor force. Hired to teach a specific course or two, provided no benefits, often given no office space, and expected simply to show up to teach a class, part-timers are the *ronin* of traditional Japan—the masterless samurai who traveled the countryside offering their services and hoping to be chosen as apprentices. These *ronin* have all the qualifications of samurai—they lack only a sponsor (permanent employer). Part-timers are exploited in the sense that they are paid very modestly on a per-course basis. Not surprisingly, part-time faculty feel little loyalty to the institution.

The implications of this emerging caste system for American higher education are significant. The structure of the academic profession will be fundamentally altered. One of the traditional strengths of the American pattern of academic organization has been its relative lack of hierarchy, especially when compared to Europe or Japan. The American academic department is a community of equals, with participation dispersed among all faculty. This is in sharp contrast to the Japanese "chair" system, where basic academic power resides with a small group of full professors, with academic power emanating from them.[203]

The changing structure of the profession also has implications for the future of research in the universities. Only the full-time faculty have the time, commitment, support, and professional obligation to engage in research and publication. Indeed, many universities permit only full-time faculty to serve as principal investigators on grants. In the research-oriented universities, academic work is arranged so that research is an integral part of the career of most academics. If one believes that teaching and research are related, and that teaching benefits from the engagement of a faculty member in active research, the new hierarchy places fewer researching faculty in the classroom, and the quality of teaching, at least in top-tier schools, may suffer as a result.

The new structure of the professoriate will affect the various sectors of the American higher education system differently. The top-tier research universities and selective liberal arts colleges will be least affected, at least in terms of traditional academic work. The new category of full-time non-tenure-track faculty will likely expand significantly at these institutions, while part-time staff may be cut back. The greatest alterations will likely take place at the less-selective colleges and comprehensive universities, where reliance on part-time and non-tenure-track faculty will grow in order to meet student demand in a context of diminishing fiscal resources and the need for institutional flexibility. These differential changes will exacerbate the already considerable variations in academic prestige and quality. The quest of many of these institutions, as well as individual professors to join the top ranks of academe may be ended as a result of tighter controls on professorial time and greater institutional accountability.

Some examples from other countries can help us understand certain changes taking place in the United States. In Germany and a number of other European countries, an academic category of full-time non-tenure-track academic employees has long existed with responsibility for teaching or research.[204] These appointees have no possibility of obtaining regular (permanent) positions, and in general their terms cannot be extended. They often circulate to different universities on term appointments, and compete for regular positions away from their home institutions. In recent years, this "underclass" of academics has again become a growing feature of the German university system. Since full professors are seldom promoted from within the institution, the term-appointment *Mittelbau* staff do not seriously alter the academic balance in the German academic system.[205]

The Latin American academic profession, where a majority of those teaching in the universities are part-timers, is also a useful point of comparison for the United States. There is a long tradition of the "taxi cab" professor who rushes from his or her professional job to teach a class at the university.[206] The large proportion of part-time staff has helped to shape the ethos of the Latin American university, and has hindered the emergence of a modern academic culture. Contemporary reformers have argued that a full-time professoriate is a prerequisite for a competitive and effective academic system. Indeed, countries such as Brazil, Mexico, Chile, and Argentina have expanded their full-time staff. Reliance on part-timers has meant that university governance is in the hands of a very few senior faculty, little research takes place, and teaching is limited to lectures given by busy professionals who have little interaction either with students or colleagues.

While it is generally agreed that research and innovative teaching and curriculum development cannot be built on the basis of part-time staff, reliance on part-time faculty has, as noted earlier, given the universities much-needed flexibility, and has permitted higher education to be offered at a low cost. Tuition levels are very low in the public institutions, and government allocations to postsecondary education are modest when compared to international norms. The public universities in Latin America have expanded their enrollments in order to meet increasing demand through the use of low-cost part-time staff.

The growth of private universities in Latin America and elsewhere has significant implications for the academic profession. Although the prestigious older private universities in Latin America, largely sponsored by the Catholic Church, maintain high standards and have many full-time professors, most of the newer institutions rely almost exclusively on part-time faculty. In Latin America as well as in the formerly Communist countries of Central and Eastern Europe, private institutions are educating an increasing segment of the student body. The quality of many of these new universities has yet to be measured—and the implications of their employment patterns for an emerging professoriate are similarly unmeasured.

TENURE

The tenure system is once again under attack. As a result of difficult economic circumstances, a perceived need by academic institutions to increase staffing flexibility, and the perennial complaint that professors who hold tenure are not accountable to anyone, the tenure system has come under widespread criticism.[207] This has ranged from attacks on putative faculty "deadwood" or professorial laziness to issues relating to institutional priorities.[208] The Minnesota case, mentioned earlier, shows the strong feelings on this volatile issue. The faculty ultimately won that struggle, although tenure rules were slightly modified. Professorial job security is an increasingly volatile issue in other countries.

The central issues in the current debate relate to accountability, post-tenure review of faculty, and institutional concerns about financial and programmatic flexibility. The interplay between the imperatives of the tenure system and the very idea of tenure and its linkage to academic freedom set against pressures for change will result in some alterations in traditional arrangements. However, in most institutions, tenure will be probably be retained with only modest modifications.[209] The important point is that there will very likely be, for the first time in close to a century, a number of modifications in the tenure system.

Post-tenure review is one likely reform. Pressures for institutional accountability are being extended to individual faculty members. Moves are afoot to hold tenured faculty accountable for their teaching, and to measure both teaching and research productivity more closely. Clearly, the era of unfettered professorial autonomy following the award of tenure is coming to a close. Another possible change is that fewer faculty members will receive tenure. A cadre of full-time non-tenure-track faculty is emerging. This class of faculty will not have the protection of the tenure system. Some will have the possibility of periodic renewal of contracts, while others will be appointed for a limited period without any prospect of renewal.

It should be kept in mind, of course, that at most colleges and universities tenure in American higher education has never been ironclad. Tenured faculty members can be dismissed in times of financial exigency or for reasons of programmatic restructuring (such as the closing down of departments). While relatively few institutions have resorted to such measures, some have, and their actions have been upheld in the courts. During a financial crisis in the 1970s, the State University of New York dismissed several faculty members when specific academic programs were being eliminated, and although the American Association of University Professors censured the administration for this action, the courts upheld it. Top-tier institutions have been less likely to resort to firing tenured staff at times of restructuring or fiscal crisis.

International trends regarding academic employment and tenure present a mixed picture. Permanent employment after a probationary period is the norm worldwide, although this varies and some policy changes are under way. American professors undergo perhaps the longest probationary period and one of most rigorous evaluations of performance prior to awarding tenure found anywhere in the world. In Europe, young scholars are appointed to university posts, "confirmed" after a relatively short probationary period of approximately three years, and given permanent appointments—if performance in teaching and research is satisfactory. The evaluation conducted is not nearly as rigorous or elaborate as that which is standard practice in the United States. Salary increases are typically based on longevity and are not performance based. Once a scholar is appointed to a "permanent" post, tenure is often protected not only by university statutes but by civil service regulations and, as in the case of Germany, the constitution itself.

Promotion to a higher rank, however, is not automatic and often involves a rigorous evaluation. In some countries, promotion to the rank of full professor requires open advertisement and competition, and the promotion of a person already in the university is not assured. In countries with the tradition of the chair system, a relatively small number of academics are promoted to this high rank, and it is by no means certain that most academics will end their careers as full professors. As European academic systems experience financial problems, fewer senior professorships are authorized, and as a result a growing proportion of the academic profession either cannot be promoted to a senior academic rank, or must be content with temporary appointments.[210]

There are even some countries where formal tenure does not exist. In Taiwan and South Korea, for example, there is no formalized tenure system, and it is possible for professors to lose their positions. Yet, virtually all academics hold "de facto" tenure and few, if any, are actually fired. England is undergoing a dramatic experiment with the modification of permanent appointments. Traditional tenure was abolished by the government for new incumbents in the academic profession during Margaret Thatcher's prime ministership, and the country is currently witnessing considerable change in the nature of academic careers.[211] At the time it was implemented, the government's policy was universally condemned by the academic profession.

Patterns of academic appointment, security of tenure, and provisions for the guarantee of academic freedom vary considerably. Legal as well as administrative arrangements differ. In India, for example, most full-time academics have permanent appointments, but weak legal and administrative protections mean that institutions can violate tenure with relative impunity.[212] Even in the United States, policies vary.

In Minnesota, protection for faculty at the University of Minnesota has been iron-clad, while in New York, tenure regulations, even in a unionized environment, are much weaker.

In the United States, academic freedom has traditionally been protected by the tenure system as well as specific institutional guarantees.[213] While few of the attacks on the academic freedom of professors match those experienced by the profession during the McCarthy period of the 1950s, American faculty feel somewhat ambivalent about the state of academic freedom. According to the Carnegie survey, 81 percent believe that academic freedom is strongly protected, but only 49 percent say that there are no political or ideological restrictions on what a scholar may publish.[214] Scholars in most of the 14 other countries included in the survey felt more secure in what they can publish—indeed, only Koreans, Brazilians, and Russians were less sanguine.

It is perhaps surprising that even one-fifth of the American professoriate feels that academic freedom is not well protected and that almost half worry about ideological restrictions on publication. This may reflect concern about "political correctness" or other debates in recent years over the ideological basis of the curriculum (although 71 percent of American academics feel that this is an especially creative and productive time in their fields—among the most favorable ratings in the 14 country Carnegie study).[215] Or it may relate to unease about the tenure system, a difficult job market, or other uncertainties.

SCHOLARSHIP RECONSIDERED AND ASSESSED

Among the most important implications of the fiscal and institutional pressures discussed here is a significant reconfiguration of academic work. The debate that began with the publication of Ernest Boyer's *Scholarship Reconsidered* continues, and may be starting to have an impact on the profession.[216] Boyer's argument that the professoriate should pay more attention to teaching and learning and that the definition of scholarship should be broadened so that it goes beyond traditional publication of research findings and analysis came at a time when academic institutions were seeking more productivity and accountability from the faculty. A sense that the emphasis on research that has characterized the top tier of American higher education may have gone too far has increasingly entered the debates about higher education in the 1990s.

Financial reality, institutional necessity, and the ideology of reform have come together in the movement to reemphasize teaching as the central responsibility of the academic profession. As it happens, the American professoriate itself is committed to teaching as its central role. When asked if their interests were primarily in teaching or research, 63 percent of American academics respond that their commitments are primarily or leaning toward teaching. This compares with 44 percent in England, 28 percent in Japan, and 33 percent in Sweden. In these nations, and others in the Carnegie survey, faculty are more focused on research.[217] Not surprisingly, American faculty members in the research cadre because of their publication records are more focused on research, yet even these individuals indicate a strong commitment to teaching.

American academics do express dissatisfaction with many of the conditions for teaching and research. For example, 42 percent feel that the pressure to publish reduces the quality of teaching at their institutions, 71 percent believe that research funding is more difficult to obtain now, and 75 percent believe that it is difficult to achieve tenure if they do not publish.[218] Half or more are critical of library, computer, and classroom facilities for their teaching. They also judge many of their students to be insufficiently prepared for their studies. But their views are by no means inimical to the teaching role in higher education.

While there is a perception that things are modestly deteriorating in academe, no groundswell from the professoriate for greater emphasis on teaching, new procedures for assessment, or a reorientation of American higher education is evident. Yet, it is unlikely that most faculty would be adverse to a renewed emphasis on teaching and a diminished focus on research. Most academics produce relatively little published scholarship or research, and most express strong loyalty to teaching. Many, as the Carnegie survey indicates, feel that they are under too much pressure to do research. Assessment, mainly in the form of student evaluations of teaching, is nearly universal in the United States. Additional assessment, if not too time consuming or intrusive, is unlikely to be strongly opposed.

Critics often overemphasize the innate conservatism of the professoriate. While it is unlikely that the academic profession will press for drastic change, a commitment to teaching and to the goals of higher education will make the professoriate receptive to proposals for change. The American professoriate, more focused on teaching than their colleagues in Europe or Japan, is likely to be more favorable to reform. Even in England, where the professoriate was united against the Thatcher changes and expressed traditional views on a range of issues, the academic profession adjusted to a new academic environment that introduced assessment of teaching and research and a greater emphasis on accountability at all levels of the academic system.

In the United States, the next step in the effort to place more emphasis on teaching and to expand the concept of intellectual work as well as to assess the totality of academic work is a Carnegie report entitled *Scholarship Assessed*.[219] The focus is on better means of assessing teaching so that it can be evaluated along with research, as an element of academic work. Guidelines are provided for covering service as well as teaching. This initiative is part of an ongoing effort in higher education to assess, measure, and evaluate all academic work. The outcome of these efforts is at this point an open question—the techniques for effective measurement of teaching and learning remain much debated. The widespread acceptance of modified norms of professorial performance will also require something of a cultural shift in the profession.

The research cadre, and indeed most faculty at the top-tier research-oriented institutions, will see relatively little change in their working lives. Those in less selective colleges and universities will probably be most affected, coming under increasing pressure to emphasize teaching and to downplay a commitment to research. Most colleges already emphasize the teaching role, although they may benefit from greater sophistication in the measurement of teaching effectiveness. Assessment and accountability are at the top of the institutional agenda. So far, the financial and governmental pressures on American higher education have been felt largely at the institutional level but have not touched on life in the classroom, but this is about to change.

In a few other countries, mainly in the English-speaking academic community, there has also been an emphasis on assessment and evaluation. Britain has been most active in this field, where policies have been implemented to measure academic performance in both research and teaching, and there are plans to ensure that those who enter postsecondary teaching have some preparation in pedagogy specifically relevant for university teaching.[220] The British approach is to provide training for postsecondary teaching and then to assess the quality of academic performance. Australia and Canada have also paid attention to issues of assessment.

MORALE

In general, the professoriate feels good about itself. There is little sense of crisis among academics, and most are unaware of the magnitude of the problems facing American higher education.[221] Overall, most faculty are remarkably content with their careers. They are less pleased with their institutional surroundings, increasingly critical of their students, and especially alienated from the administration of their institutions. Nevertheless, more than 75 percent are happy with their job situation as a whole and express satisfaction with the opportunities they have to pursue their own ideas. A majority feel that this is a good time to become an academic, and only 11 percent say that if they had to choose careers again, they would not choose academia. Faculty report that they are generally content with their colleagues, and 79 percent are satisfied with their job security, although only 61 report that they are tenured. Faculty are even relatively happy with their salaries—46 percent describe their salaries as excellent or good. This is a surprisingly high proportion in view of the reality of relatively stagnant academic salaries during much of the 1990s.[222] Ninety-six percent are satisfied with the courses that they teach, although they are somewhat critical of their students. A quarter of the faculty reported that their students are less qualified now than they were five years ago. Overall, they believe that academic freedom is protected. In short, in their departments and in the classroom, the professoriate expresses general satisfaction. Faculty are content with their overall professional autonomy. The Carnegie data suggest that if an academic feels professionally autonomous, secure in his or her job, and respected by campus colleagues, he or she is likely to give a positive rating to the job situation as a whole, even if some other, less central aspects of the job are seen as unsatisfactory.[223]

It is interesting that there is little worry over what some have called the crisis of "political correctness" on campus. The Carnegie survey shows that most faculty are comfortable with the level of academic freedom and feel few constraints in their teaching and research. However, 34 percent are of the opinion that there are some restrictions on what a scholar can publish, perhaps reflecting a concern about "P C" There is, however, scant evidence to support the claims of conservative analysts that the campus is seething with conflict over the nature of scholarship, the "canon," multiculturalism, and other issues.[224]

The faculty do report dissatisfaction in a number of key areas, most notably, as indicated, with the administration, with a number of institutional arrangements, and to some extent with students. Unhappiness with academic administration is a near universal phenomenon.[225] In all of the 14 countries in the Carnegie survey, alienation from administration was a strong theme among the faculty. Only in Brazil and Russia did even half of the respondents judge relations between faculty and administration to be good. In the United States, 57 percent of the professoriate rate relations as fair or poor. Thirty-four percent of American academics do not feel that they are kept informed about what is going on at their institution, and 64 percent state that they have no say at all in shaping academic policies (only 14 percent consider themselves very or somewhat influential). Fifty-eight percent have the opinion that the administration is often autocratic, 45 percent report that communication between faculty and administration is poor, and only 39 percent say that top-level administrators are providing competent leadership. American faculty are rather typical in their attitudes toward institutional leadership when compared to the other countries in the Carnegie survey.

This alienation from administrative authority tells us a good deal about attitudes within the academic profession. While faculty express satisfaction with their colleagues at the department level, they are deeply unhappy with institutional governance and policy. Similar dissatisfaction is expressed with governmental involvement in higher education. Only 10 percent of American faculty agree that the government should have responsibility for defining overall purpose and policy for higher education. Thirty-four percent feel that there is far too much governmental interference in important academic policies. Faculty are alienated from the people who run their colleges and universities, and from the governmental authorities who provide the funding as well as shape broad approaches toward research, student aid, and affirmative action. There is a large gap between the satisfaction felt about the "local" aspects of academe and discontent with the broader policy direction of higher education.

The faculty would like to be permitted to pursue teaching and research unfettered by governmental interference or administrative restrictions. Most academics enjoy what they do, believe that they do their work well, and consider themselves reasonably well prepared for their jobs. There is a vague sense of unease with the institutional climate and with trends in higher education, and this seems to be reflected in negative feelings toward institutional leaders and their policies.

FUTURE REALITIES AND PROFESSORIAL PERCEPTIONS

The full-time American academic profession remains largely insulated from the broad changes taking place in higher education. Not only that, the professoriate seems to have little understanding of these trends. The majority of tenured faculty have been unaffected by the deteriorating academic labor market, although their job mobility has become limited. When colleges and universities have been forced to cut their budgets, the faculty have been largely protected. Only in a few cases has tenure been violated due to financial exigency. For a long period in the 1970s and 1980s, faculty salaries did not keep pace with inflation. However, the last few years have seen a modest improvement, although in 1996 there was slippage again.

In some respects, academic work has changed. Classes have become larger. Research funding is more difficult to obtain, and enrollments in many schools have increased while full-time faculty numbers remain steady or have even declined. Part of the slack has been taken up by part-time staff, graduate student instructors, and an increase in class size. The full-time professoriate has become somewhat more "productive" in terms of numbers of students taught. Although there is little hard evidence, most academics are of the opinion that obtaining tenure has become more difficult, especially at the research universities.

Among those who have experienced the current realities, in many fields, new doctorates cannot find full-time positions and must content themselves with insecure part-time teaching and repeated postdoctoral assignments. Some have been forced to leave academe altogether. Competition is fierce for the positions that do exist. Assistant professors find working conditions increasingly difficult and experience increased obstacles on the road to tenure.[226]

Most academics do not see these trends as a crisis, and do not recognize them as part of a permanent change in the landscape of American higher education. They have not yet experienced the new realities for themselves. Presidents and other leaders have not communicated the idea of faculty responsibility for institutional adjustment and survival in the current period, and have not involved the professoriate in responding to the new financial and other realities. Faculty members do not yet realize that if institutions are going to survive and the traditional prerogatives of the professoriate maintained, the profession will need to take an active role in ensuring institutional well-being.

The professoriate is faced with difficulties and diminished circumstances almost everywhere. The Carnegie survey portrays an academic profession that has a vague sense of unease rather than of crisis. It is instructive and even relevant to examine some of the trends evident abroad. Britain has seen the most far-reaching reform, with the abolition of the tenure system, the amalgamation of the polytechnics with the universities to more than double the size of the university system, and most recently, the imposition of performance measures for teaching and research and the allocation of funds to universities based on these measures. These policies have had considerable impact on the professoriate, as indicated by the low morale of the British respondents to the Carnegie survey.[227] The British academic profession has been significantly affected by these structural changes, as well as by forced retirements and deteriorating conditions of teaching.

There has also a less dramatic deterioration in the conditions of the professoriate in most Western European countries, where little structural change has taken place. Most pronounced in Germany, but also evident in France, Italy, and to some extent in the Netherlands, increases in student numbers have not been accompanied by growth in the professoriate, and the conditions for teaching and learning are declining. Few jobs exist for younger scholars, and research funding has been cut or at least has not kept up with costs. There have been few, if any, initiatives to reform the universities or the basic terms and conditions of the academic profession.

Eastern Europe and the former Soviet Union, on the other hand, present a dramatic picture of decline and deterioration. In all of these countries, higher education has come under severe financial pressure with cutbacks in government funding for the universities. Support for research has been especially hard hit. The establishment of new private universities has changed the equation since few, if any, of these new institutions offer tenured appointment. The Russian universities have suffered severe financial declines so that the conditions necessary for research and advanced scholarship no longer exist. The professoriate has had to adjust to a changed environment. Many have left the universities, pursuing careers in other fields or finding positions abroad. Others find that they cannot survive financially, and take extra part-time academic jobs. The universities and the academic system remain in a period of transition, with the future unclear.

In a trend most evident in China but also seen in other countries (including the United States, to some extent) universities are increasingly asked to generate their own revenues. Chinese universities are now charging many of their students tuition and other fees. The universities have also established consulting departments, profit-making laboratories, and even businesses in many fields. Peking University, China's most prestigious academic institution, runs a successful software company and other enterprises. Many professors are involved in these enterprises, and in private consulting as well. As a result, they naturally pay less attention to campus life and to their students. The professoriate is increasingly seen as a source of direct income for academic institutions. In the United States, university-industry collaboration has an element of Chinese-style academic entrepreneurs.

In very few countries is the academic profession secure in its traditional role. Even in Hong Kong, which may have the highest academic salaries in the world, new performance evaluation and accountability standards are being implemented. Many faculty are also worried about the impact of the transition to Chinese sovereignty on academic freedom and on higher education as a whole. In Australia, the new conservative government's promises of significant cuts in higher education funding, have the professoriate profoundly worried. In Japan, current reform efforts aimed at improving undergraduate education may affect the traditional autonomy and insularity of the Japanese professoriate. The implications of heavy reliance on part-time faculty, which has been part of the Latin American academic system for a century or more, have some lessons for the United States as the balance steadily shifts.

CONCLUSION

The American professoriate is part of an international academic community that now faces diminished circumstances, decreased autonomy, and threats to the perquisites and even the traditional roles of the professoriate. While each academic system is embedded in its own national issues and circumstances, there are some common realities, especially in the realm of fiscal problems and demands for accountability, making it possible to learn from the experiences of other countries.

The largest and arguably the most powerful in the world, the American academic profession is faced with unprecedented challenges. Its world scientific and research leadership is reasonably secure because of the size of its academic system. At the same time, it must function in an increasingly multipolar world in which international skills and connections are important, and it is ill prepared for this role. American scholars and scientists remain remarkably insular in their attitudes and their activities. Domestic challenges also abound, and again the professoriate seems poorly prepared for the future. There is little understanding of the complex realities facing American colleges and universities. Attitudes reflect little sense of crisis. Indeed, the distrust felt by many academics toward the leadership of American higher education makes innovation more difficult.

At the same time, the academic profession has weathered difficulties in the past. The wave of creative energy that resulted in the establishment of the American research universities at the end of the nineteenth century and the professionalization of the academic profession shortly thereafter prove that reform and change is possible. Academics also met the challenges of the economic depression of the 1930s and the expansion of the postwar period creatively.[228] With leadership and energy, there is no reason why the early twenty-first century cannot be as creative a period for higher education as was the early twentieth century.

6

Professors and Politics: An International Perspective

Colleges and universities are seen to be bastions of truth and knowledge, seemingly immune from politics and contention. This is the idealized fiction of higher education. The fact is that universities are often politicized institutions, full of dispute and debate. Further, key components of the academy—faculty and students—are frequently involved in politics, on campus and off. Indeed, politics is an integral part not only of the governance of academic institutions but of the creation and dissemination of knowledge. This chapter discusses one element in the politics of higher education, the activism and political involvement of the academic profession. Professors are an extraordinarily important group in every society. They control one of the most important institutions in modern societies—the university. They determine, for the most part, the curriculum, degree requirements, admissions standards, and the other central intellectual functions of the university. The academic profession also constitutes probably the largest single group of highly educated people in many societies, especially those with relatively few highly educated people. While the professoriate is seldom in the economic elite of a country, it is part of the social and prestige elite. Professors are influential through their teaching and through their academic research and writing. They may also be more directly involved in politics and in the intellectual life of the nation. It is this extra-academic activity with which this chapter is concerned.

The politics of the academic community has had a remarkable impact on society.

Student activism on occasion has toppled governments and has frequently caused disruption and focused attention on political matters of concern to the students.[229] Faculty activism has in general been more indirect, expressing itself through professorial writings and utterances. At times, however, professors have organized themselves for political purposes as well, but these have been fairly unusual occasions. Academic political involvement has extended over a wide range of activities, including running for public office, serving in advisory capacities to political leaders, providing expertise on issues of political and economic importance, serving in government as well as in oppositional movements and organizations, writing for newspapers and magazines, and appearing on television. Professors sometimes also participate in politics at the local or regional levels as well as nationally. This activity goes back many centuries and was present in many countries.

Students and faculty are uniquely able to express ideas, and the activism of the academic community is very often the activism of ideas and ideologies. Ideas are at the center of the academic enterprise. The academic community deals with ideas and concepts within the confines of the academic disciplines, relating them to teaching and research. On occasion, however, these concerns spill over into the realm of society and politics. Academic activism is often directed toward expressing ideas and shaping public debate on a topic. This is often done through publication, in scholarly journals and books, and sometimes to a broader audience. It can also be done through public speaking and increasingly through the mass media. Activism sometimes expresses itself through demonstrations and agitation. The impact of academic activism on society can be considerable. University-based intellectuals and experts often frame the discussion on topics of public importance—from the environment to medical ethics. The role of campus activists in determining the debate on issues in the early stage of consideration is of special importance. The opinion pages of major newspapers in many countries are filled with articles by professors on topics of emerging societal importance and discussion.

Direct action can be very effective in focusing public attention on societal issues. In the United States, debate and then activism concerning the Vietnam War emerged from the campuses and later became a matter of public concern, eventually convincing a president to step down.[230] Students were most directly involved, but many professors were also engaged in writing, teaching, speaking out in public, and providing moral support to student activists. While not often on the barricades, concerned professors were a key cadre in the antiwar movement. It should be noted that even on campuses with the most ferment, only a minority of the community was generally politically engaged. But this minority is of special influence, not only because of its involvement but because it frequently represents a wider section of the campus community, as well as reflecting wider social concern.

The university, in almost every society, is a kind of sanctuary where individuals have more freedom (and usually more leisure) to reflect on ideas—even political ideas. Even in societies that are repressive and authoritarian, the campus still offers somewhat more freedom. Governmental authorities sometimes shut down academic institutions entirely to root out political activism. Because of its tradition of freedom of teaching and expression, the university is able to harbor dissident ideas and people more easily than other institutions. The tradition of academic freedom and autonomy, however vitiated in practice, is a powerful idea that has an impact on both society and the academic community.[231]

It would be a mistake, of course, to assume the campuses are seething with agitation and political concern. This is not the case, except in very unusual circumstances. In general, the academic community is engaged in the normal pattern of teaching and research. Nonetheless, ideas of social importance are constantly percolating in the universities, and from time to time, these take on a broader societal importance. It is at this intersection of ideas and political debate and practice that campus activism arises.

THE IMPACTS OF ACTIVISM

Campus-based professorial activism may affect society and the university itself. The societal impact is often subtle and indirect. It has most to do with ideas and expertise. The role of the "academic as expert" is common, and often has political implications. Nonscholarly publications with significant participation from academics frequently have an impact on society. In the United States, journals like *Foreign Affairs*, the *Bulletin of the Atomic Scientists*, *Commentary*, and the *Public Interest* are examples of publications that focus on public policy issues, and have limited circulations, but are taken seriously by elites and have had an impact on policy and politics. In Britain, the *New Statesman and Society* and *Granta* play a similar role. Japan's *Sekai* and *Bungei Shingu*, and the *Economic and Political Weekly* in India, are other examples. *Science* in the United States and *Nature* in Britain not only provide analysis of scientific developments but are also influential in debates about science policy. In these publications, new ideas—originating frequently from the universities—are expressed. These are examples of publications that are circulated beyond the academic community and are taken seriously.

Academics also write for publications with a wider circulation. In some countries, Britain and Japan among the more prominent, academics frequently appear on television to discuss their ideas and interpret events. "Op-ed" pages of newspapers worldwide are filled with the writings of professors—analyses of contemporary issues, often based on research findings. Academics, because of their access to data and their connections with the media, are able to place their ideas before both the public and policymakers. The ideas and interpretations from the campuses are quickly brought into the mainstream of thinking.

It is also sometimes the case that publication in scholarly journals may be influential. In the United States, the *New England Journal of Medicine* has an impact not only on medical research and practice but also on policy discussions relating to health. Professorial publication of this kind represents a link between the role of "professor as expert" and "professor as politician." In virtually every society, regardless of the level of freedom of expression or complexity of the media system, the academic community is expected to play a role in the generation of ideas and in reflecting on public issues. It is clear that the ideas expressed by professors have consequences that go far beyond the classroom or the laboratory. The professor, serving as an "expert," may have significant influence on policy and politics—sometimes in entirely unanticipated ways.

The academic community is also indirectly involved in government—in a variety of contexts—and again reflects the linked roles of expert and politician. Most professors, even in relation to controversial matters of public policy, see themselves as experts, providing information and research-based analysis rather than directly participating in political disputations. The role of professor as expert or politician has a very long history. Professors at the University of Paris, in the medieval period, provided the expertise that solved one of the most volatile political disputes of the day—the division of the papacy between Avignon and Rome.[232] The theological ideas coming from the academic community during the Reformation had a profound influence on religious thinking, and directly affected the politics of Europe, the rift between Roman Catholics and Protestants, and the bitter conflicts that this split engendered. Martin Luther, it should be remembered, was a professor of scripture and theology.

German scholars in the nineteenth century not only assisted the development of Germany through their scientific research but also through their advice to the government on a range of subjects.[233] It was in newly unified Germany after 1872 that the idea of the "professor as expert" became an important part of the academy. Professors also had access to government funding for research, and the results of this research were expected to contribute to the economic growth of the society. Two other rapidly developing countries at the time, the United States and Japan, found the German academic model appealing, and the idea of linking the universities to national development was adapted in both countries.[234] In the United States, professors have a long tradition of providing expertise to governmental agencies. For example, the faculty at the University of Wisconsin played a key role in framing the progressive social legislation that shaped the state's social policies early in the twentieth century.[235] From the late nineteenth century to the present, academics have been providing their expertise to the government, on many issues and in different contexts.[236] Indeed, the emergence of professional associations in the social sciences was stimulated in part by a desire of the professors to play a prominent role as experts.[237]

Professors are not only experts, they are sometimes direct participants in government. At the least important but probably most common level, professors are frequently appointed to commissions and committees set up to advise governments or to solve specific problems. These appointments are made to take advantage of professorial expertise and to utilize the skills of qualified individuals who are not directly involved in an issue. The professor, in his or her role as "expert" is also often appointed to government posts that require high levels of expertise. For example, in the United States, the President's science adviser, the chair of the Council of Economic

Advisers, and other senior posts of this sort, are very often filled by professors. The architect of the deregulation of America's airlines was a professor who served as head of the Federal Aviation Administration. Former professors, Henry Kissinger, foreign policy adviser and later secretary of state, and William Bennett, secretary of education in the Reagan Administration, were appointed because of their specific expertise but gained wide political influence. Many Western European countries frequently recruit professors for policymaking positions in government.

Other countries make similar use of academics in advisory or indirect policy-making positions. The Indonesian economy, for example, was restructured after 1968 by a group of U.S.-trained academics, commonly referred to as the "Berkeley Mafia," who were appointed to policy positions in the government. Nicaragua's leftist Sandinista government had a former professor as minister of foreign affairs, and other academics also served in powerful positions. Chile's military rulers in the 1970s relied on academics trained at the University of Chicago to restructure the economy. It is not unusual in Third World countries for professors to serve in government positions—occasionally as presidents or prime ministers, but more often in jobs that require specific expertise such as education or economic affairs—in part because the pool of highly qualified people is small. Many of the intellectual elite naturally take jobs in higher education, and find that their careers take them in and out of the university.

Professors sometimes assume a direct role in elective politics, in a few cases becoming presidents or prime ministers. Several of Italy's postwar premiers have been professors, and academics have served in many senior ministerial positions. Professors have served as presidents or prime ministers in the United States, Thailand, Benin, Greece, Czechoslovakia, Portugal, Taiwan, the United Kingdom, and Canada. Academics serve in significant numbers in many legislatures. Several U.S. senators and representatives have been academics, and a large number of parliamentarians in France and Italy are professors. When the Socialist Party is in power in France, more than a quarter of the Chamber of Deputies consists of teachers or professors. In some instances, faculty members must resign their academic positions when they enter politics, while in others they can fulfill both roles.

It has been said that intellectuals have a propensity toward oppositional thinking. There is an interesting contradiction here. It is true that many professors have positioned themselves in general opposition to established authority, but overt political activism is rare.[238] Many professors, especially in the humanities and social sciences, feel themselves part of an informal oppositional intelligentsia.[239] Faculty members in such fields as management studies, agriculture, and the natural and biomedical sciences do not, generally, share this perspective. There are also significant national variations.[240] Faculty members in developing countries are more likely to be highly politicized than those in industrialized nations. Further, the academic atmosphere was more politicized in the 1960s than is the case in the 1990s in most countries. While an important minority of professors see themselves as an oppositional intelligentsia, most faculty, even during periods of activism, are politically uninvolved. It is quite unusual, although by no means unprecedented, for professors to become active in radical or revolutionary politics.

Professors, on some occasions, have been involved in direct oppositional political activism. Professors were instrumental in the nationalist movements of 1848 in Europe, and they formed a significant number of the members of the nationalist parliament that was dubbed the "Professors Parliament."[241] They not only stimulated students (who were also deeply involved in the movement) through their teachings but also became directly engaged in politics. Professors in the German-speaking countries provided the intellectual sustenance for emerging nationalism and, some have argued, the groundwork for fascism and Nazism. In later periods, significant numbers of academics were involved in antiwar movements on several occasions—in England prior to World War II for example.

In a few instances, professors have been involved in revolutionary movements in the Third World. In Peru, for example, the imprisoned top leader of the ultraradical *Sendero Luminiso* guerrillas was a professor. More often, professors have been involved in more moderate movements for civil liberties and political change. American professors were instrumental in the early oppositional movements to the Vietnam War—they organized teach-ins and other intellectual activities. When the antiwar movement turned more militant at a later stage, most academics withdrew. A significant number of the architects of the "velvet revolutions" in Central and Eastern Europe were academics. In such countries as Poland, the former Czechoslovakia (where a number of the liberal Charter of 77 signatories were academics), Hungary, and even Romania, professors provided intellectual leadership, and then assumed prominent positions in the new postcommunist governments. It might be added that several of the ultranationalist leaders in the former Yugoslavia were professors. These leaders were instrumental in precipitating civil war and the breakup of the nation. In China, Fang Lizhi, a professor of astrophysics, was one of the most prominent spokespersons for democratization.

Occasionally, when professors engage in political activism, they lose their jobs or are jailed. This happened in Burma in 1988, in Argentina, and Chile—where a significant number of academics were imprisoned and many others were forced into exile in the aftermath of the military takeovers of the 1960s—and at different times in Eastern Europe. Authoritarian regimes keep a close watch on the academic community, seeking to limit its independence. Indonesia demands that university teachers join the ruling political party, while Singapore supervises the kind of research and publication that academics engage in. Governments, particularly in the Third World, take professorial activism very seriously because they feel that academics have the potential to provide leadership to oppositional movements.

Professors can also provide political leadership locally. It is generally the case that the academic profession has a high level of social prestige—academics are respected and admired in their societies. Most sociological studies of prestige place professors near the top of the rankings. They often have influence on local affairs. In developing countries, professors are often asked their opinions on a variety of issues. In most societies, their participation in a range of civic affairs is welcomed and valued. The concerns of academic activists vary quite a bit. In some contexts, they have sought to form academic labor unions for ideological reasons or to ensure higher professorial salaries or better working conditions. Academic activists may wish to change university policies—to provide better assurance of tenure or to force the university out of certain kinds of research. They may wish to protect academic freedom from either external threat or internal interference. Academic activists have on occasion pressed the university to change its orientation—to focus more attention on research or to reform the curriculum.

The professoriate has at times had an impact on the university through its activism. This may take place within the established processes of governance—by, for example, organizing groups of professors to influence the vote in academic bodies. Such internal organizing can significantly politicize the academic community. On rare occasions, activist professors may go outside the governance structures altogether. They may go on strike, organize professorial labor unions, or directly appeal to the public or to governmental bodies. On very rare occasions, political parties may become involved in campus affairs—this has become an endemic problem in India in recent years.[242] In the aftermath of the 1960s reforms in the West German universities, elections to faculty and administrative posts became highly politicized, with groups of professors, academic staff and students supporting warring political factions.[243] The debate in the United States concerning political correctness and multiculturalism in the curriculum is, in considerable degree, an intellectual conflict among sections of an ideologically divided academic profession.[244]

PERSPECTIVES ON FACULTY ACTIVISM

Professorial activism is more subtle and less dramatic than student activism. It includes involvement in political affairs on many different levels—from providing expertise to government and commentary on current affairs in the mass media to direct participation in oppositional politics on and off of the campus. The vast majority of professors are not concerned with activism of any sort and simply teach their classes and do research. While research on professorial activism in particular and on the academic profession generally, is very limited, it is possible to provide some generalizations concerning the phenomenon.[245]

Alvin Gouldner divided the academic profession into cosmopolitans, those who look mainly to their disciplines and to the wider world of scholarship, and the locals, whose links are mostly to their home academic institutions.[246] The most visible professorial activists are cosmopolitans. These professors tend to be at the top of their disciplines, on the staff of the prestigious universities and most involved in research. They have reputations and visibility that permit them to function outside of their home institutions. They are called on to provide expertise, and they have the contacts in the media and elsewhere to project their voices to a wider audience. Faculty members with a local orientation seldom are engaged in activism outside of their own institutions and probably have less propensity to be involved with societal activism, regardless of academic discipline, although as Gouldner pointed out, these individuals provide the backbone of the campus governance process and serve on university committees and the like. Locals frequently dominate campus-based activism, serving not only on academic committees but also providing the leadership for campus unions and other faculty pressure groups. Faculty unions, which are active in many countries (e.g., India, Britain, France, and in some public colleges and universities in the United States, among others), tend to be led by locally-oriented faculty. These unions are concern themselves with campus-based activism and politics, and on rare occasions extend their interest to off-campus issues.[247] Locally oriented academic staff are in the majority in their universities. Their reputations seldom spread beyond their campus. However, during periods of campus turmoil and crisis, cosmopolitan academics may also concern themselves with local issues.

Activist "experts" can be found in most disciplines but predominate in fields that have relevance to public policy such as, in recent years, environmental science, area studies, nuclear physics, and of course applied economics. Economists may be most in demand at present, providing both policy advice and public commentary on issues ranging from the national debt to unemployment rates. Crises in China or Bosnia will bring relevant professorial experts before the mass media and to the attention of governmental leaders. A nuclear accident or a terrorists attack will also require relevant professorial expertise and commentary.

Professors of classics or analytic philosophy are less likely to be called on for their expertise, although even in these cases there are examples of "public expertise." Philosophers have been frequent participants in public debates, bringing a philosophical perspective to public policy issues. Recently, issues in medical ethics have involved experts from philosophy, law, and other fields, as well as from the biomedical sciences. With the growing concern about educational quality and standards, professors of education have become embroiled in public debates concerning the future of the schools, and have been joined by sociologists and political scientists. Ideally, academic experts contribute research data and analytic insights on issues of public concern or social policy.

Academic activists who are critics of established social or political institutions or policies are more controversial than those who provide expertise or who are involved in campus-based politics. They are mostly cosmopolitans who have access to the media and have a claim to expertise in their fields. They may be senior scholars at key universities. They have the self-confidence to speak out on issues and the security of tenure and reputation. Such critical scholars disproportionately come from the social sciences and, to some extent, from other policy-relevant disciplines. They often have some political experience as well, frequently as alumni of student political movements or in other political organizations. Critical scholars are often more ideologically oriented than their compeers and have a broader political perspective on society and government. Traditionally, professors have been to the left of the political spectrum in their societies, although with the collapse of the Soviet Union and the rise of "market-oriented" policies in China and other countries, mapping the ideological spectrum is more difficult.

Few critical scholars seem to be directly involved with political parties in any activist sense. These critics are a very small proportion of the professoriate, but they are often among the most visible. They speak out in the mass media, sign letters of protest in newspapers, and are even occasionally arrested for their activities. Noam Chomsky or, in an earlier period, Nobel prize winner Linus Pauling are examples of critical scholars and scientists. Generally, however, critical academics, unlike student activists, work within the confines of accepted political discourse in their countries. They are seldom willing to expose themselves to possible political sanctions.

Professorial activism, like its student counterpart, is very much a minority phenomenon. The socialization process of academics in most countries emphasizes detached scholarship and teaching rather than activism. For junior staff, there are frequently sanctions against involvement in politics, especially in critical activism. In some countries, the professoriate is seen as an influential group and is watched closely by the authorities. Yet, academics, particularly in the senior ranks, have high prestige and job security. The tradition of academic freedom also provides some procedural protections, as well as an ideology that supports speaking out on issues.

The traditions and structures of the academic profession and of contemporary universities present some contradictory pulls and pushes in terms of professorial activism. Cosmopolitan academics, however, are increasingly pulled into the mainstream of debate on important societal issues because of their expertise. The universities are increasingly the repositories of knowledge and expertise on most topics affecting society, and the professoriate, especially those senior academics at the major universities, have become a kind of mandarinate of expertise.

CONCLUSION

Campus activism has a long historical tradition. Campus-based activism has had significant effects on society and on the university and it will continue to do so. Student political movements have toppled regimes, created political crises, and highlighted major social issues. Student activists have frequently acted as the "conscience of their generation," speaking for significant segments of the population. Professorial activism is a more complex phenomenon. The role of the academic as expert has grown increasingly important. Academics also play a key role as social commentators and critics, helping to shape discourse on important topics. Academics occasionally are directly involved in politics, sometimes serving in government and sometimes in oppositional activities. As information and expertise become increasingly central to contemporary societies, those involved in the knowledge industries and especially in higher education—largely students and faculty in universities—will inevitably play a key societal role. For the most part, that role is limited to the direct concerns of higher education, but in important ways the academic community is affected by and sometimes influences the wider society. Activism, by both students and professors, is inherent in the nature of the academic community. The combination of academic freedom and relative professorial autonomy in universities, the place of ideas (and sometimes of idealism) in higher education, the power of the expertise of the universities, the relative ease of organizing campus-based activism, and the increasingly central place of the academic community in a knowledge-based economy guarantee that academic activism will continue to be at least an occasional force on campus and in society.

7

Student Political Activism

Student political activism is difficult to explain and even more problematic to predict. It is not surprising that there is no overarching theoretical explanation for it. Yet, understanding the complex phenomenon of student politics is important. Political leaders would do well not only to listen to student protest movements but also to understand their dynamics, since regimes have been threatened or even toppled by student protests. The academic community also needs to understand student activism, as students have frequently been key actors in movements for university reform and have also disrupted academic institutions. Moreover, the activists themselves should be fully aware of the history, politics, and potential of student protest movements since, as has often been said, those who do not know the past are doomed to repeat it. This chapter will posit some general perspectives on student politics although it will stop short of developing a comprehensive theoretical framework for understanding student movements.

It is difficult enough to understand the saga of student movements in a single country—it is far more problematic to focus on the phenomenon worldwide. Yet, we will consider student movements in a comparative context. Student protest is a national phenomenon, or even an institutional one, for the most part, but there are nonetheless some useful cross-national comparisons to be made. Further, the experience of one country may well be valuable in understanding the situation in another.

THE HISTORICAL CONTEXT

Student political activism did not start in the 1960s, although much of the research and analysis on the subject dates from that turbulent decade. There is a long history of student involvement with politics. Students, for example, have long been drawn to the cause of nationalism, and some of the earliest student movements were part of broader nationalist movements. Students were an important force in the revolutionary movements of 1848 in Germany.[248] While the 1848 struggles were not primarily student movements, students, professors, and intellectuals played key roles. The academic community was particularly concerned with pressing for democratic rights against absolute monarchies and developing a broader nationalist focus for the movements, especially in the German states. Indeed, the nationalist ideology that developed out of the 1848 movement provided a very powerful force in the drive for the unification of Germany later in the nineteenth century and strongly influenced the movement for Italian unification around the same time. Student organizations were supportive of the nationalist-based fascist and Nazi movements in the 1920s and 1930s in Italy and Germany. Indeed, German student organizations were among the first groups to support Hitler.[249]

Nationalism was also a key motivating force during the colonial period in Africa and Asia. A strong component of virtually every nationalist and independence struggle involved student participation. In some instances, the university community was in the leadership, articulating a vision of an independent nation and culture, while in others students were key players in the movement.[250] Frequently, students who were educated abroad were actively involved in the articulation of nationalist sentiments. The development of the concept of Indonesian nationhood and of a national language for the country emerged from a group of student intellectuals and became the basis for a successful nationalist struggle.[251] Students in countries as diverse as India, Kenya, Vietnam, and Burma were central to efforts to free their countries of colonial rule. China, while never under direct colonial rule, was pressed by foreign powers. In 1911 and on several other occasions, students spearheaded nationalist and revolutionary movements with the intention of modernizing China.[252] While it is true that students were not the primary leaders of any of the anticolonial nationalist movements, they were deeply involved and active in them.[253]

Student activism is generally oppositional in nature. This opposition to established authority may be from the left or right, or it may express itself in cultural or religious form. In the cases of Germany and Italy, students supported rightist nationalist causes. In the Third World, nationalism often has been leftist in nature. Students at times were "cultural nationalists," concerned with ethnic or cultural issues and not so much with ideological politics. In recent years, religious activism—especially in the Islamic world—has been a powerful force on campus.

Students have also been involved in academic matters. The most influential university reform movement was led by students—the Latin American reform movement of 1918. The movement, which began in Argentina and spread throughout the continent, reflected the growth of the Latin American middle class. It had far-reaching consequences for society and for the university, which was transformed to include the students in the process of governance.[254] The tradition of the 1918 reform movement continued as a powerful force for half a century.

In the West—with the exception of the student role in the revolutionary struggles of 1848—students did not appear as a major force in politics until the 1960s. The occasional upsurges of student political activism were sporadic and while they had a considerable impact in the universities, the political system as a whole was not affected. Students were active in some European countries during the Depression years of the 1930s—on both the left and right. The rightist trends in Germany and Italy have been noted, and some French students were also involved with right-wing student movements. In most industrialized nations, however, students leaned towards the political left. In the United States, which experienced a major student political movement during the 1930s, student organizations were exclusively liberal or radical.[255] Students were much more of a force in some Third World nations in the historical as well as the contemporary context. They were engaged in nationalist movements and considered to be a legitimate part of the political equation.

THE IMPOSSIBILITY OF A "PERMANENT REVOLUTION" IN THE UNIVERSITY

One notable characteristic of student movements is their sporadic nature. Student movements last only a short time—even a year or two is unusual although there are instances of more sustained activism. Just as it is difficult to predict the rise of activist movements, it is as great a challenge to predict their demise. There are a variety of structural and perhaps psychological reasons to explain the lack of longevity of student movements. The rhythm of academic life both helps and hinders activist movements. Student life, in most academic systems, permits a good deal of free time that can be devoted to politics. In the traditional European systems examinations were infrequent and the pace of studies were almost entirely determined by the student. This meant that student leaders could devote themselves exclusively to politics and still maintain their student status. In the more regulated American system with its frequent examinations and the course-credit system, sustained activism becomes more difficult.[256] In the American system, the "permanent student" syndrome, which is common in some European and Third World nations, is not easy to do and student leadership, as a result, is more transitory. It is clear that the structural realities of academic life in an academic system can control the nature and longevity of student movements.

Student "generations" are short and thus make sustained campus political activist movements unusual, since both leaders and followers change. Undergraduate generations change every three or four years. Further, even in the most laissez faire academic system, pressure to pass examinations and complete degrees is intense toward the end of the program—at which time students are less likely to be involved in activist movements.[257] The rapid turnover of participants makes it difficult to sustain a movement. Further, succeeding campus generations may have quite different orientations and interests, and the "tradition" of activism is sometimes transitory. Student movements may be impatient for results precisely because the leadership realizes that the movement may be short-lived. On issues relating to university reform or campus conditions, there is often an urgent desire to achieve results so that the current student generation can benefit from the change.

Sociological factors also militate against sustained student movements. In most countries, university students come from relatively affluent sections of the population. In the industrialized nations and to some extent in the Third World as well, broad political questions—sometimes related to ideological matters—stimulate student political activism. Often, students are not struggling for their own direct benefit but rather for idealistic causes. This may make them less deeply committed to the struggle than if they were fighting for an issue that would directly affect their lives. The often idealistic nature of student movements may be both a stimulus and a limiting factor for sustained student activism. Student activist movements seldom last more than one or two years and seldom lead to the establishment of permanent organizations or political parties. Further, although student movements frequently try to link up with political parties, labor unions, or other organizations outside the universities, these links rarely succeed or are very short-lived.

RESPONSES TO ACTIVISM

One of the reasons that student movements are not sustained relates to the outside response to activism. Student movements seldom function in a purely campus environment.[258] They are often concerned with broad political or social issues and consciously try to influence developments beyond the university. Even when the movement is campus-focused, the impact frequently extends beyond the university. Student movements depend, to some extent at least, on the reaction of the society to activism. As noted earlier, in the Third World, campus activism may focus on key political issues in society and lead to significant social unrest—sometimes contributing to the downfall of the regime. This is unusual in the industrialized world. However, student movements are affected by the reactions of the mass media, by key social groups outside the universities, and by other extracampus factors.[259] When the students focus on an important social concern—such as, for example, the issue of civil rights in the United States in the early 1960s—they are likely to attract both the attention of the mass media and the support of significant segments of the population. American students helped to stimulate both the civil rights movement and the struggle against the war in Vietnam in the 1960s precisely because they were articulating wider social concerns.[260]

Where student activism is traditionally accepted as a legitimate element of the political system, it is more likely that activism will have an impact on society. In many Third World nations, where students were a part of independence movements and had established a place in the society's political mythology, activist movements continue to be seen as a "normal" part of the political system.[261] In the industrialized nations, student movements are not considered as legitimate political actors, and society and the established authorities react with less sympathy to student activism. Thus, historical traditions of activism play a role in how society responds to student movements.

The relationship between the mass media and student activism is a complex and important one. In the industrialized nations, the response of the mass media to activism has been a factor in the impact of student movements. During the 1960s, the media highlighted student politics in many countries, and student demonstrations were featured in the press and on television. The message of the activists was widely disseminated. At other times, the media have ignored student politics, relegating it to a phenomenon relevant only to the universities. In such a situation, it is very difficult for activists to extend their influence beyond the campus. It is not easy to predict the nature or scope of media attention. For example, student efforts to force universities to give up their investments in South Africa in the 1980s were widely reported in the mass media, while campus protests against United States foreign policy in Central America did not attract as much coverage. It helps if the protests take place in the capital—as was the case in France when students demonstrated against proposed educational reforms. Student activist leaders often try to stimulate media attention since they recognize that they need media coverage.

Government response to student activism has considerable influence on the nature of student movement. Such response can range from ignoring student protests entirely to violently repressing demonstrations, including killing activists and closing universities for extended periods. In the West, the general predilection of government authorities is to ignore student protests and let university authorities handle them. Only when demonstrations are very large or disruptive do they stimulate a response. Western governments, in general, do not accept student protests as legitimate political expression and try to ignore them. Government authorities generally try to deal with student protests in the least confrontational way possible. When violence takes place, it can lead to increased militancy and attract added public sympathy.

Violent repression of student activism is more characteristic of the Third World, where student movements are seen as a direct threat to the political system and have in fact toppled regimes. Repression can sometimes stifle a movement, but it may also increase both the size and the militancy of the activist movements. For example, repression of student demonstrations in Argentina and Uruguay contributed to the rise of urban guerrilla movements, which caused considerable disruption and unrest. Governments—for example, in Nigeria, Kenya, and Burma—have closed down universities and sent students home in response to activism, occasionally for long periods. Sometimes, this brings activist movements to an end, but sometimes the students simply export activism to the countryside, engendering even more widespread unrest.

There are many examples of violent repression of student movements, with leaders being jailed, tortured, and sometimes killed.

Repression has sometimes been used against student movements in the West with mixed results. Efforts in France and West Germany to stop student movements in the 1960s resulted in the deaths of students at the hands of the police, and this increased the scope, size, and militancy of the movement.[262] In the United States repression took several forms in the 1960s. FBI and other police authorities attempted, with some success, to infiltrate student movements in order to disrupt them from within. Authorities also took action against demonstrations, sometimes in violent confrontation—as at Kent State and Jackson State universities in 1970.[263] The killings of students by police and troops during protests against American incursions into Cambodia during the Vietnam War resulted in nationwide student protests. These protests closed down several hundred universities and colleges and had a significant national impact.

University authorities must respond to activist movements, since they are often focused on campus issues and take place on campus. However, with few exceptions, university authorities are seldom prepared to deal effectively with student protest. Academic decision making is a slow process, and activist movements are not perceived as "normal" parts of university life. Conflicts between different factions among the faculty sometimes make response difficult. Academic disciplinary procedures are not geared to respond to protest movements. In some instances, campus academic authorities may prefer to move slowly to try to avoid confrontation, but are pressed by government officials, the media, or others in society to resolve the situation quickly and decisively. Such prompt and sometimes violent action against protests frequently stimulates activism and sometimes escalates students' tactics to include building takeovers and other illegal actions.

In many instances, campus authorities seek to negotiate with student activists and reach accommodation with them. These negotiations may reduce campus violence and the destruction of property. In a few cases, activism involving university issues has resulted in change. This was notably the case in West Germany, where student demands for reform resulted in structural changes in some of Germany's universities that gave students participation in most aspects of university governance in the 1960s.[264] These reforms were later modified or even reversed. More commonly, students achieved very little in terms of lasting change in higher education procedures or policies. In the United States, for example, the massive student protests during the 1960s produced little lasting reform in American higher education.[265] In some countries, however, student activism has resulted in campus change. In India, protests have frequently resulted in the removal of university administrators or the improvement of local conditions.[266] In the 1980s, the campaign to convince American universities to divest themselves of stocks in South Africa–related corporations yielded significant success. Thus, institutional response to protest, while difficult to predict, has sometimes resulted in the enactment of some of the changes demanded by students, although full success has seldom been achieved.

WHO ARE THE ACTIVISTS?

Just as it is important to analyze the historical circumstances and the external reactions to student politics, understanding the participants in student activist movements is also necessary. This section looks at activist leadership in a comparative context. While there has been some sociological research concerning student leaders in the United States, several Western European nations, India, and Japan, the data are very limited, and thus the general comments made here are quite tentative in nature.[267]

Leadership cadres constitute a tiny minority of the student population. Moreover, with few exceptions, the entire movement remains a minority of the total campus population. Even in the most dramatic upheavals—such as at the University of California at Berkeley in 1964 or during the 1968 events in Paris—most students did not participate in the demonstrations. In such major activist movements, the proportion of students involved is large, but usually under half of the total. For most movements—including the most successful and the ones receiving considerable attention from the mass media—only a minority of the student population is directly involved. Activist participation is made up of three "rings": core leadership, which is a minority and is generally significantly more radical than most participants; active followers, who are well aware of the issues involved, committed to the movement's goals, and willing to be involved in demonstrations; and a much larger group of students who are sympathetic to the broad goals of the movement but who are rather vague about the specific aspects, and who are only sporadically, if at all, directly involved. Outside of these rings are a large group of uninvolved students, some of whom may oppose the movement and many of whom are apathetic. The dynamics of student movements are not unlike those of other social movements although the specific aspects of campus life—an age-graded population, the close-knit community, common social class backgrounds, and other elements—make student movements unique.

The core of student leadership tends to be politically aware and often ideologically oriented. Student leaders are more likely than their less active colleagues to have already been members of political organizations prior to their involvement in activism. Activist leadership is often politically engaged during periods of campus quiet, and in many instances, student political leaders are part of an existing political community. Activist leadership has several general characteristics:

- Student activists tend to study in the social sciences and, to some extent, in the humanities. There has also been a propensity for students of mathematics to be involved in activist movements. Overall, the political attitudes and values of social science students are more to the left than those of students in many other disciplines—especially those in the applied professional fields. There seems to be a kind of self-selection of activist students into the social sciences. The social sciences' concentration on the study of society and social problems may create a critical perspective in some students. Social science faculty members also tend to have more radical views than do members of the academic profession in general, and these critical views may affect students.[268]

- Activist leaders tend to come from somewhat more affluent families than those of the general student population. University students overall come from wealthier families than the norm in virtually every nation, and activists tend to come from the top families in terms of income and status. This factor is magnified in the Third World, where income differentials are great.

- Leaders also come from families that are very well educated and in which mothers as well as fathers have a fairly high level of education. The families tend to be more urban in orientation and background, a key factor in Third World nations. In short, the families are more cosmopolitan than the norm.

- It has been argued by some that the child rearing and general attitudinal patterns of the families of activists are more liberal than in the general population. However, most of the data for such research have come from the United States and there is very little corroboration from a comparative perspective.[269]

- In the United States and Western Europe, using data from the 1960s, some scholars have found that activist students tend to be among the best students, earning very good grades in their studies.[270] The data on this, however, are not very extensive.

- Activist leaders often come from minority groups in the population. In Japan and Korea, the small Christian populations have contributed a disproportionate number of student leaders. In France, Protestants have been disproportionately involved in activism. In the United States, Jewish and liberal Protestant students have been significantly engaged in activism.[271] It may be that socially conscious and fairly affluent minorities, to some extent, tend to become involved in social movements.

There are many variations in the patterns of activist leadership and participation outlined here. For one thing, this description holds mainly for activists of the left—and since left activism has predominated in most countries since World War II, this pattern of leadership has received the most attention. It may not hold true for the strong fundamentalist Islamic student movements in the Muslim world or for campus-based student groups in India, where the concern is often with local issues rather than ideological questions. As noted earlier, available data are largely from the industrialized nations and relate to the era of the 1960s, a decade of abnormally high levels of activism.

THE ACTIVIST IMPULSE

We know relatively little about the nature of activist leadership. We know even less about why students become involved in activism and what precipitates student demonstrations and movements. Indeed, analysts and officials alike are generally surprised by outbreaks of activism in the universities. Further, there are significant variations by country and historical period. Nonetheless, it is useful to look at some of the factors that may contribute to the outbreak of student activist movements.

A variety of psychological motivations have been discussed. Lewis Feuer argues that "generational revolt" plays a key motivating role in student activism and that activist movements are acting out the "struggle of the children against the parents."[272] Most scholars find little validity in the generational revolt theory. Others argue that students have a propensity for "antiregime" attitudes because of the nature of the campus culture, youthful idealism, and the like.[273] Kenneth Keniston believes that student activists have a higher moral sense than do their uninvolved compeers since they have a commitment to act on their values.[274] On the other hand, one of the few cross-national studies of student activists found that there is a complex set of attitudes and values that contributes to activism.[275] While there is considerable disagreement concerning the psychological motivations for student political activism, it seems clear that psychological dispositions and orientations as well as the sociological factors discussed earlier must be part of the activist impulse.

Militant student activism is generally stimulated by salient events in society. In an earlier period, nationalism was a central force—both in Europe in the nineteenth century and in the Third World during the pre-1945 colonial era. Students participated in large-scale social movements, sometimes playing a major leadership role. In the United States, students were involved with foreign policy issues—in opposition to American involvement in European conflicts and concerned about the deepening world economic depression during the 1930s, a period of intense political activism on campus.[276]

In the contemporary period, broader political issues have been the main stimulants for large-scale student activist movements. Issues such as nuclear war, civil rights and liberties, and of course the war in Vietnam were the main motivating forces for American student protest during the 1960s.[277] In Europe, societal politics were also the main focus during the turbulent 1960s. French students reacted against the authoritarianism of the DeGaulle regime, while in West Germany, students organized an "extraparliamentary" opposition to the coalition government of the conservative Christian Democrats and the leftist Social Democrats.[278] In most of the other European nations where activism was a major force, extracampus political issues were also the major motivating force.

In the industrialized nations, educational and campus-based issues are sometimes relevant to student activism, but such questions do not usually stimulate mass movements. In the United States, a feeling in the 1960s that the American "mass university" was not meeting student needs was clear, but there is no evidence that this discontent contributed significantly to the emergence of massive student activism. Educational reform was also a minor element on the agenda of the movement. Reform issues were more important to activists in Western Europe than in the United States.

The underlying motivating factors contributing to student activism are complex. No doubt, psychological proclivities play a role. So too do economic realities. Students worry about future jobs and about their role in the upper strata of society after graduation. It is evident that, at least in the industrialized nations, major student movements have been stimulated not by campus issues but rather by broader social and political concerns. The development of activism is, thus, the product of many forces and factors.

THE IMPACT OF ACTIVISM

Despite the fact that student political activism is largely a minority phenomenon, that it is sporadic in nature, and that student leaders do not reflect the rank-and-file of the student population, the impact of student movements has been immense. While the most dramatic possible outcome of student activism is the overthrow of government (limited largely to the Third World), many other less volatile but nonetheless important results deserve careful attention.

In July of 1988, Burma's authoritarian ruler stepped down after 26 years in power. His resignation was precipitated by two months of student demonstrations during which many students were killed.[279] These efforts proved ultimately to be unsuccessful, however, since the military again seized power. The universities were shut down for an extended period, and many students were forced to flee the country. Student protests in South Korea led to concessions by the government that later resulted in elections and significant political change. However, Korean students remain in opposition to the elected government, although there is much less activism since democracy was established.

Such student-induced changes have been most evident in the Third World. However, students in the industrialized nations have occasionally directly influenced politics. A few examples will illustrate the point. In 1968, French students forced President DeGaulle to flee the country for a French military base in West Germany and brought the political system to the verge of collapse.[280] A few years earlier, in Japan, student demonstrations against Prime Minister Kishi forced his resignation. And in the United States, student dissent against the war in Vietnam was a key factor in Lyndon Johnson's decision not to run for a second term as president.[281] More frequently—as in the case of the extraparliamentary opposition in West Germany in the 1960s—student activism does not force political change but rather focuses attention on social or political problems. Thus, the direct and indirect political impact of student movements is considerable, if infrequent.

Since the 1960s, however, there has been relatively little activism in the industrialized countries. There have been few sizable activist campaigns. French students have, from time to time, successfully opposed university reform legislation proposed by the government. American student protests against the former Apartheid regime in South Africa yielded some results.

Student activists frequently serve as a social and political barometer of their societies. Through the issues that they focus on, they sometimes point to flashpoints of concern, sometimes before these issues reach a social boiling point. This may be particularly true for authoritarian societies, where political free expression is not permitted, and for Third World societies, where students are among the best organized and most articulate groups in the country. Campus-based organizations are frequently given more latitude than would be the case elsewhere in society, and students are often more interested in social issues in any case. The concerns expressed by student organizations may well spill over into society later.

Students have also had a considerable cultural impact. Student attitudes about cultural norms are frequently more liberal than is the case for the broader society, and the trends on campus may influence society later. In the United States, trends evident on campus later spread to the middle classes and to some extent to the society at large. For example, concerns about race relations and civil rights were expressed first in the universities in the early 1960s. Students have since been involved in efforts to improve race relations in society, and on the campus as well.[282] The feminist movement first gained strength on campus and then spread.[283] Permissive attitudes concerning abortion, marriage, and drug use first found acceptance among university students and then spread to the broader society. Indeed, it can be argued that one of the most important legacies of the activism of the 1960s in the United States was not political but rather cultural and attitudinal. Similar trends were evident in Western Europe. What are often seen as avant-garde campus ideas eventually spread beyond the universities. Frequently, but not in all cases, student activists are responsible for these trends and are most active in spreading them beyond the gates of the campus. The cultural impact of student activism is hard to assess, but it is nonetheless important.

The educational effect of student activism has, in most countries, been modest. As noted earlier, in a few countries, such as West Germany, students articulated perspectives about university reform and were able to ensure that their ideas were partially implemented in the 1960s. In France, while students did not propose specific reforms, they agitated for change in higher education and were a catalyst for major reforms that resulted in student participation in governance, among other changes. Generally, however, while student activists may complain about the conditions in the university, they have few concrete ideas for change and do not see the university itself as a major battleground. Thus, their impact on the academy has been limited. In the United States, there was much criticism of higher education during the 1960s, but only one set of changes was strongly influenced by the student movement—the growth and institutionalization of women's studies, black studies, and, later, ethnic studies programs in American universities. Student activism has frequently disrupted the normal functioning of universities and has sometimes subjected academic institutions to significant external pressure. One of the legacies of the activism of the 1960s in several Western countries was societal discontent with higher education institutions, in part engendered by public reaction against student activism. In the United States, this contributed to declines in some state budgetary allocations for public higher education.

In a few instances, the impact of student activism has been dramatic and immediate, but more often, activism has had a less direct influence. It has contributed to the development of public opinion or has raised public consciousness about certain issues. At times, students have precipitated actions that they did not favor, such as the seizure of power by the military in South Korea or repression of dissidents in Argentina. There is often a tendency to judge student movements on the basis of the direct impact that students have. But this is too simplistic because the results of student activism are often less direct or immediate. Students might contribute an idea that does not have influence until years later. For example, complaints by a minority of activist students against the policy of in loco parentis in the 1950s and early 1960s in the United States led to the virtual abandonment of the practice a few years later. The styles in culture, attitudes, and music evident on the American campus gradually spread to the rest of the youth culture and beyond. As student generations mature they frequently bring some of the values and orientations learned on campus to the broader society. It is virtually impossible to quantify these less dramatic trends, but they are nonetheless quite important in assessing the impact of student activism.

THE INDUSTRIALIZED NATIONS AND THE THIRD WORLD

While largely ignored in the literature, the dramatic differences between student activism in the Third World and the industrialized nations reveal key analytic variables. Third World students have overthrown governments and have frequently had a direct political impact. This has not been the case in the industrialized nations, where students only rarely have created political change.

Third World student activism is difficult to categorize. Student involvement in nationalist movements was a key factor in many nations in the independence struggles. In Latin America, students forced a major reform in higher education in 1918 that has influenced the university up to the present time. Students have been instrumental in overthrowing governments in many nations in the Third World.[284] Despite their ability to precipitate political upheaval, students have never been able to impose a government that reflects their views. Indeed, student activism often has led to military or other repressive regimes. For example, in both Korea and Thailand, student dissent in the 1960s caused the downfall of regimes, but the military assumed political power rather than groups favored by the students. In Argentina, student unrest led not to a leftist government but rather to right-wing repression of students and others. In Uruguay, Burma, and other countries, student-led activism was met with massive military repression. In other cases, students, while unable to seize power for themselves, were nonetheless successful in precipitating political change that was generally in a direction that they favored. In 1987, student demonstrations in South Korea forced the government to call elections and the result was a significant move toward democracy. While student activists did not feel that the change was large enough, most Koreans saw it as highly significant. The pattern of student unrest in India and a few other Third World countries has focused on the universities themselves in an effort not only to express opposition to established policy but also to win improvement of difficult campus conditions and poor job prospects for graduates.[285] Indian student "indiscipline" has frequently resulted in campus disruption. On occasion, Indian students have also demonstrated against political officials and have sometimes forced them to resign. Thus, the spectrum of Third World student dissent is very broad. Ideologies range from the most revolutionary Marxist theories to Islamic fundamentalism. Sophisticated ideological rhetoric characterizes some student movements, while others have no discernible overall perspective. Some movements aim at the overthrow of the government while others are concerned with poor conditions in the dormitories.

There are many reasons why Third World students have been successful in politics, especially when compared to activist movements in the industrialized nations. While it is not possible in this chapter to develop a comprehensive theoretical explanation for Third World student politics, it is worthwhile to point to some of the key factors.

- Third World nations often lack the established political institutions and structures of the industrialized nations, and it is thus easier for an organized group, such as the students, to have a direct impact on politics.
- Students have, in many cases, been involved in independence movements and have been a recognized part of the political system. Thus, in contrast to the West, where activism is seen by most people to be an aberration and an illegitimate intrusion into politics, Third World students are expected to participate directly in politics and activism is seen as a legitimate part of the political system.
- Third World university students constitute a kind of incipient elite and have, in many countries, a consciousness that they are somehow special. They are members of a small minority with access to postsecondary education. Their prospects for later success in careers are very good.[286] The advantages, real and imagined, accruing to those who have a university degree and the historical sense of elite consciousness are a powerful combination.
- The location of the major universities of the Third World contributes to the efficacy of activism. Many are located in the capital cities, and a large proportion of the student population is within easy reach of the centers of power. This simple fact of geography makes demonstrations easier to organize and gives students a sense that they are at the center of power and have easy access to it.
- Relatively few Third World nations have effective, functioning democratic systems. As a result of this, and of the widespread problems of illiteracy and poor communications, students are often seen as spokespersons for a broader population. They have, in a sense, an authority exceeding their numbers, and for this reason those in power often take student demonstrations and grievances seriously. In many cases, small student agitations have acted as a catalyst for larger social movements or have had a surprising impact on the authorities. In a sense, Third World students act as the "conscience" of their societies.
- Because Third World students, on the average, come from higher socioeconomic groups than their compeers in industrialized nations, they have an added impact.

While there are significant national differences and changes in terms of social class background as higher education expands, much of the student population in many Third World nations is drawn from urban elite backgrounds, and these students have, through their families, direct access to powerful segments of society.

These factors are a partial explanation for the relative effectiveness of student activist movements in the Third World in the past several decades. While students in industrialized countries, particularly during the 1960s, had an impact on their societies, their role pales in significance when compared to the Third World student movements. Further, Third World students have continued to be a force—they did not disappear after the decade of the 1960s.

CONCLUSION

There are many variations because of historical circumstance, level of sociopolitical development, and political and educational systems. Student movements are difficult to predict. Further, effective movements depend on external circumstances for their success—on the media and on acceptance by key social groups of the legitimacy of the activist movement. Student movements, by themselves, are never powerful enough to overturn a government. The movement depends on its goals and tactics and on the perception of legitimacy that it manages to create.

Student movements seem to go through cycles. Since the 1960s, in most industrialized nations, student movements have been neither active nor successful. In some Third World nations, activism has continued although overall the trend has been toward quiescence. In many ways, it is just as important to study student politics when it is at a low ebb as it is during a militant phase. Both phases can provide insights into the nature of student politics and perhaps into broader political realities. The collapse of Communism had a profound effect on leftist student activism. Marxism was one of the main ideological backbones of many student movements, and it was largely discredited by the failure of most of the world's state socialist regimes. No left ideology has emerged to replace Marxism. Conservative governments came to power in much of Western Europe in the 1980s and early 1990s, and this too had a negative influence on student activism. There will inevitably be an upswing in activism and a recovery of the ideological and idealistic basis of student activism. However, neither the timing nor the nature of the next wave is clear.

8

Student Politics in the Third World

Student political activism remains a key issue for Third World universities as well as for governments.[287] Students continue to be politically active, on occasion contributing to political unrest. The scope and pace of student politics change over time and across national boundaries, but the issue remains one of the most important for higher education administrators, planners, and government officials. Since the end of the 1960s, the contrast between continued political activism among students in the Third World has provided a dramatic contrast to the relative quiet in the industrialized nations of Western Europe and North America. This chapter examines this contrast as well as the main characteristics of student activism in the Third World—a complex phenomenon with implications for both the university and society.

The definition of the Third World itself has become more problematical in recent years. At one time, the term Third World was applied to all the nonindustrialized countries of Africa, Asia, and Latin America. Now, dramatic political and economic changes have blurred economic distinctions and transformed the political landscape. Economic growth in many countries—especially on the Pacific Rim, but also including Brazil, Mexico, and Argentina in Latin America—and the rise of the petroleum-based economies of the Middle East have brought more regions relative economic prosperity. Singapore and South Korea, for example, are now wealthier than Portugal. Social changes have dramatically increased literacy rates and educational standards in much of the Third World. The collapse of Communism has also brought fundamental political changes to Central and Eastern Europe and the former Soviet Union, with implications for the rest of the world. Nevertheless, it is still useful to discuss the countries of the Third World as a group, recognizing that the differences among the nations of the Third World are now as great as the similarities. We are concerned, in this chapter, with the traditional countries of the Third World—Africa, most of Asia, and Latin America.

Student politics is generally viewed by those in authority as a negative factor—something to be eliminated from academic life. It is not enough to condemn student politics as a negative force. It is useful to understand the factors that impel student political activism and to examine the results of this activism. In some respects, student political involvement can contribute to the processes of nation building and political socialization. Student activism contributes to social change in the Third World and focuses national attention on political and social questions that might otherwise be ignored by the political system.

Student political activism may differ greatly by country, region, and historical period. The most dramatic difference at present is between the industrialized nations and the Third World. There are variations among Third World nations as well. In India, much student activism tends to focus on campus-based issues that are occasionally linked to broader political and ideological questions. Typically, however, student activism is motivated by political and social forces in society, with attention focused away from campus. Countries with a strong tradition of student activism—often stemming from student participation in independence struggles—are likely to have active student movements. Government policies concerning activism affects the viability and the tactics of student movements. In political systems that permit the relatively free functioning of social organizations and movements, students are likely to be politically active, but such activism is less often revolutionary in nature. Social and economic conditions also affect student political movements and organizations. Conversely, poor campus conditions, as in India, and in recent years in Africa, have stimulated activism and protest. On the other hand, an "elite" campus environment can also promote student political consciousness. Variations in levels by academic field and discipline can also be noted, with students in the social sciences and humanities in most countries more politically involved than those in the natural sciences and professional fields.

With such a diverse phenomenon, it is not surprising that there is no widely accepted theoretical perspective concerning student activism. The purpose of this chapter is not to create such a formulation, but rather to examine the nature of student politics in Third World nations. This is particularly important since most of the theories relating to student politics refer mainly to the experience of the industrialized nations.[288] The literature on student activism is a curious blend of the descriptive and the theoretical. The 1960s saw a massive outpouring of publication when Western nations were disrupted by student activist movements. Since then, the topic is seldom discussed in Western academic circles. Much of the literature reflects the concerns of

Western social scientists and university officials impelled in considerable part by a desire to understand and to cope with the activist movements that had arisen so suddenly. The paradigms used were largely Western in orientation. The political models reflected the realities of North America and Western Europe. This literature is not necessarily directly relevant to the Third World. While academic institutions have similar roots worldwide, Third World realities are distinctive. Further, the cyclical pattern so evident in the West does not necessarily hold in the Third World. In most Third World nations, there was no dramatic upsurge during the 1960s and no dramatic decline in the mid-1970s. National variations in the scope and timing of student activism in the Third World exist. In many respects, the Western "bias" of the literature has distorted analyses of student politics in the Third World. While it is possible to utilize conceptual frameworks from the Western literature and even some of the general research trends, it is necessary to look at Third World student activism as a relatively independent phenomenon.

THE POLITICAL FRAMEWORK

Universities do not function in a vacuum. They are integrally linked to social, political, and economic realities. This is especially true in the Third World, where traditions of autonomy are weaker. Students are also attuned to societal developments, and student political activism in most Third World countries is directly related to broader political forces. It is rare for a student movement to be fully campus based and concerned mainly with university issues. There are many reasons for this close relationship between students and the political system.

Third World political systems are typically less "dense" than those in the industrialized nations. There are fewer competing political forces, and this permits students to play a more direct and powerful role. The mass media are weaker; parliamentary systems are often ineffective or nonexistent; trade unions, consumer groups, and the myriad of interest groups typically found in the Western industrial nations are missing; and the educated middle class is small. University students, as one of the few easily mobilized and politically articulate groups in society, play a crucial role in politics. It has been said that student movements constitute something of a "conscience" for their societies, as they often articulate the concerns of broader segments of the population that are unable to voice their discontent.

Students are a uniquely mobilizable group in the Third World. In many countries, the major university is located in the capital city, often a short distance from the seat of political power. Students are located on the campus and generally have their own newspapers and journals. Politics touches the lives of students more directly than is the case in the industrialized countries. The decisions of government have an immediate effect on the direction of the economy, including employment prospects for graduates in countries where a very large proportion go into the civil service or other government employment. Students take politics very seriously, in part because it affects them very directly and in part because they have, in many places, a consciousness of their unique role in society. Students see themselves as a kind of "incipient elite" destined for power and responsible for exercising their political power even while students.[289]

While there are a number of Third World nations that have exhibited considerable political stability, in general political systems are less stable than in most industrialized nations. The basic political fabric of society can be torn apart by disputes concerning language policy, social reform, or other issues. Many Third World societies are multiethnic, and this presents further potential for unrest and contestation. Many of the major political and social questions facing society directly affect students. Language policy, for example, often has implications for the medium of instruction in the educational system. Disparities in the treatment of ethnic groups also affect student populations. Students are often more ideologically aware than the population generally. Ideological awareness comes from a variety of sources, including the nature of university education and the psychological propensities of students.[290]

The reaction of the political system to student activist movements helps to shape their actions, orientations, and, of course, the impact they have on society. Many Third World political systems are relatively intolerant of political activism, fearing that the students may generate political instability or cause disruption. A growing number of countries have sought to ensure that the universities will be relatively free of political activism. In some countries, a "certificate of suitability," aimed mainly at checking for political dissidents, is required for anyone wishing to attend university. Nations as different ideologically as China and Singapore use this means of controlling dissent. Those denied such certification may not enroll in postsecondary educational institutions. In the Chinese case, such measures proved ineffective at the time of the Tienanmen Square demonstrations in 1989, proving that when political consciousness is at a high level, it is very difficult to keep it bottled up permanently. Legislation concerning the operation of universities has sometimes included restrictions on political expression on campus by both students and academic staff. The traditional concept of university autonomy has, as a result, been weakened.[291] In many Third World nations, campus unrest is dealt with harshly by political authorities, with repression of organizations, jailing of student leaders, and severe limitations on freedom of movement imposed on activist organizations. The traditional insulation of the university campus from external interference, honored most strongly in Latin America, has lost its force in most countries, and police or military authorities are willing to come onto the campus to deal with unrest or perceived disruption.[292] Malaysia's University Act, which was stimulated by student unrest and widespread rioting in 1969, severely limits university autonomy. Restrictions in many other countries—including Thailand, Singapore, Indonesia, South Korea, and the Philippines—have limited the scope of student activism and indicate the concern political authorities have about the potential force of student activism.

It would be tempting to develop or posit a hypothesis that the more democratic and civil libertarian a regime is in the Third World, the more likely it is to permit a fairly high level of activism. In general, this seems to be the case, although political regimes can change quickly and tolerance can evaporate. It is perhaps significant that in those countries where activism is most widely tolerated, it generally has the least impact on the political structure, precisely because there are other competing political forces at work, or because the regime itself is quite stable.

Governments consider students a potentially powerful political force and have in many instances moved to ensure that activism does not become a political threat. Despite these efforts, students have been influential in politics, and efforts at repression have not been completely successful. The fact is, however, that student activism is more difficult when restrictions are placed on it by external authorities, although governments have been unable to eliminate activism completely. In fact, repression sometimes leads to renewed commitment and public sympathy. Given a sufficiently severe social crisis, strong pro-activist student opinion, and a desire to participate, activism cannot be completely repressed without disrupting the academic system and closing universities. Where governments have felt themselves sufficiently threatened, universities have indeed been closed and in some cases entire student populations dismissed. Nevertheless, even such dramatic action has sometimes failed to quell student activism. Without question, in the Third World, students are a key political force—one that must be reckoned with by governments. Students are not necessarily involved in all political struggles, but when they become mobilized, they are a powerful force.

THE ACADEMIC ENVIRONMENT

Students live and work in academic institutions and the environment, curriculum, and policies of the university affect student activism. Although students are generally concerned about societal politics, the institutional milieu plays a significant role. In order to comprehend student politics, it is also necessary to understand the nature of the university and its culture.

Universities are unique institutions in many ways. They have a degree of autonomy rare among large social institutions, even if this autonomy has been under attack in recent years. The educational culture of the university is important also. The process of learning and the nature of the curriculum can contribute to political consciousness. For students in the social sciences particularly, the study of social forces contributes to an understanding, and sometimes to criticism, of established institutions and policies. Universities have unique cultures, histories, and practices that form student political consciousness and make academe a uniquely fertile ground for political movements.[293] Universities are meritocratic institutions and emphasize promotion and advancement by merit alone. This concept often contrasts with more traditional practices in Third World societies, where family, ethnic group, or tribe is more central. The meritocratic ideal is part of an academic value system often at odds with traditional norms and values and helps to engender an oppositional consciousness among students.

The university as a community also contributes to the political consciousness and organization of the students. In the Third World, independent and autonomous groups of young people are unusual. The subculture of the university is unique in the freedom that university students have from their families. Further, in many countries, the subculture of the university (and of intellectuals generally) is frequently an oppositional subculture, which examines carefully and critically the society of which it is a part.[294] The professoriate often adds to the sense of intellectual ferment by encouraging students to ask difficult questions and by displaying critical political and social views. The campus community is more cosmopolitan than its surrounding society and inevitably comes into some conflict with it. While student populations come from relatively privileged strata of the population, they have greater opportunities to interact with compeers from different social groups. Traditional barriers of caste, ethnicity, tribe, and religion seem less important in the meritocratic atmosphere of the university.[295] The ethos of the university community tends to contribute to interest in social and political questions and to make it easier to express these interests and to organize for political discussion and action.

The university, in almost all countries, is a more autonomous, independent, and liberal environment than its surrounding society. The professoriate, while seldom revolutionary in its political orientation, is usually somewhat to the left of the general population.[296] Even in countries where there are significant limitations on freedom of expression and action, the campus is allowed a greater degree of freedom than the rest of the society. To some extent, political authorities recognize that a university requires a free environment in order to provide quality education and research. Political authorities have always found it difficult to enforce total conformity in the universities. The balance between the requirements of a quality educational institution and the demands of government for political loyalty is a delicate one. Student activism is often able to flourish in the confusing middle ground between freedom and enforced conformity.

Universities contribute in other ways to student activism. Student newspapers are able to ensure that students are quickly informed of events and are able to create an atmosphere that stimulates activism and political consciousness. In this environment, organizing a demonstration at the center of political power is relatively easy. As universities have grown in size, it becomes easier to mobilize a large number of individuals on a variety of political issues. Even a small minority of 10 percent of a student population of 10,000 is a large crowd of 1,000 students. While student demonstrations are almost everywhere minority phenomena, large groups can be relatively easily organized.

In a few countries, campus issues and conditions stimulate student activism, and this activism sometimes spills from the campus to the society. The most dramatic example of campus-based activism is India, where poor, and in many cases deteriorating, conditions combined with an interest by external political groups in campus politics often stimulate activism that links campus and society. The Indian case may be relevant to other countries if standards of education decline or unemployment of university graduates becomes endemic.[297] In India, most activism in the past several decades has been campus based and stimulated by local issues—such as examinations or complaints against administrators or faculty. Poor and deteriorating conditions in the hostels (dormitories) and a general feeling, supported by statistics, that graduates (except in a few fields) are in a difficult employment market are underlying factors. The unrest that emerges is often violent and disruptive of academic life. The University of Bombay and many other Indian universities have had their annual examinations disrupted or postponed by student unrest. India's most prestigious university, the Jawaharlal Nehru University (JNU), has been closed down on a number of occasions due to local campus disputes. JNU was closed for several months after rioting damaged several staff houses during a dispute relating to hostel regulations. In India, external political groups frequently attempt to gain support in the universities and then contribute to local, and largely nonideological, student unrest. The combination of a tradition of local student politics, off-campus political groups, and deteriorating conditions in the universities is a powerful one. While India is almost unique in the scope and intensity of local student activism, campus conditions contribute to student activism and to a generalized feeling of disaffection among students throughout the Third World.

The organization of studies has an impact on student activism. Academic systems that permit long periods of time between examinations, that have centralized examinations, and that leave students relatively unsupervised and without direct academic responsibilities are more prone to student activism than are the more regulated academic systems. Students in systems with relatively few requirements have more time to participate in political movements. The sense of constant responsibility for academic work is not strong and in general lectures and other assignments are not compulsory. In contrast, academic systems that are organized according to the American course-credit system, in which students are examined regularly by their teachers, seem to instill a greater sense of responsibility. Further, there is less time for extracurricular activities of all kinds because of the constant assessment of academic work. There has been a trend in the Third World to shift to an academic organization that provides more supervision and continuing assessment.

The academic environment is a complex one. It is based on traditional approaches to higher education, on patterns of administration, on sets of expectations for academic work, and on particular locations and cultures of academic institutions. These factors have a profound impact on the nature and orientation of student political activism. Perhaps the most important force, however, is the very nature of a university education. It is not surprising, therefore, that university students sometimes take their newly found understanding seriously and translate their knowledge into action.

HISTORICAL TRADITIONS

Although universities stem from a common Western institutional model, nations have different academic histories. Historical circumstances and traditions have quite a bit to do with the nature and scope of student activism in a national context. Perhaps the most important general difference in this regard between the industrialized nations and the Third World is the role played by the academic community and students in independence struggles in many Third World nations. This key political role has legitimated the participation of students in national politics.[298] Because students participated in the national struggles, they have achieved a place in history and their contemporary political role is considered legitimate. Governments have attempted to eliminate this legitimacy, but it remains a powerful force. If students are somehow expected to play a political role, their actions and opinions carry a greater weight. In the Third World students, as representatives of the middle classes, have been expected to play an active political role.

In Latin America, there has been a strong tradition of student activism that continues to the present, although at a significantly diminished level in recent years as democratic governments have taken power throughout much of Latin America. Stimulated by the famous reform movement of 1918, which transformed the Latin American university and placed students in the governance process, Latin American universities have long been sanctuaries for student radicalism. Repressive military-led regimes in the 1970s managed to limit activism by jailing students and sometimes closing universities. The traditional autonomy of the public universities was severely weakened during this period. In the past decade, the reestablishment of democratic governments throughout the continent has also led to diminished activism, perhaps because the new regimes have been seen as legitimate by most people in Latin America. There has also been a shift from public institutions to private universities, and this has further diminished activism.[299] Without question, the historical tradition of student activism in Latin America remains strong and students continue to be involved in university governance in a number of countries as well as in politics.[300]

Students were active in independence struggles in a number of countries—including, among others, India, Indonesia, Bangladesh, and Egypt. In countries where students were active at such important points in national development, they have often maintained a sense of their political efficacy and there has been an acceptance of students as legitimate political actors, in part based on their involvement in the national struggle. With the exception of Latin America, there are no Third World nations with a tradition of student involvement in academic governance and in university reform. Student political participation has, in general, been on the national level and with ideologically based political movements.

Students have historically been involved in cultural and linguistic reform movements, and have been instrumental in shaping the cultural traditions of the modern period. Students, for example, were at the forefront of the struggle to use Bahasa Indonesia as the Indonesian national language, and they provided the intellectual underpinnings of the national movement. Muslim students in India were active in the intellectual movement that led to the founding of Pakistan, and Indian students were involved at all stages of the nationalist movement.[301] Historically, the universities have been places of cultural ferment and debate. This is not surprising considering the small size of the intellectual class in most Third World nations prior to the growth of modern universities in the postindependence period. When the history of the growth of nationalism and of cultural ferment is written in many Third World nations, the academic community—both students and faculty—will emerge as an important force.

In prerevolutionary China, students played a central political and cultural role. The May 4th movement of 1919 was spurred by students and marked the emergence of students as a significant political force.[302] Students demanded radical solutions to the many problems facing China at the time and contributed to the intellectual and political ferment that culminated in the 1949 revolution that brought the Communists to power. In Burma, students were active in creating a nationalist movement in the 1920s, and they remained politically involved until the military government put an end to all political activity in the 1960s.[303] This pattern was repeated in Vietnam and elsewhere. While there were a few international contacts among students in Third World countries during the colonial period, most of these movements emerged in isolation.[304] Where there was contact, it was between the universities in the colonial center with students and intellectuals in the colonies.

Historical traditions function in different ways in different countries. In some, students were directly involved in the independence struggle. In others, students played an intellectual and cultural rather than a political role. In Latin America, students were involved in campus reforms, but this was generally not the case. In almost all cases, the intellectual influences of the West—the ideology of nationalism, and later of socialism and Marxism all permeated academic and intellectual communities in the Third World. Special ferment occurred after World War I, as the ideology of colonialism came under attack and the Russian revolution produced an electrifying impact among intellectuals and nationalists. While the historical tradition differs from country to country, there is no question but that history remains a key factor in understanding contemporary student activism.

SOCIOLOGICAL CURRENTS

Student political activism does not occur equally in all types of postsecondary educational institutions or among all segments of the student population. Student politics, even in the most troubled environment, is almost always a minority phenomenon— the majority of students do not participate in student movements. In order to understand student activism, it is useful to consider some of the sociological variables that seem to affect activism. Unfortunately, the largest amount of sociological research has been conducted in the industrialized nations, particularly in the United States, but some generalizations relevant to Third World nations can be made.[305] National differences are very important, yet there are some common themes that emerge from observation of a large number of student activist movements in Third World nations.

Much has been written about Third World university students as "elites," either present or future. It is almost universally true that university students come from the upper strata of societies throughout the Third World. Further, student populations tend to be largely urban in countries that are predominantly rural. Student populations in many instances contain disproportionate numbers of young people from minority groups with a tradition of education or have achieved a certain level of affluence. Thus, Third World student populations are often distinct from the general population.

In most industrialized nations students are not fully representative of national populations. Students come from more affluent and urbanized backgrounds than does the general population. In general, the larger and more comprehensive the postsecondary education system, the more representative the student population. In small academic systems that enroll a limited proportion of the age-cohort, there is usually a high level of elitism. In the United States, for example, the student population is more representative of the general population in its socioeconomic characteristics, although even there the elite sector of the system is disproportionately affluent in terms of student background. In the Third World context, those countries with larger academic systems—such as the Philippines, India, and to some extent, Nigeria—have a relatively more "democratic" pattern of access to higher education, but even in these countries, students are hardly typical of the general population. Third World students come from more elite backgrounds than students in industrialized nations.

As student populations are generally not typical of national populations, this naturally has some implications for both student activism and for the role of the university in society. The role, for example, of such groups as the Chinese in Southeast Asia, the Ibos in Nigeria, the Brahmins, Christians, or Parsis in India, the Christians in Indonesia, and the Indians in East Africa all reflect the importance of minority communities in higher education. Relatively affluent backgrounds give university students a certain confidence in their future social roles and expectations concerning the way they should function while in the university. There are, in many countries, further variations concerning field of study. Students in the sciences and professional fields tend to come from more privileged backgrounds than those in the social sciences and humanities, although the differences are often not very great.

Student activists are atypical of the general student population in many countries. Activists tend to come disproportionately from the social sciences and the humanities, and very seldom from fields such as agriculture, engineering, or medicine. There are a number of reasons for this phenomenon. Social science students, in almost all countries, are among the most liberal (or radical) in their ideological views and the most interested in societal problems and issues. Thus, there is an element of self-selection and propensity toward social concern prior to entry into the university. In addition, the content of the social sciences is focused on societal issues and on an understanding of the problems of modernizing societies. In the Third World particularly, the gulf between reality and a desired social goal is often wide, leading students to question the efficacy of existing political arrangements. Social science faculty are the most liberal (or radical) in the university in most countries, and it is possible that the sometimes critical stance of the professoriate has some influence on the students. Social science students are, of course, not the only students interested in politics. Next in concern are generally students in the humanities. In some countries, especially in Latin America, law students seem to exhibit a high degree of concern for politics.

Student activist leaders tend to come from the most affluent and cosmopolitan sectors of the student population. In many instances, they are the sons (less often, the daughters) of politically or economically powerful families in their societies. They have, in other words, connections to the elite. These students have an understanding of the way power works in their society and a willingness to attempt to use it. Their backgrounds give them a feeling that their families will protect them from the risks that sometimes come with participation in activist movements. In other words, the perceived risks of political involvement—for example, possible disciplinary action by the universities or arrest by the civil authorities—may not seem too formidable to students from affluent backgrounds.

Student activists are often among the most able students in terms of academic performance. Although the sociological studies of student leadership have mostly been carried out in the industrialized nations, this generalization seems to hold true for many Third World nations as well.[306] Relatively few student leaders who come to public attention have poor academic records. In some countries, such as India, there seems to be a pattern of "permanent student leaders," and these individuals are often marginal academically or no longer even enrolled in the university. This pattern exists in some other Third World nations as well, but it is unusual.

IDEOLOGICAL ORIENTATIONS

Student movements are assumed to be leftist in their ideology and nationalist in direction, with a strong ideological interest and an anti-establishment perspective. These generalizations, which stem largely from the militant decade of the 1960s and relate to the experience of North America and Western Europe, are applied throughout the world and in all historical periods. While it is true that the majority of contemporary student movements are probably left-of-center in their orientation, there are considerable variations among student movements. Edward Shils has argued that student activists—as well as intellectuals generally—tend to be "anti-establishment" regardless of the orientation of the ruling authorities.[307]

Student politics, with some exceptions, is the politics of idealism. Students look for consistent, just, and far-reaching solutions to the many problems of society. They tend to be more interested in ideological issues since ideologies offer "complete" solutions to problems. Compromise and accommodation, practiced in most political systems, do not appeal to student idealism. Student leaders are particularly interested in complete solutions to problems and often embrace political (or religious) ideologies that offer a total program for society. Marxism has had a great appeal for student activists for this reason. However, the collapse of Communism in the Soviet Union and Eastern Europe and the adoption of a "market orientation" in China has significantly diminished the appeal of traditional Marxist ideas. It is fair to say that leftist ideologies of all kinds have been called into question by these developments, and the ideological moorings of student movements are less secure.

Despite the largely leftist ideology of student movements, there are significant variations in ideological currents and growing diversity in the Third World. Historically, student movements in Europe were occasionally rightist in their orientation. Both Mussolini in Italy and Hitler in Germany had student support.[308] The nationalist student movements in Europe in the nineteenth century could not be classified as "left" in their ideology—and these influenced early Third World student movements. In the Third World, nationalism and socialism were in many countries intertwined. Further, the influence of the Russian revolution of 1917 on the emergent Third World nationalist and student movements was considerable. In countries like the United States, Britain, and France, where liberal and left opinions have characterized student activist movements, there have been influential rightist student organizations as well.

The situation in the Third World is increasingly complex. Radical ideological currents remain strong in student movements and organizations. In Latin America, left ideological sentiments continue to dominate, although there are some changes. For example, during the radical Allende period in Chile, students at the Catholic University expressed opposition from center or right-wing positions.[309] In the 1990s, the conservative Catholic Opus Dei movement has strength on campuses in some Latin American countries. On occasion, extreme leftist student groups oppose democratic regimes. Virulent nationalism occasionally attracts student support, and this trend is usually allied with rightist political groups. Student activism has declined in sub-Saharan Africa.[310] Students have often protested against the deteriorating conditions in most African universities, but have been less directly involved with broader politics. Nigeria, which has had a strong tradition of student political involvement, has been relatively calm as well, due perhaps to a repressive military regime which does not tolerate campus dissent. In general, however, student opinion and orientations seem to be leftist, and even where campus conditions and issues have been the primary focus of activism, as in Nigeria, radicalism is the dominant mode.

The situation in Asia and in the Islamic countries is varied. Although students played an active role in the Cultural Revolution in China, their participation seems to have been as an adjunct to the dominant faction in the Chinese Communist Party at the time. The participation of Indonesian students in the movement that overthrew the Sukarno government in 1965 was a reaction to the leftist orientation of the ruling authorities at that time.[311] Egyptian students have not been politically militant, although campus support among some Egyptian students and intellectuals for the orthodox Islamic Muslim Brotherhood is significant. Similarly, in countries like Malaysia and Pakistan, there is growing support in the universities for an Islamic revivalist political movement and a stress on Islam as a political current. In Iran, the Islamic forces that overthrew the Shah had strong support on campus, and the militant Islamic Taliban forces which have been a powerful force in Afghanistan have had strong student support and participation. In Saudi Arabia, students oppose the monarchy from both left and Islamic perspectives, while Islamic militancy is a strong current among Palestinian students. Governments that are secular minded or those that must deal with populations not fully in favor of the new religious revival have been faced with a dilemma in dealing with these "rightist" student movements.

Thus, in the contemporary Third World it is no longer true to point to campus activist movements as uniformly leftist in their orientation. A revival, particularly in the Islamic world, of religious orthodoxy, in part perhaps as a reaction to the predominant secularism and Westernization of the universities, is an important element. Students remain an anti-establishment force in many nations, criticizing entrenched political regimes for their failings and sometimes leading antigovernment movements. In recent years, students have been a key force in antigovernment movements in South Korea, the Philippines, Thailand, Chile, Argentina, Brazil, Malaysia, and other countries. In each of these instances, there are recognizable ideological differences. Students were instrumental in the popular movements that contributed to the downfall of Communist regimes in Central and Eastern Europe. In Poland and Czechoslovakia, especially, students were a key part of the dissident coalition.

THE FUTURE

Students are and will remain key political actors in the Third World. While students may not be a political power in all countries at all times, the conditions that make for effective student political participation exist in the Third World and are likely to continue. One cannot make the same prediction for the industrialized nations, where the emergence of student activism is the result of rather special circumstances. Despite the continuing importance of student activism, it is difficult to predict where activism will play a major political role. Further, student political involvement varies from country to country and over time, often due to external political stimulus. Thus, a left-wing movement may collapse and the next wave of activism might be religious or conservative in focus.

Third World students have not in general been interested in university reform or change and, when they have, they have as often as not actually opposed such reforms. In Latin America, for example, students have consistently opposed changes in admissions policies, finances, examination procedures, and the like. Students in India have also often agitated against reforms in higher education. Thus, Third World activism has in the main been less of a threat to the functioning of academic institutions than to the political system itself. In a few countries, such as India, students have been concerned with campus-based issues, but usually to correct an injustice or express frustration rather than to attack the academic system itself. The one major exception to this generalization was the university reform movement in Latin America early in the twentieth century, which resulted in major academic change. Students have, on occasion, taken an interest in issues that affect higher education, such as language (and by implication the language of instruction), but there have been few university reform movements in the Third World. Students have been surprisingly tolerant of academic systems that sometimes produce neither a high quality of instruction nor jobs for graduates. As a general rule, however, those Third World academic systems that are able to provide a reasonable level of upward mobility for the graduates of universities and jobs for graduates will probably remain relatively free of activism directed at the institutions themselves.

It is more difficult to predict the ideological direction and the tactical orientation of student movements. There is some tendency in the Third World for student activist movements to look to traditional cultural and religious values—particularly in the Islamic countries. The trend toward anti-establishment politics remains strong. The student predilection toward ideologies, particularly those that offer "total" solutions to societal problems and models for social reconstruction has continuing salience.

Student movements do not emerge from a vacuum but are produced by the social and political environment and by government (and sometimes academic) policies concerning student activism. Evidence shows that repression, legal or otherwise, does work, at least in the short run. In Argentina, Uruguay, and several Central American nations, right-wing governments used a combination of repression against the universities and jailing (and sometimes torturing) activists as a means of controlling student unrest. In Malaysia, legislation placed restrictions on student activists as well as on the functioning of the universities. In many countries, universities or entire academic systems are closed down by the authorities in response to activism. Such draconian measures are usually effective, at least temporarily, in stifling dissent in the universities. The long-term result may be damaging to the universities, creating a deeper sense of alienation among young people, and perhaps stimulating an "underground" oppositional movement. Repression, while often effective, does have implications beyond the simple snuffing out of dissent. Repression, in some cases, can trigger even more massive social unrest. Authorities have occasionally tried to co-opt student movements and organizations in order to control them and to ensure campus calm. Student leaders have been brought into the government and authorities have listened to student grievances. Such tactics sometimes work to defuse dissent.

III

Exchanges:
People and Ideas

9

Gigantic Peripheries: India and China in the World Knowledge System

At first glance, China and India seem to be well positioned for scientific leadership, and in fact they have achieved considerable success. They have relatively well-developed scientific infrastructures today, including scientific laboratories, universities, a network of scientific journals, and large numbers of scientists and researchers. India is, in fact, the Third World's scientific superpower in numbers of qualified scientists, and China is not far behind. Both have a long scientific tradition—dating back many centuries—in indigenous science and scholarship and well over a century for Western-oriented science and higher education. Both have, in the years following World War II, promulgated scientific plans and have taken scientific development seriously. India has become a major force in computer software, based on its tradition of excellence in mathematics. Both are nuclear powers and have a growing high-tech industrial base capable of producing sophisticated products, although not on the cutting edge of world technology.

This chapter has at its core a surprising contradiction: its basic argument is that the world's two largest countries, at least in terms of population, are now, and will remain for the foreseeable future relatively unimportant in international science and scholarship. They are, and will continue to be, influenced by scientific developments external to them. They will not have equal access to the major elements of scientific communication such as international scholarly journals and databases. In basic scientific research in most fields and disciplines, these two countries will remain behind the world leaders, and they will be dependent on ideas and discoveries from abroad. They are, and will remain, peripheral in the world scientific system.

Why must these two large and powerful countries be relegated to peripheral status in world science and technology? The truth is that world science is highly centralized, that its infrastructures are located in a small number of industrialized countries, that advanced science requires large investments of funds and highly sophisticated laboratories, and that top scientific personnel are concentrated in a small number of countries and at the key academic and research institutions within those countries. It takes a tremendous investment to break into the "major leagues" of world science, and it is unlikely that either China or India will have the resources to accomplish this.

This is not to say that these two important countries cannot play a significant scientific role, or that science and research cannot help to contribute to national development. Both already play a role and have used science for development. By focusing on maintaining a scientific base, supporting scientific research and higher education, and ensuring that the best scientific personnel do not leave the country, scientific research can be sustained at a reasonable level.[312] By targeting specific areas of science as essential to national development and generously supporting these, it may be possible to build up world-class science in a few fields. China and India need to be realistic about their position in the world system of science and technology. By recognizing what is, and is not, possible, they can make the best use of indigenous potential and develop effective strategies for functioning in the world scientific system.

There are also distinctions to be made between the development of universities and of ancillary research capacity for internal purposes, and involvement in research at the international level. Both countries have built up large and differentiated academic systems that serve their domestic needs. Both countries have a number of universities as well as research facilities that approach or meet international standards. Advanced training in universities is necessary for expanding economies. Thus, the peripheral positions of these two countries in world research is not an argument against developing higher education. However, effective planning for higher education must take into account the nature of the international knowledge system and the place of the country in that system.

Countries cannot free themselves of the international knowledge system. Both the basic institutional structure of modern higher education and science and the intellectual underpinnings are Western in nature and have come to dominate the world. All contemporary universities are based on the Western model, regardless of their location.[313] No developing country has made a serious attempt to build a new university model. Further, the scientific communications networks—journals, databases, and the like—are also Western in orientation and controlled by the West.

This discussion has relevance to developing countries generally, since all have seen higher education as a central part of nation building, and many have stressed research as a function of higher education. The points made in this chapter apply to all developing countries, since all face similar problems in their efforts to build up scientific capacity and to work in the context of the world knowledge system. With a much smaller population and resource bases than China or India, each developing country faces distinct circumstances, and their higher education and scientific development will be determined in considerable part by these realities. Many countries, such as most in sub-Saharan Africa, will find it impossible to build up a research infrastructure able to function at an international level, and universities will need to adjust to this reality. Others, such as the newly industrializing countries of East Asia, do have the financial and personnel resources to build up a research base in selected areas.[314] However, many of the issues that affect China and India are also relevant for the NICs despite their greater wealth.

Adjusting to the realities of the international knowledge system is not solely a matter for the developing countries. Small industrialized nations or those outside the mainstream must survive in this context of limited resources due to size and position. Norway, for example, despite its high per capita income, must adjust its educational and scientific priorities to fit its place in the international knowledge system. Many Norwegian scholars obtain advanced degrees in other countries and use English as the language of scientific communication—and sometimes of teaching. The experiences of the largest and best developed of the Third World nations—China and India—provide relevant lessons for other countries.

THE INTERNATIONAL KNOWLEDGE SYSTEM

It is beyond the scope of this chapter to discuss the international knowledge system in detail, but we should look at some of the key elements of the system as they affect China and India.[315] By international knowledge system, we mean the people and institutions that create knowledge and the structures that communicate knowledge worldwide. There are, of course, many different kinds of knowledge. Our focus is on research-based scientific knowledge that is circulated internationally. This knowledge is both basic in that it relates to the advancement of the scientific disciplines and applied in that it is used for technological and industrial products and innovations. While the natural, engineering, and biomedical sciences are perhaps most central, we are also concerned with the social sciences and even the humanities. The knowledge system affects all of the scholarly disciplines as well as applied fields. We are less concerned here with the areas of indigenous science and scholarship because these are not generally circulated internationally, although the example of acupuncture in China shows that there are some exceptions to this generalization. Fields such as religious studies, domestic history, music, and art have strong local roots and are much less dependent on external forces, but even these fields often look abroad for the latest methodological approaches or for scholarly legitimation in the West.

In the international knowledge system, the means of production and distribution are both centralized. The bulk of the world's research and development expenditures are made by a small number of industrialized countries. Developing nations, including China and India, account for under 10 percent of the world total. The United States, the European Union, and Japan dominate. Russia (the former Soviet Union), at one time a research power, is no longer very active in research at the international level. Both basic and applied research is dominated by the major industrialized countries. Basic science depends on funding from governmental sources, the existence of a large and well-trained university-based academic scientific community (or in a very few cases government-sponsored research laboratories), and a competitive scientific culture that stresses research productivity for career advancement and prestige. Increasingly, basic science requires expensive laboratories with the most up-to-date equipment and access to libraries and databases. Only the large, research-oriented universities in the industrialized countries offer these resources. Further, new interdisciplinary or subdisciplinary specialties are increasingly at the frontiers of science, and these tend to emerge in large and well-equipped academic institutions. Basic science also depends increasingly on networking—the personal and professional contacts that are helpful to scientific advancement. Being at the center of scientific development is crucial to involvement in these informal networks.

The scientific communications system is also centralized and dominated by the research-producing nations. A few examples will indicate the elements of this network. While there are between 60,000 and 100,000 scientific journals worldwide, only about 3,000 are indexed by the Institute for Scientific Information, which keeps track of "significant," internationally circulated journal publications. Most of these influential journals appear in the major international scientific languages—predominantly English and to a lesser extent French and perhaps German and Spanish. These are the publications that communicate the significant discoveries in the scientific disciplines, are read by scholars and scientists throughout the world, and are cited by other scholars. Most of them are edited by senior scholars in the United States, Britain, and to a lesser extent Canada, Australia, and other major Western countries. These editors are the "gatekeepers" of science.[316] The norms and paradigms that are influential in the academic and scientific systems of the United States and the large industrialized countries dominate the world. Scholars in other parts of the world with different orientations find it difficult to get published in these international journals. Journals from other parts of the world are not often circulated internationally. The publishing system for books is quite similar. The recognized publishers and editors are located in the industrialized world, as are the main markets for books (as well as journals). English dominates international scholarly publishing. The most recent innovations in scientific communications, databases, and information networks are also located in the industrialized nations—especially in the United States. The nations that produce scientific research own the data networks, control what goes into them, and manufacture the hardware and software that permit these systems to work.

It is clear that developing countries are at a particular disadvantage. Not only are their scientific systems generally small and poorly equipped, they do not have easy access to the communications networks. They are, at best, consumers of knowledge. And it is often difficult even to obtain access to needed information because it is too expensive or utilizes high-tech networks that Third World nations do not have readily available. Third World scholars may not be able to write easily in English and may not have access to the latest fashions in science or scholarship. Thus, they tend to be excluded from the top journals and are not part of the "invisible college" of science that works through personal contacts, international conferences, seminars, and the like.[317] It is in this context of inequality and scarcity that even countries as large and powerful as India and China must function.

THE THIRD WORLD SCIENTIFIC SUPERPOWERS: INDIA AND CHINA

India and China both have large and relatively productive academic and scientific systems. Both have taken science and higher education seriously. Both see science and higher education as important to national development, and desire both to build research capability and harness it to technology and industry. The two countries exhibit many similarities and some differences. Together, China and India constitute close to one-third of the total population of the globe. This, in itself, is a significant factor because they are key consumers of scientific knowledge. Both countries have large and growing academic scientific systems. Both have increasingly sophisticated technology-based industries that seek to be linked to the global economy through trade and export.

China and India show some important similarities. The countries have made a significant commitment to higher education, but they enroll only a small proportion of the relevant age group. India enrolls about 5 percent of the relevant age group, while about 1 percent attend postsecondary institutions in China (4 percent of the secondary school graduating cohort). This compares with close to 50 percent in the United States, 35 percent in Japan, and around 20 to 25 percent in Western Europe. However, in the context of the developing countries, both India and China enroll a relatively high proportion—many countries in Africa, for example, have only 1 or 2 percent of the relevant age group in postsecondary education, although Latin America educates a much higher percentage, as do most of the rapidly developing economies of the Pacific Rim. South Korea enrolls 35 percent and even the Philippines has a similar proportion in postsecondary education.

India has over 140 universities and 7,000 colleges. It also has a large number of specialized postsecondary institutions—such as the internationally recognized Indian Institutes of Technology, several Institutes of Management, the Tata Institute of Fundamental Research, and others. India's higher education is highly differentiated, with the quality of teaching and research high at some of the apex universities and specialized academic and research institutions. However, the vast majority of undergraduate students in India's 7,000 colleges receive instruction that is well below international norms. India also has a network of government-funded research facilities in a range of disciplines, from atomic energy to coal technology.[318] In addition, Indian private industry has sponsored a few research laboratories in several fields such as silk technology and pharmaceuticals. In some fields, such as computer software development, India has a large and sophisticated research apparatus, both in some of the universities and research institutes and in the private sector. India also claims one of the world's largest scientific communities—including researchers and postsecondary level teachers. It is often said that India ranks third in the world in terms of the number of scientists, after the United States and Russia.

China, similarly, has a large, differentiated, and complex academic and research system, with well over 1,000 colleges, universities, and other full-time institutions of higher education. More than half of this number are colleges of engineering and colleges of education. Only 4 percent are comprehensive universities, which have the highest prestige. There are 2 million undergraduates and over a quarter million graduate students in institutions of postsecondary education, as well as 189 doctoral granting universities.[319] Like India, China's higher education system is highly differentiated, with a large number of institutions sponsored by provinces, cities, or other local authorities, which are often of moderate or low quality, and a small number of "key point" universities, generally sponsored by the central government, at the top of the system. In addition, China has a large number of research institutions in a variety of fields, some of which function at international levels of excellence. While Chinese science is much less visible internationally than is Indian science, China has a large and active scientific community and a significant number of scientific journals.[320] Chinese scientists have produced nuclear weapons and satellites. Except during the period of the Cultural Revolution in the 1960s, China has emphasized scientific research and higher education as a part of its plans for modernization and development. Chinese higher education is undergoing significant change, as greater emphasis is placed on private initiative and funding, and links with industry are being encouraged.[321]

There are also some differences in the academic and scientific development of these two countries. India has permitted market forces and the private sector (although with considerable state subsidy) to determine the rate of growth of higher education. The large majority of Indian students attend private colleges that are subsidized by public funds and controlled, to an extent, by public authority. The Indian academic system has grown steadily—sometimes at a rate of close to 10 percent annually—for more than three decades, and efforts to control growth by government authority have largely failed.[322] Most agree that academic standards for the majority of students have declined in recent decades. There are massive problems of unemployment among college graduates. China, on the other hand, has tightly controlled higher education expansion. During several periods, most notably the Cultural Revolution in the 1960s, expansion was stopped. Indeed, at that time the entire academic system was closed for almost a decade, with disastrous consequences for higher education and research. Higher education in China has been rigidly planned by the central government, although the situation is now changing to some extent and provinces are playing a more active role in higher education development. In India, the majority of college and university students focus on the social sciences and humanities—despite unemployment of graduates in these fields—while China's planned academic development has emphasized engineering and science and, recently, the study of management, with a modest proportion in the social sciences.

While the legacy of foreign influences and colonialism is significant in both countries, the specific impacts have been quite different. The modern academic and research systems of both countries have Western roots, although both have rich ancient cultural and educational traditions. China's early Western-style academic development was influenced by Western missionaries and by modest government efforts to build a few universities. The language of instruction was Chinese, for the most part, and the institutional models were American, German, French, and Japanese.[323] China's higher education development went through a number of quite distinct and disjointed phases, with significant disruptions during the war with Japan during the 1930s and 1940s and during the struggle between the Nationalists and Communists, which culminated in the establishment of the People's Republic of China in 1950. During the first phase of Communist rule, the Soviet academic and scientific model was introduced into China, displacing other influences.[324] This was followed by the break with the Soviet Union and the Cultural Revolution when higher education came to a complete halt, many academic and scientific facilities were damaged, and most scientists and scholars were forced to stop working. Since the 1970s, China has again been open to Western academic influences, with ever closer ties interrupted to some extent but not stopped by the Tienanmen Square incident in 1989.[325]

India, in contrast, was under British colonial rule for two centuries, achieving independence at approximately the same time as China's revolution. India's academic development proceeded without the disruptions that characterized China's. The British imposed an academic model—the University of London—and imposed the English language as the main medium of instruction and scholarship.[326] The colonial language and the colonial academic models remain, with some significant modifications, as the main features of the Indian academic system to the present. India's academic and intellectual ties have always been with the English-speaking Western countries, especially Britain and, in recent years, the United States. India's academic journals and books are published in English.

China's academic life has, since 1950, not only been tightly controlled in terms of academic growth and development, but also in terms of research focus and intellectual and ideological directions. India, in contrast, has had a significant measure of academic freedom and consistent contacts with the outside world. India's scientists and scholars, at least in the major universities and research laboratories, have long been a part of the international scientific community. At the same time, Indian higher education development has been guided more by market forces than by any effective planning. Chinese academics have had much less contact with the outside world, limited by the constraints of language, government policy, and funds, and only in the 1980s joined the international scientific community.

THE BRAIN DRAIN AND THE CHINESE AND INDIAN DIASPORAS

Large numbers of students and scholars from China and India have studied abroad—mainly in the industrialized nations of the West. Many remained overseas, while others returned home. In both cases, these foreign-educated Indians and Chinese have had a profound influence on the two countries. Foreign study is by no means a recent phenomenon. Students began going abroad in large numbers in the nineteenth century, and foreign-returned individuals played a great role in creating modern China and India. One need only mention Sun Yat-sen and Chou En-lai as examples of Chinese who studied overseas and profoundly influenced modern China. Jawaharlal Nehru, B. R. Ambedekar, and many other Indians also studied overseas, mostly but not exclusively in England. It should be noted that these returnees not only bring foreign ideas back, they also reinterpret their own culture and society. For half a century, India has been one of the main "sending" countries among the developing nations. India has been among the top five countries sending students to the United States since the 1950s—it is likely that 200,000 Indians have earned academic degrees in the United States and probably a similar number in other countries over the past 40 years.

China's foreign study experience has been somewhat different. Prior to the establishment of the People's Republic of China in 1950, the large majority of Chinese students studied in the West or in Japan. Between 1950 and the mid-1960s, most Chinese students went to the former Soviet Union—and the total numbers also decreased. After the Sino-Soviet split, the Soviet Union was no longer open to Chinese students. When China cut itself off from the outside world during the Cultural Revolution, virtually no students went abroad to study. However, beginning in the mid-1970s, when the country committed itself to the "four modernizations" and reopened the universities, students began studying abroad in unprecedented numbers. By the late 1980s, more than 25,000 students from China were studying in the United States, with perhaps an equal number enrolled in all other countries.[327] In 1995, almost 40,000 Chinese students were studying in the United States. China had overtaken India (with 34,000 students in the U.S.) as a major sender of overseas students. As is the case for India, a significant number of Chinese students have not returned home after completing their degrees. Nonreturn rates went up after the Tienanmen Square incident, when many Chinese students abroad became disillusioned with their government, and foreign countries, especially the United States, loosened immigration rules.

Foreign scholars are also of considerable importance in the process of knowledge transfer and intellectual contacts. A large number of established scholars from China and India have visited Western countries and Japan and have returned with ideas and orientations influenced by their sojourns abroad. For example, more than 10,000 foreign scholars from China were in the United States in the early 1990s and about 6,000 from India. Typically, foreign scholars are established academics who remain abroad for periods ranging from a few months to several years, to pursue research. Many are sponsored by universities or other agencies in the industrialized nations (such as the Fulbright program in the United States or the DAAD [German Academic Exchange Service] in Germany).

What is important about foreign students and scholars in the context of this discussion of the academic and scientific development of China and India is that this very large group of individuals is profoundly influenced by their experiences abroad. They learn about science, research, and scholarship in the industrialized countries and bring this knowledge back with them. Their orientations to science and scholarship are shaped by what they learn abroad. Further, they are also frequently influenced by the academic models, the lifestyles, and perhaps the products and social ideas of the countries in which they study. Because of their expertise, and sometimes also because of the prestige of a foreign academic degree, these returned students and scholars frequently achieve positions of leadership in science, higher education, the arts, or in politics or business. All of this is inevitable. The flow of people who have been trained abroad is one element of the continuing set of relationships between China and India and the industrialized nations. There has been a significant brain drain from both China and India over the years. In one sense, this talent has been lost for the economic and social development of these countries. On the other hand, these populations serve as a point of ongoing contact and exchange.

Significant numbers of Chinese and Indians live outside of India and China. These populations are an important point of contact between India and China and the industrialized world. The full extent of Chinese and Indian populations living in the West is not clear, but they number in the millions. Many occupy positions in science, education, and the professions.[328] The number of Chinese and Indians holding academic posts in American universities is large—probably more than 10,000. Many of these scientists and scholars maintain contacts with colleagues in their countries of origin and frequently work in these countries.[329] They serve as consultants, visiting professors, and participate in conferences. In India, these people are called "nonresident Indians" and they constitute an important source of investment, knowledge, and contacts with the industrialized world. Similar populations of Chinese are equally engaged.[330]

There are also populations of Chinese and Indians settled in other parts of the world, and these groups are also very important to consider. Chinese living in Hong Kong and Taiwan—technically parts of China but in the case of Taiwan not currently under the jurisdiction of the People's Republic of China—are of special significance because of their wealth and high levels of scientific productivity. They are a source of knowledge, investment, and contacts with the West and Japan. The economies as well as the scientific and academic systems of these two areas are also of importance to China in the long run. Other Chinese populations living in countries such as Singapore and Malaysia may also play a role. There are also established

Indian populations settled in such regions as Southeast Asia, East Africa, and Guyana in Latin America, but these communities are less important in terms of India's international relationships.

Chinese and Indian populations settled abroad are sources of contact, ideas, and relationships with industrialized nations. Because they understand the home culture and society and because they speak the home language, they have special advantages. Many feel a sense of kinship as well. However, these populations are, in a sense, a source of continuing peripherality as well because they reinforce the importance of the ideas, products, and practices of the industrialized world. They are, rather, serving as points of access for foreign ideas, practices, and institutions. They are not, for the most part, reinterpreting Indian or Chinese traditions. From the perspective of this essay, these diasporas serve as a source of continuing peripherality. Their influence is considerable and very probably it is a positive one in terms of commerce, science, and industry. The Chinese and Indian diasporas are among the most important in the world because the groups are so large, well educated, and widely dispersed.

THE FUTURE

Despite their size and relatively high levels of scientific and educational accomplishments, neither India nor China can avoid participating in the world knowledge system. This participation will necessarily be unequal. World science and scholarship will continue to be dominated by the West and Japan for some time to come for the reasons that have been discussed in this chapter. Thus, even India and China will, to a significant extent, remain peripheral in the world knowledge system. The industrialized nations simply have such large scientific infrastructures and spend so much on research and development that it is not possible for developing countries to catch up. Nor is it possible to opt out of the system—China tried this during the Cultural Revolution, to its great detriment.

The structural factors that have been discussed to a very large extent determine the place of a nation in the knowledge system. These factors are not only relevant to low per capita income countries. The wealthy nations of the Arabian Gulf, for example, also face a situation of peripherality. Their wealth does not permit them to play a central role in world science. In these cases—such as Kuwait and even Saudi Arabia—the problem is one of the size of the scientific and academic communities and the development of a culture of scientific research.[331] Even smaller highly industrialized nations with well-established academic traditions—such as Norway or Finland—find themselves in a peripheral position in the world academic system and must rely on research initiatives and publication outlets in the larger centers of academic power.

For the foreseeable future, India and China will depend on other countries for charting the basic direction of scientific research, for the means of obtaining information about the latest scientific developments, and for training in the most advanced scientific specialties. The basic paradigms of research will take place abroad and will necessarily affect the local scientific community. Scientific products, including the most advanced laboratory equipment, advanced computers, and of course, books and journals will continue to be imported. These products are not designed with China and India in mind, nor are they priced so that countries with a low per capita income can easily afford them. Training in some advanced scientific fields will also take place abroad. These are some of the elements of peripherality that will continue to affect science and higher education in China and India.

Nevertheless, these two countries have already achieved a certain level of scientific and academic independence, and they can continue to build on established strength and, by careful allocation of resources, achieve many of their academic and research and development goals. Indeed, in some areas, both countries have already made impressive progress, sometimes against major obstacles. Both countries have built up a significant capacity in military-related research and production and possess nuclear weapons and the means of delivering them. While Chinese and Indian technology in these areas does not meet world standards, it seems adequate for their purposes, and it has apparently mostly been developed indigenously.[332] This example is relevant for our broader discussion because it exemplifies the challenges, the opportunities, and the problems of targeted research. Both countries have invested considerable sums in military and nuclear research and development. They have, despite considerable problems and a lack of cooperation from the international scientific community, been able to build up capacity in this applied area.

China and India have the capacity to target specific areas of research for priority development. India has, for example, achieved considerable success in computer technology at all levels, from basic research building on India's long and distinguished research tradition in mathematics to applied areas such as software development. Significantly, Indian scientists work closely with colleagues abroad and are very much part of the international scientific community. Indians working abroad in this field, especially in the United States, have contributed significantly to India's development in computer science. These nonresident Indians have even invested in the Indian computer industry and have encouraged direct collaboration between firms in the United States and those in India. They have even helped to build up an Indian "Silicon Valley" in Bangalore as a center for research and development in computer science and in applied computer applications. Much of the initiative for this development has come from the private sector, but the Indian government has also assisted by making research funds available and promoting work in this field. The late Prime Minister Rajiv Gandhi had a special interest in applied research and development generally, and in computer technology, in particular. There are other examples of successful targeting of research and the application of this research to development. India's successful "green revolution" dramatically improved agricultural production in the 1970s. This was done by a combination of using, and sometimes adapting, research developed in other countries—especially in this case by the International Rice Research Institute in the Philippines; applying this research to local needs in Indian scientific institutions; and then disseminating information and providing resources for the use of the new technologies. Similar examples can be provided for China.

One strategy available to China and India is targeting specific areas for intensive research and development investment. These areas are generally in fields that can directly benefit the economy and that build on existing strengths in the country. The strategy requires a coordinated effort among the academic and research communities, and the targeted industries or agencies, and the ability to ensure that research and development can be translated into applied products, innovations, or developments. However, it is also necessary to support a capacity for basic research as well because applied research cannot be built on a foundation lacking in scientific community or infrastructures. Several of the Asian newly industrializing countries have successfully targeted applied research areas and have used these to support economic growth. Taiwan's support for a science-based industrial park at Hsinshu, and the links between several universities involved in the park and the Taiwanese computer industry, have yielded major success.[333] India has been more successful in building up basic scientific capacity through the large number of scientists working both in the universities and in government laboratories, many under the aegis of the Council of Scientific and Industrial Research, which is supposed to support and monitor applied research. However, the links between actual industrial and technological productivity and these scientific efforts are often not fully exploited. While China has a significant scientific infrastructure and strong ties among research institutions and industrial enterprises, it would seem that highly productive relationships between research and industry are less common, although recent policy initiatives have moved strongly in this direction.

India and China are tied to an international knowledge system that places them at a significant disadvantage, and it is virtually impossible for these two large and educationally well-developed Third World nations to achieve full parity and independence in this system. It is necessary to recognize the nature of the system and the realities that guide it. Nonetheless, it is possible for China and India, as well as many other Third World countries, to assess their scientific strengths carefully and to build on them. It is appropriate to conclude this discussion with ideas that may be useful to these two Third World scientific superpowers as they contemplate the use of research and development for national development:

- Scientific links and cooperation between China and India may significantly strengthen both countries. Political differences have kept them apart for many years, but with the end of the Cold War and other changes, it may be possible for these two countries to work together in areas of mutual scientific interest.
- Ensuring that at least a segment of the university system achieves international levels of teaching, research, and scholarship is crucial because applied research and development must have a base in domestic science. Careful choices of institutions, fields, and specialization can be made.
- Decentralization of decision making may be useful, especially in countries as large and complex as China and India. Initiative at the state or provincial levels, perhaps

supported by central government funding, may yield results. Careful coordination between enterprises and academic and scientific institutions may be easier and more effective at a more decentralized level.

- At the same time that many decisions are decentralized, it may be useful, at the national or perhaps regional level, to target specific areas for research and development. Even countries as large as China and India cannot be strong in every scientific field.

- Cultivating the scientific diaspora is of importance because these scientists can be linked to the home country productively.

- Long-term linkages with academic and scientific institutions in other countries may be helpful in maintaining international contacts and access to the most current innovations and knowledge. These linkages may be largely in the West and Japan, but in some instances could be in the newly industrialized countries.

- Policies that encourage multinational companies with manufacturing or commercial facilities in the country to do some of their research and development in the country as well can help to build up infrastructures and provide current scientific information that will be valuable to local industry. Multinational firms may also be encouraged or in some cases compelled to share some of their technologies.

Research, development, and science are linked not only to the higher education system but also to broader issues of industrial and trade policy, to the place of the country in the international world of science and scholarship, and to ideas about the nature of research and higher education. While both China and India have built up impressive academic systems in the past half century and have also made considerable progress in industrial development, they have not pondered the interrelationships of these elements. The first step is to reach a clear and unemotional understanding of the nature and functioning of the world knowledge system. After that, it is possible to focus on how a nation that is not at the center of scientific power can make the best possible use of its own academic and scientific resources. An important part of a successful strategy may be cooperation among countries that are in similar positions.

10

The New Internationalism: Foreign Students and Scholars

Academic institutions are international. They are linked across international boundaries by a common historical tradition. They are connected by an international knowledge network that communicates research worldwide through books, journals, and, increasingly, databases.[334] Scholars are part of an "invisible college" that constitutes disciplines and specialties. The role of the major world languages, especially English in the late twentieth century, is also an internationalizing element. More than any other major institution, the university is by its nature international. At the center, major world-class universities, scholars, and scientists are directly involved in the international network. Those at the periphery may not be directly engaged, but they are nonetheless affected. In a world where international relationships in commerce, science, and technology are seen as crucial to "competitiveness," the international role of academe is ever more important.

Foreign students and scholars are among the most visible aspects of the internationalism of higher education. They are the concrete manifestation of the ways in which the knowledge network functions. There are now more than a million students studying outside their home countries and countless other foreign scholars who are not working on a specific academic degree. The majority of the world's foreign students are from the Third World, and they study in the advanced industrialized nations. The United States is the largest "host" country, with more than 450,000 foreign students and 60,000 foreign scholars.[335] France, Germany, and the United Kingdom each host more than 50,000 foreign students. Russia, once a major host country, no longer admits large numbers.

Foreign students and scholars sometimes join the scientific community of the host country by remaining in that country after completing their studies. In a much larger number of instances, they return home imbued with the norms and values of the host country.[336] The foreign student phenomenon has important economic, political, psychological, and academic consequences for both sending and receiving academic communities. For many of the individuals involved, the experience of foreign study is one of the most important of their lives. This chapter begins with a consideration of some of the broad structural elements of the foreign student equation. It then proceeds to discuss some of the emerging issues that require both research and analysis if this topic is to be understood fully.

INEQUALITIES

Inequality is inevitably a part of the foreign student phenomenon as it is of the international knowledge system. The system is controlled by the industrialized nations. The ideas, products, books, and journals and the methodologies and orientations of the industrialized nations dominate the system. The publishers in the industrialized world issue the vast majority of the world's scientific literature. More than 90 percent of the world's research and development expenditures take place in the industrialized nations. The large majority of the world's scientific journals are edited in the industrialized world. English, and, to a much lesser extent, French, Spanish, and German serve as the major internationally used scientific languages. The international knowledge system is characterized by inequalities that place many smaller nations and those at the periphery of the system, and this includes all the developing countries of the Third World, at a considerable disadvantage.

It is not surprising that the foreign student phenomenon is also part of this nexus of inequality. Recognizing the structural problems of international exchanges is needed to ensure a maximum degree of equality and communication. Too often, structural inequalities are forgotten as people of goodwill try to implement programs and formulate policy. Foreign students study the curriculum of the host country, in the language of the host country.[337] The policies of the host countries determine the configuration of foreign study. For example, when the British government increased fees for foreign students in the 1980s, nations that were sending students to the United Kingdom reassessed their policies and in some cases made changes.[338] The number of foreign students in Britain significantly dropped when full fees were introduced, and the momentum of growth was never reestablished.[339] Malaysia, for example, cut back temporarily on the number of students sent to Britain. There is, of course, an interplay of actions and reactions, but in general the industrialized nations retain control.

Foreign students and scholars are among the most critical parts of the international knowledge system. In many ways, they are at the center of that system. They are the "carriers" of knowledge across borders. Foreign students learn skills abroad and take them home. They are the embodiment of the cosmopolitan scientific culture. Foreign students perform some very important roles during their sojourn overseas. They frequently constitute a key cadre of researchers and teachers for the academic systems of Western countries in their capacities as research and teaching assistants. In the United States and the United Kingdom, foreign graduate students in such fields as engineering and computer science literally keep academic programs functioning due to the absence of sufficient numbers of home students. When students graduate, they return home with the values, training, and ideas that they acquired in the West. Even if they do not return home, they frequently keep in close contact with the academic communities in the countries from which they came and constitute a kind of bridge between cultures. Indeed, it is likely that the brain drain is a much more complex phenomenon than once thought since many scholars from the Third World who settle in the West eventually return home, either temporarily or permanently, bringing skills and ideas with them.[340] Foreign students and scholars are one of the most visible and important parts of the worldwide exchange of ideas.

FOREIGN STUDY AS A PHENOMENON

Foreign study is a complicated issue, with many ramifications. This section looks at specific aspects of the foreign student phenomenon. Although this analysis is by no means exhaustive, it will provide a sense of both the parts and the whole.

Knowledge Transfer

Knowledge transfer is one of the most important elements of foreign study. Knowledge is imparted directly through the formal curriculum. Many have argued that, in some cases at least, the standard curriculum in Western academic institutions is not entirely relevant to the needs of foreign students and that modifications should be made.[341] With very few exceptions, the curriculum has remained unaltered. Foreign students must make the appropriate "translation" themselves. Many argue that students studying for advanced degrees, regardless of nationality, should have access to the most advanced knowledge possible and that foreign students should not be offered a special curriculum. However, the picture is not entirely one-sided. It is often the case that doctoral dissertations by foreign students are tailored to topics of relevance to them. There are a small but growing number of degree programs designed specifically for foreign students in the Netherlands, Germany, Japan, and several other countries. These programs usually use English as the medium of instruction. The fact remains, however, that the knowledge imparted through university study is chiefly Western knowledge.

The nature of the knowledge transmitted to foreign students has broad implications. Degree holders return home and take up academic and research positions, often rising to posts of authority—in part because of their foreign qualifications. The knowledge that they have obtained overseas becomes a key element of the home curriculum and often dominates the research agenda. The methodological paradigms and topics of current interest in the West are frequently the focus of research and attention in Third World universities. To some extent, this is inevitable since the major scientific advances are made in Western universities and research laboratories, but it is also due to the fact that the scientific values absorbed while studying abroad become embedded in the Third World even when research and teaching needs would require different approaches.

Knowledge is also transferred through more subtle means. Foreign students learn about books and journals as well as about scientific equipment while studying overseas. These orientations frequently have a lasting impact on them when they return home. The impact of the books and journals published in the industrialized nations remains strong in part as a result of the habits developed during the foreign sojourn. There are many instances of foreign-trained university professors teaching from textbooks and other research materials that they themselves used during their studies abroad. Third World universities try to gain access to the major Western databases so that they can keep up with the latest scientific literature. They are often much more oriented to Western science than to academic developments in their own regions. While most scientific literature is published in the industrialized nations, there are some valuable Third World journals and textbooks published in such countries as India that may be useful elsewhere. Such materials enter the mainstream only rarely.[342]

Foreign Scholars

A large but virtually ignored element of the international study equation is the growing foreign scholar population. There are probably well over 100,000 foreign scholars worldwide, half of whom are studying in the United States. Foreign scholars include professors and researchers pursuing nondegree study abroad. Some remain abroad for extended periods of time, while others have sojourns of short duration. As with foreign students, the overwhelming majority of foreign scholars are from the Third World and pursue their studies in industrialized countries. They sometimes have formal teaching or research responsibilities as part of their work. Foreign scholars are financed from a variety of sources, including universities and governments in the industrialized nations, home government and institutions, and individual resources.

Foreign scholars generally have a close working relationship with a specific faculty member or academic department at the host institution and frequently work on topics of mutual interest with their hosts. However, because many academic institutions in the West have only rudimentary facilities for foreign scholars, it is possible for them to be ignored. As the number of foreign scholars has grown and as they have been recognized as an important element in international exchange, more attention is being paid to them. The relationships built up by foreign scholars are often quite productive not only for them and their research but also for developing institutional links and long-term collaboration. Agencies such as the Council for the International Exchange of Scholars in the United States (CIES), the British Council in the United Kingdom, and the German Academic Exchange Service (DAAD) in West Germany have long recognized the importance of the visiting scholar experience. Australia, Singapore, and Canada have traditionally provided generous sabbatical arrangements, often linked to study overseas.

Foreign scholars obtain research experience. They also learn something about the academic systems in which they are located. The inequalities that characterize the international knowledge system are present in foreign scholar relationships. It is generally the case that foreign scholars from the Third World come to the industrialized nations to "learn" from their hosts. They are likely to be influenced by the academic systems that they encounter as well. The relatively small number of scholars who go from the industrialized nations to Third World universities go more to teach than to learn, although both teaching and learning generally take place. Such scholars are not as greatly influenced by the research trends and academic systems they encounter.

The nexus of influences and relationships is obviously very complex. Given the importance of foreign scholars as an element in international educational exchange, it is surprising that so little research and analysis has been devoted to them. We need to learn about the motivation for involvement in foreign scholar programs, the impact of the problems and experiences, the nature of research and teaching, and the unanticipated consequences of the experience.

Foreign Study Policy

Policies of governments and academic institutions play a crucial role in determining the nature of foreign study opportunities and in shaping the realities of the experience.[343] Only in recent decades has foreign study policy been seriously considered by either government or academic officials. Previously, arrangements tended to be ad hoc and informal. With the rapid growth in the number of foreign students, both government and academic officials have been faced with difficult policy decisions. Host countries (largely in the industrialized world) have been increasingly concerned about foreign student numbers from several points of view. In the United Kingdom, fiscal stringencies led governmental authorities to favor subsidizing higher education for domestic students rather than foreign students. A belief that subsidies should be targeted toward specific groups led to the imposition of the "full-fee" policy and resulted in a drop in the number of foreign students in the country.[344] The decline, however, proved to be temporary, and foreign student numbers have begun to move back towards their pre-"full fee" levels. It should also be noted that students from the European Union (EU) are not required to pay the full cost of their education in the United Kingdom.

Foreign study policy has also received a great deal of attention in the EU as countries open their universities to students from the member countries as part of a coordinated internationalization policy throughout Europe. One of the key elements of European policy is the ambitious ERASMUS project. ERASMUS has meant large increases in foreign study within the EU, and some adjustments have been necessary. At the same time, study in some European countries became more costly to others from outside the EU.

A number of the major host nations have examined their policies relating to foreign students and several have implemented changes—usually in the direction of restricting access and raising costs. Britain is the most dramatic example. Canada and Australia have also looked into the costs and benefits of foreign students and have restricted access and/or increased costs.[345] The United States does not have a "national" policy concerning foreign students, although immigration regulations set parameters. Advisory groups, including the National Association for Foreign Student Affairs (NAFSA), the CIES, and others, attempt to shape government policy, but often without notable success. In the United Kingdom, the Overseas Students Trust has tried, again only with limited results, to influence the government.[346]

In the United States, access by foreign students and scholars to colleges and universities remains quite open. Japan, after a national study, has placed more stress on international education, with the goal of attracting 100,000 foreign students by the year 2000—a goal that will probably be reached, but with the large majority of these students coming from neighboring Asian countries.[347] As foreign students have grown in number and become a visible part of the higher education systems of several key industrial nations, those countries have carefully examined the impact. Many industrial nations host few foreign students—in Norway, the Netherlands, Finland, and Japan, for example, less than 1 percent of the student population is composed of foreign students. For the nations of the Organization for Economic Cooperation and Development, the proportion of foreign students is 3.4 percent, but the proportion for Belgium is 20.7 percent and for France 13.6 percent. By contrast, under 3 percent of the American postsecondary student population consisted of foreign students, although that group was not equally distributed throughout the country or in the various disciplines.[348]

There are many reasons for student flows, including government and institutional policy. However, countries like Norway and Japan, which teach in nonmetropolitan languages, will naturally attract only a limited number of foreign students, while France, Belgium, the United States, the United Kingdom, and other countries that offer instruction in "world languages" will be more attractive.[349]

While the research on foreign students reports mainly on the policy debates of the industrialized nations, the policies and orientations of the "sending" nations, largely in the Third World, are also very important. Recent policy changes in China and in Taiwan, both very large sending countries, may have significant effects on foreign student numbers in the coming period. For several years, China has had an "open door" policy in terms of permitting students who gained entrance to overseas universities and could obtain funding to go abroad. A large number of scholars, perhaps as many as 15,000, are also supported by the Chinese authorities. The Chinese government has been rethinking its policies as they have noted a growing nonreturn rate and some dislocation for graduates who have returned to China after their studies. The Taiwan government, which for many years refused to permit undergraduate students to study abroad, relaxed its policy. This decision led to an increase in the number of Taiwanese students going abroad (mainly to the United States)—and Taiwan is already one of the largest sending nations in the world. The Malaysians have traditionally funded large numbers of Malay students for overseas study.[349] Some government programs have kept many of these students within the country, at least for the first two years of study. The fact that Malaysia does not provide funding for Malaysian Chinese students in large numbers has probably contributed to nonreturn rates among this segment of the Malaysian overseas student population. In general, Third World nations seem to have less clearly articulated policies concerning foreign study. Demands by the educated segment of the population and lack of access to local academic institutions swelled demands for opportunities for overseas study. A few countries, such as Nigeria and Venezuela, cut back on government funding for overseas study when these countries encountered serious economic problems after the drop in oil prices. India has also from time to time restricted foreign study opportunities to save scarce foreign exchange and because the Indian authorities felt that adequate advanced study opportunities were available within India in many disciplines.

Policies developed by academic institutions relating to foreign students and international study are also a key element in understanding the nature of foreign study. Foreign students have their greatest impact at the institutional level. They are in classrooms, are involved in research, participate in extracurricular activities, and in many other ways affect universities. Universities generally control their admissions criteria and procedures as well as the content and orientation of their teaching programs. In the industrialized nations, many academic institutions have developed policies that relate to foreign students. Relatively few universities have addressed the curricular issues with respect to foreign study, but this is a topic of increasing concern among academic leaders. Universities have also been slow to regulate the flow of foreign students into particular subjects and disciplines. In the United States, there was for a time a worry that graduate programs in such fields as engineering and computer science had enrollments that were at least half foreign. This concern was not translated into restrictive policies. Universities have in many instances attempted to integrate foreign students into the life of the institution by providing an organizational framework for social activities and through housing policy and other efforts. In the 1990s, American universities began to see foreign students as a part of their efforts to internationalize.

Economic Realities of Foreign Study

Despite the major economic importance of foreign study, there is remarkably little research on this topic. Economic factors have received considerable attention in the past decade, and major policy decisions have been made with economic issues in mind. The basic rationale for the United Kingdom's full-fee foreign student policy was based on the government's view that the cost of educating foreign students was too high. There was considerable argument in the United Kingdom concerning the actual cost of educating foreign students in the context of enrollment trends and fixed costs as well as the contributions of foreign students to the local economy. The economic factors relating to foreign study are at present a matter of concern, but at the same time there is a lack of consensus concerning the relevant factors, the appropriate means of measuring these factors, and the implications for government and for academic institutions. We do not seem to know the "realities" of foreign study despite the sophistication of economic science.[351] While there are problems with addressing educational costs (especially relating to foreign students), it may be possible that with more sophisticated tools more accurate and useful data can be obtained so that the real costs, to institutions, government, and individuals, can be ascertained.

There is a "macroeconomics" and a "microeconomics" of foreign study. The larger economic realities—such as policies regarding fees for foreign students and costs and benefits to institutions—have received the bulk of attention. As higher education budgets in the industrialized nations have been cut, efforts have been made to reduce expenditures while maintaining the "core" functions of universities. In the United Kingdom, Australia, and Canada, policymakers have felt that foreign students were being subsidized to too great an extent, and cuts were implemented. The motivating factor was largely economic. The macroeconomics of foreign students is quite complex. Economists such as Gareth Williams and Lewis Solmon have sought to analyze the various elements of the economic equation, but it is fair to say that the economic analysis of the costs and benefits of foreign study is still in its infancy.[352]

The "real" cost of foreign students to a host country and academic institution is very complicated. Even the "direct" costs of study may be misleading. For most countries, the cost of higher education is subsidized, usually by the state, and foreign students are subsidized to the same extent as domestic students except, of course, where they are charged higher fees.[353] Yet, it is also the case that the cost of "additional" foreign students may in reality be fairly low as these students may not require additional academic staff or equipment. This is particularly true where foreign students are taking places that would otherwise be unoccupied by domestic students. Academic institutions would continue to function, and most academic staff would be kept on the payroll. In this situation, foreign students may be "place-holding" in low-demand fields. Graduate study in fields like engineering and computer science in the United States constitutes such an example since domestic demand is quite low and foreign students keep the programs functioning. Foreign students, in this example, also provide low-cost teaching assistants and permit the high-demand undergraduate programs to function. There are, of course, major differences among the academic disciplines in terms of costs, with medical education being much more costly than the humanities. These costs also must enter into the economic equation of foreign study.

The "microeconomics" of foreign study has received even less attention in large part because it is a matter of individual concern rather than governmental policy. In the United States as well as in most European countries, the large majority of foreign students, especially those at the undergraduate level, are self-funded. It is estimated that foreign students bring considerable economic benefit to the host country in direct spending for living expenses as well as for tuition. The economic problems faced by foreign students have received little attention in the literature. Indeed, the detailed economics of individual foreign students is little understood despite the fact that a majority of the world's foreign students are privately funded. True living costs are not well understood. Many foreign students remit funds to their families at home, particularly to countries where "hard" currency is difficult to obtain. The problems faced by the families of foreign students, including family members accompanying the students and those back home, are also not understood. The nature of financial transfers from families and individuals studying abroad is important as well. We know little about just how much money foreign students spend and thereby contribute to the economies in which they are studying. In human terms, we know little about the economic problems of individual foreign students and the solutions found to these problems and hardships.

There are also long-term economic implications of foreign study that are little understood. The economics of the brain drain, for example, is related to the costs of foreign study. For that fairly substantial segment of the foreign student population that does not return home, the "host" country benefits to the extent that the student's education up to the graduate level has been paid for by the "sending" country. Further, the subsidy provided by the state in the host country for the student's education is often paid back through the productivity of the degree holder in the economy of that country. For this segment of the foreign student population, there is very likely a subsidy given to the industrialized nations by the sending Third World country. We also know virtually nothing about the economic costs and benefits of foreign degree holders who return home. We have, for example, no information concerning how the networks built up with the country in which they studied might have implications for purchasing scientific equipment or computers.

The economic factors relating to foreign study are not yet fully comprehended. Because key policy decisions are being made on the basis of economic concerns, it seems essential to know the real costs and benefits of foreign students. As noted, most of the limited research and debate on economic factors has concerned issues relating to host countries and institutions. There is virtually nothing known about the impact of foreign study on Third World nations, about the immediate and long-term costs of foreign study, or about the implications for local economies. In some countries, more students are studying outside the country than inside, and the economic factors relating to this large number of students are of considerable importance. The microeconomics of foreign study also have implications for individuals and families in the Third World.

Individual Perspectives

We need to know more about how foreign study affects the individual and about the individual experience of foreign study, although there is research on "adjustment problems" and related factors. It is, after all, true that all of the many economic, political, and sociological repercussions of foreign study ultimately reflect on individuals. We know something about "push" factors that stimulate individuals to wish to study abroad and about the "pull" factors of education that attract students from the Third World to the industrialized nations. Nevertheless, we know relatively little about how the foreign study experience affects individuals.

So far, most of the psychological studies have been of groups of individuals and the effort has been to discern general factors and trends. For example, the famous (and now largely discredited) U-curve adjustment hypothesis held that foreign students went through an initial period of favorable reaction to the host country, followed by a period of dissatisfaction, and then a positive period at the end of the sojourn.[354] It did not take into account individual reactions and perspectives.

The characteristics of the foreign student population need understanding. Social class, ethnic, religious, and other background factors will explain quite a bit about roles, reactions, and performance of foreign students. Too often, foreign students are treated like an undifferentiated group. In most cases, the major breakdown is by national grouping. It is clear that other factors may be just as important as nationality in understanding the realities of foreign study. Gender, for example, has only recently been recognized as a salient variable. As female foreign students have increased in numbers, it is particularly important to learn more about their experiences and orientations. Ethnographic studies of foreign students are necessary to understand more about the experience of individuals and also in order to make informed generalizations about specific nationality groups. At present, basic national statistics and trends are about all that is available concerning foreign students along with questionnaire-based studies of attitudes and values of specific foreign student groups.

The individual motivations for foreign study, individual reactions to differing academic organization and research styles, and individual health and adjustment variables are all important to understand. The foreign student population is, after all, a highly differentiated one, not only by nationality groups but also within those groups. Sometimes, students from different countries but from a similar religious background may have much in common. And of course groups of foreign students from different nationalities but in the same field may have much in common. In sum, there are strong arguments for understanding foreign students—not only in a broad societal and economic context, but also at the level of individuals.

Foreign Students from Industrialized Nations

While the large majority of the world's foreign student population is from the developing countries of the Third World, a significant number of students from industrialized nations study abroad. For example, about one-third of the foreign students study-ing in the United States are from industrialized nations, and some 84,000 Americans studied abroad in 1995. It is worth noting, however, that fewer than 10 percent of America's overseas students studied in Third World nations—the large majority went to Europe. The European Union has dramatically increased the numbers of students in the member states studying in other EU nations. The ERASMUS project, lavishly funded by the EU, has significantly expanded cross-border student flows in Europe. Planners, however, work against some obstacles since the number of intra-European students has actually decreased somewhat in recent years, probably in response to a more difficult job market in Western Europe. In Japan, a major effort is under way to "internationalize" Japanese higher education. While the major component of this effort is to increase the number of foreign students studying in Japan, another aspect is the internationalizing of the curriculum and a further element is encouraging Japanese students to study in other countries.[355] A national commission in the United States stressed the internationalization of American higher education, including strengthening foreign language training and courses relating to other parts of the world. An important element is encouraging study abroad programs as well.

The last two decades have seen a growing consciousness in the industrialized world of the importance of an international perspective in higher education. The EU's initiatives are the most widespread and effective in terms of stimulating cross-border study in the industrialized world. The numbers quadrupled over two decades, but from a very modest start. Fewer than 1 percent of American undergraduates go abroad, and only a handful study in the Third World. In order to increase the popularity of foreign study among students in the industrialized nations, such study must be stressed more as an integral part of the educational experience and better coordinated with normal academic studies. At least in the United States, foreign language training needs to be improved and expanded so that Americans will have the necessary linguistic skills to study abroad. The number of students studying foreign languages has not been increasing very rapidly.

THE FOREIGN STUDY INDUSTRY

Foreign study is one of the growth industries in the higher education systems of the industrialized nations. New careers and specializations have developed to serve the needs of foreign students and scholars, and to assist universities in the international arena. Such an arcane but necessary task as the evaluation of academic credentials from other countries has become a speciality of a significant number of employees in university admissions offices, government agencies, and a few private credential eval-uating firms. Assessing the academic qualifications of a foreign applicant accurately requires a knowledge of comparative education and the nuances of the grading sys-tems in different countries, and a "feel" for the higher education system in question. Twenty years ago, there was hardly any need for such detailed knowledge. Today, credentials specialists not only assist in the admission of foreign students but also evaluate the qualifications and degrees of professionals wishing to practice in fields such as medicine or architecture in another country. Other areas include foreign student advisement, specialists on immigration rules, administrators of international education programs, and, of course, a very large group of professionals concerned with second-language training. An ancillary speciality concerns the testing of foreign students. The administration of examinations such as the Test of English as a Foreign Language (TOEFL) is now a significant part of the work of the Educational Testing Service.

A somewhat less-well-regarded subspecialty concerns the recruitment of foreign students.[356] This too has become a growth industry—and it has also been a concern of both host and sending countries. As recruitment has become more competitive and an economic necessity for some hard-pressed academic institutions in the United States, the United Kingdom, and elsewhere, concerns have been raised about ethics and practices. In the United Kingdom, questions have already been raised about these matters. Recruitment efforts by Western academic institutions in such important sending countries as Hong Kong, Taiwan, and Malaysia are intense and sometimes questionable. Recruiters are subject to increased regulation in the sending countries and are being more carefully scrutinized in the industrialized nations as well.

What might be called the "English-language industry" is by now ancillary to foreign study. The impetus for this industry is clear—the growth of English as the major language of science and technology and its importance as a means of international communication in both business and scholarship. The majority of the world's foreign students study in English-speaking academic institutions. English is the main "second language" in most educational systems throughout the world. However, the standard of instruction in many of these foreign language programs is not very high. It is actually estimated that there are more people studying English in China than in the United Kingdom. India is probably the third-largest English-speaking country in the world, with more English speakers than Australia or Canada. Despite the ubiquity of English training, it is often necessary for individuals who seek entry to English-speaking universities to obtain additional training in English.

As a result of these factors, there has been a great deal of interest throughout the world in English-language programs within academic institutions and also specialized language training separate from the academic curriculum. A major industry has developed to meet these needs. There are many approaches to the study of English as a second language (ESL). Private firms, usually based in Western countries, have set up branches in many Third World nations to provide training in English for applicants to Western universities. There is an immense, and largely unregulated, trade in English tutoring, sometimes done by individuals or by business firms or government agencies. Many Western academic institutions have set up special programs for providing foreign students or others with training in English, usually aimed at passing the TOEFL test or some other admissions requirement. The English-language industry has developed its own curricula, books, and educational aids. There are academic programs in ESL in many universities, aimed at providing professionally trained personnel for language training programs, both in academic institutions and in the private sector.

There is a substantial literature on the linguistic and pedagogical aspects of foreign language training and, in the recent past, on specialized training such as ESL.[357] But very little is known about the nature of the training programs. There are no firm data on how many people are enrolled in such programs, the nature or extent of their financing, the overall qualifications of their staff, or other details. The fact is that training in English—and to a much lesser extent French, German, Chinese, and Japanese—is a major growth industry. It is a key element of the foreign study equation.

Training programs for the various subspecialties of foreign study have developed in academic institutions in recent years. ESL programs have expanded considerably. There are also programs for training foreign student advisers, for sensitizing personnel to cross-cultural issues, and for advisement for those aiming for foreign study, among other specializations. However, many of those involved in the field have no direct professional training. Organizations like the National Association for Foreign Student Affairs (NAFSA), which represents professionals involved in foreign study programs, have helped to offer short courses in order to provide some training to people appointed to positions that relate to foreign study.

The foreign study industry has grown in response to the clear need for services on the part of foreign students worldwide and uncounted others involved in visiting scholar programs, language training, and other international programs. The institutions and organizations providing these need to be staffed by competent professionals. For a small segment of the industry, the promise of quick profits may have stimulated activity.

CONCLUSION

Foreign students and scholars are a central part of academic life, reflecting a growing internationalism in higher education worldwide. Foreign students and scholars constitute an important academic resource in that they provide valuable expertise and a cross-cultural perspective. They are the manifestation of internationalism on the campus. They are also a challenge for policymakers, professionals who have the responsibility for serving the foreign students and scholars, and the academic community that interacts with them. Flows of students and scholars will continue and probably increase in today's global environment.

11

The Foreign Student Dilemma

Universities are international institutions. Knowledge is without boundaries, and universities have traditionally welcomed individuals from many nations to study and teach. Indeed, the very origins of the universities were international. The early European universities used an international language, Latin, and from the first had an international student body. One aspect of the internationalism of academic institutions—foreign students—has become an issue of considerable controversy in the modern world. Foreign students constitute an important element of the world higher education system. Well over one million students study outside the borders of their home countries, with 450,000 in the United States, 136,000 in France, and 106,000 in Germany—the top three "receiving" nations. The bulk of the world's foreign students travel from the developing countries of the Third World to the industrialized nations of the "North."

The impact of foreign students is significant. It has been estimated that more than $4.5 billion is devoted to the education of foreign students in the United States, and in France, over 10 percent of total university enrollment is foreign. In the United States, graduate study has been especially affected by foreign students, with half of graduate enrollments in fields like engineering and computer science comprised of foreign students. Debates over appropriate policies on foreign study, the economic impact of foreign students, curriculum, and ideological ramifications are on the rise in many countries.[358]

This chapter looks at the policy, curricular, and economic factors relating to foreign students in a broad comparative context.[359] To a surprising degree, the issue of foreign students has largely been neglected, given that it has broad ramifications for higher education. In many ways, the issue is symptomatic of international relationships in higher education—relationships based on deep-seated inequalities, shaped by educational factors and by broader economic and political forces. Policymakers on both sides—in the sending and host countries—must fully understand the complexities of the situation. Too often, decisions regarding foreign students and international study have been made by default, by the "market forces" of Third World students eager for higher education overseas, by political leaders concerned with maintaining national influence through educational diplomacy, or by academic institutions in the industrialized nations wishing to fill their classrooms with students, regardless of the relevance of the academic programs being offered.[360]

THE WORLD BALANCE OF STUDENTS

It is often assumed that the flow of students across international borders is directed exclusively from the Third World to the Western industrialized nations. The bulk of foreign students do flow in this direction.[361] However, significant numbers of students go from one Third World nation to another to study. For example, India, Egypt, and the Philippines are among the top 20 host countries. Thousands of European students come to the United States and Canada to study, and many North Americans study in Europe. Thousands of American medical students study in Mexico, the Caribbean, and other parts of the world and contribute to the flow of foreign students. Two more important changes in the foreign study equation in the past two decades are the implementation of the study abroad policies of the European Union (EU) and the collapse of Communism in the former Soviet Union, and Central and Eastern Europe. The EU's several programs to promote study within the EU have dramatically increased the number of students crossing European borders to study. Programs such as ERASMUS, TEMPUS, and SOCRATES have provided unprecedented opportunities within EU nations, and between the EU and Central and Eastern Europe. The collapse of Communism caused some shifts in patterns of foreign study. The former Soviet Union was once the third largest host nation, with 63,000 foreign students, and Russia remains a large receiving country. The flow of foreign students to Russian universities has, however, slowed in comparison to other major host countries. Students from Central and Eastern Europe at one time mainly studied in the former Soviet Union. The flow is now primarily to Western Europe or, to a lesser extent, the United States.[362]

Most of the contemporary discussions concerning foreign student policy, adaptation problems, curricular relevance, and other issues relate to the flow of Third World students to the industrialized countries. Yet even here the balance sheet is far from simple. India, often seen as a major exporter of students, is in fact a major host country—India sends 33,000 abroad but takes in 12,000 overseas students. Similarly, the Philippines takes in almost as many students as it sends abroad. In both of these cases, the bulk of overseas students coming to study are from other Third World nations, while most of those who go abroad study in industrialized countries. Within the broad flow of students from the Third World to the Western industrialized countries, there are smaller but sizable tributaries among the less industrialized nations, and between the Western nations.

The impact of foreign study varies from country to country. More than 10 percent of students in France are foreign students, while in the United States, which plays host to triple the number of foreign students compared to France, foreign students constitute less than 2 percent of total enrollment. In Britain, where there has been much debate concerning policies relating to foreign students and to the relative costs and benefits of hosting such students, about 7 percent of the total enrollment is from overseas.[363]

For a number of sending countries, overseas study constitutes an even more central issue. The demands for admission to postsecondary study are intense, and one of the ways that Third World nations have dealt with the pressure is by sending students abroad. Further, academic programs and specialties are frequently unavailable in newly established Third World universities, forcing students abroad to study these subjects. The pressure can be illustrated by the fact that when Thailand opened its first "open university," which has no enrollment restrictions, 560,000 undergraduates matriculated in its seven faculties. Although scholarship holders constitute only a small fraction (8,700 of 35,000) of the total studying overseas, the Malaysian government allocated $400 million for overseas study—out of a total education budget of $1.8 billion in 1985.[364] Thus, foreign study is seen as an outlet for pent-up educational demand that cannot be met by existing educational facilities and as a means of obtaining advanced technological and other skills unavailable at home institutions.

It is difficult to predict future student flows. Many factors impinge on the scope of educational exchanges—fiscal, political, and curricular. As Third World nations build up their own higher education systems, patterns of overseas study may change. Total numbers may decline, and the flow of undergraduate students will significantly diminish. The mix of students in terms of subject specializations may alter significantly, depending on the needs of Third World nations and on perceptions of the job market. Some have argued that the major expansion in foreign students may be ending, or at least slowing down because of enhanced capacity for higher education in many Third World nations and for economic reasons as well.[365] A countervailing positive trend, however, is the increased wealth, and the concomitant desire for access to higher education, in the newly industrializing countries (NICs), such as Taiwan and South Korea, where more students are able to afford overseas study.

Iran was at one time the world's largest "exporter" of students. After the downfall of the Shah, the numbers of Iranian students abroad declined, and many of those still abroad became refugees. When Ethiopia shifted political allegiances from West to East, the numbers of Ethiopian students studying in the United States fell, and new programs tended to send students to the Soviet Union and other socialist bloc nations. Two decades later, after another political switch, small numbers of Ethiopians are coming to the West. Similar trends can be seen, more recently, for Nicaragua. Shifts in government policy and priorities can affect student flows. The Indian government moved to reduce the flow of students abroad by curtailing government scholarship programs, making it more difficult to obtain a passport for study abroad, and by limiting the amount of foreign exchange available for study. Indian authorities also restricted the number of fields of study that could be pursued abroad, arguing that many specialties were available within India. In the 1990s, Indian policy became less restrictive for those who could afford to go overseas or who were able to obtain funding from external sources.

Trends in overseas study among students in the industrialized countries follow very different patterns. In both North America and Western Europe, students who choose foreign study often do not take a degree abroad, but rather study for shorter periods of time as part of their matriculation in home universities. The number of stu-

Table 11.1. International Student Flows: Major Indicators, 1980 and 1990

Top Host Countries			Top Sending Countries		
	No. of Students			No. of Students	
Country	1980	1990	Country	1980	1990
USA	325,628	407,529	China	30,127	93,347
France	114,181	136,015	Japan	18,066	39,258
Germany	61,841	105,269	Morocco	20,876	36,595
United Kingdom	56,003	70,717	Germany	16,983	34,850
Former USSR	62,942	66,806	South Korea	n/a	32,986
Canada	32,303	35,187	India	15,238	32,972
Belgium	12,875	33,335	Greece	31,509	32,184
Australia	17,694	28,993	Malaysia	35,693	31,497
Japan	n/a	23,816	Iran	65,521	30,555
Switzerland	15,515	22,621	Hong Kong	20,625	28,954
Italy	27,784	21,416	Italy	13,848	25,647
Austria	12,885	18,434	USA	19,843	24,174
Spain	10,997	13,839	Turkey	14,606	21,460
Egypt	21,751	10,176	Jordan	17,030	20,767
Philippines	7,901	5,752	Canada	17,714	20,370
India	11,761	11,759	France	n/a	20,017
Holy See	9,104	10,938	United Kingdom	n/a	17,240
Lebanon	26,343	n/a	Indonesia	n/a	16,835
Argentina	8,649	n/a	Lebanon	15,117	16,531
Greece	8,304	n/a	Syria	13,701	13,994
			Palestine (Refugees)	15,414	12,597
			Singapore	n/a	10,720
			Nigeria	26,863	8,487
			Philippines	n/a	5,594
			Saudi Arabia	14,298	5,005
			Venezuela	17,755	4,996

Sources: UNESCO, *Statistical Yearbook 1983* (Paris: UNESCO, 1984), and *Statistical Yearbook 1992* (Paris: UNESCO, 1992).

dents in Western Europe studying outside their own country has dramatically increased as EU programs have been implemented. In the United States, foreign study has increased as well, although not as much. Russia continues to be a major host country, although conditions in its universities have seriously deteriorated. Foreign student enrollments in some of the formerly Socialist countries in Central and Eastern Europe have declined. Central and Eastern European students are now going predominantly to Western Europe under programs established by the EU. Table 11.1 shows current trends in the flow of students across international borders.

The world balance of students in terms of flows and directions is complex and difficult to portray or predict, but several generalizations are possible. The basic flow is from the South to the North and is likely to remain that way. The shift toward a more sophisticated choice of countries, institutions, and subject fields by Third World students is evident and the trend toward a higher proportion of graduate students is likely to continue. Political and economic factors can have a significant effect on numbers of students, and where they choose to study. In the industrialized nations, changing perceptions of the employment market, curricular preferences, and other factors can have an impact on the flows. Recent political changes in Europe have had a profound impact on patterns of foreign study. The magnitude of foreign study, despite changes in direction, orientation, and conditions, is likely to remain large.

THE FOREIGN STUDENT INFRASTRUCTURE

Foreign study has become big business for many countries. Governments have hired specialists to help handle the large numbers of foreign students and established offices to assist in placement, advisement, and services for foreign students. In some countries, private entrepreneurs have been active in recruiting and placing students in overseas institutions. A growing trend is the establishment of branch campuses of institutions from the industrialized world elsewhere, and an array of "twinning" and other arrangements linking established universities in the industrialized world with academic institutions or sometimes business or other firms in the NICs or the Third World. The development of a foreign student infrastructure is perhaps an inevitable result of the growth in numbers of foreign students, but it also creates a built-in pressure to maintain and even expand overseas study.

The major industrialized nations have built up service organizations relating to foreign students. In the United States, the National Association for Foreign Student Affairs (NAFSA) has a membership of more than 5,000 and not only publishes materials relating to overseas students but also acts as a lobbying group for its members and for international education generally. The Institute of International Education (IIE), headquartered in New York, is a placement agency for foreign students and frequently represents overseas governments and other agencies in placing students in academic institutions in the United States. It also provides statistical and other services relating to international education. In Britain, the United Kingdom Council on

Overseas Student Affairs serves a similar function. Similar agencies also exist in Japan, Canada, Germany, and other countries.

Third World governments have set up agencies to serve—and, frequently, also to watch—their foreign students studying overseas. For example, tiny Kuwait has a full-time office in the Kuwait Embassy in Washington that has responsibility for Kuwaiti students in the United States, most of whom are funded by the Kuwait government. Singapore, Malaysia, Saudi Arabia, and numerous other countries maintain similar offices. Each of these countries has an impressive infrastructure at home to handle its overseas students. The government of Malaysia, for example, awards several thousand government scholarships each year and has an agency to monitor student progress. A few countries have become notorious for spying on their overseas students and trying to ensure their political loyalty.

Many other organizations assist international education in a variety of ways. UNESCO has for many years collected statistics on educational trends, including study abroad, and it has encouraged a wide range of international activities in education. More recently, the EU has emphasized facilitating study in universities in Europe. For example, students who wish to study outside their home country pay their domestic tuition fees when matriculating in any EU nation. There are also places guaranteed for EU students.[366] Agencies such as the Council for International Exchange of Scholars (Fulbright Commission) in the United States, the Commonwealth Secretariat in Britain, the German Academic Exchange Service, and similar agencies in many nations support foreign study and international exchange as well.

Along with these organizational structures, a cadre of professionals has emerged that deals with foreign students in many nations. It can be estimated that perhaps 25,000 people worldwide have careers that are dependent on foreign students and international study. Some serve as administrators of foreign study programs, others as advisers to foreign students, as government officials supervising funding agencies for overseas study, and a few as policymakers. In a few countries, most notably in the United States, it is possible to obtain an academic credential in student personnel work and in a few universities to focus specifically on foreign student affairs. Those responsible for admissions of foreign students have been assisted by the American Association of Collegiate Registrars and Admissions Officers, which has published guidelines for degree equivalencies. UNESCO has also been concerned with the transferability of academic credentials from one nation to another.

The development of a nexus of organizations concerned with foreign study and international education and the emergence of a professional cadre of people whose careers are dependent on foreign study are signs of the growth of the field in recent years. This cadre also constitutes a kind of pressure group for continued growth and keeps official and academic attention focused on the benefits of international educational exchanges of all kinds. In short, foreign study has become "institutionalized," in a sense, and this provides benefits in the form of efficient administration and well-designed programs. At the same time, a self-interested professional cadre has emerged with its own concerns and orientations. The infrastructure of organizations, individuals, publications, and networks proves that foreign study and international education have become an area of worldwide interest.

CURRICULAR FACTORS AND FOREIGN STUDY

The curriculum is often considered the "black box" of higher education. This is also true for the relationship between the curriculum and foreign students. Many curricular issues are important in this relationship: the relevance of a Western academic curriculum for Third World foreign students, the transferability of knowledge, the impact on Western institutions of the presence of large numbers of foreign students, and so forth. It is generally the case that few curricular alterations have been made to accommodate foreign students in Western academic institutions.[367]

What foreign students learn in academic institutions in industrialized nations affects them, academic institutions in the Third World, and perhaps broader economic and social developments. In virtually all institutions catering to foreign students, foreign students learn side-by-side with their local compeers, with no accommodation of courses, textbooks, or content to Third World contexts. They study a curriculum that is tailored to the needs of the host country.

When asked, foreign students sometimes question the relevance of some of the things they learn in Western academic institutions, but by and large they express satisfaction with their academic experiences. Yet, there is evidence that the curriculum is not directly relevant to Third World needs. Orientations toward research and methodology naturally reflect the concerns of scholars and research agencies in the industrialized nations. Equipment is frequently highly sophisticated and expensive. The examples used in experiments, textbooks, and seminars reflect the realities of the industrialized nations. Science is, of course, universal. Yet, in many fields, particularly those that apply knowledge to the problems of the "real world," the issues of concern to the Third World are frequently not those that relate to industrialized societies. Social problems, agricultural techniques, educational innovations and practices, and many other factors differ from society to society. Research strategies and methodologies that are common in the West may not be relevant in the Third World—or may not be practicable given the funds and equipment available.[368] Not only is the knowledge learned in the West sometimes not relevant, the ideas about higher education that are learned in the West may also not be useful.[369] It is at least possible that more careful attention to the educational needs of Third World students might make the transition back to home countries easier and their orientation to knowledge and the curriculum more appropriate to Third World needs.

The issues are complex. Few would argue, for example, that foreign students should be segregated and taught a "second-class" curriculum in academic institutions in industrialized nations. Since foreign students are in any case a small minority in most departments and disciplines, this would be impossible as well as inadvisable. A few special institutions focusing largely on educating foreign students were established in the former Soviet Union and Czechoslovakia.[370] These were not replicated elsewhere. In the 1990s, a variation on this theme has been the growth of specific programs aimed at an international audience within existing academic institutions, often taught in English.

The impact of foreign students on institutions of higher education in the industrialized nations is growing, particularly in selected fields, institutions, and disciplines. Foreign students are not randomly distributed throughout the academic systems of the industrialized nations but tend to cluster in particular institutions and fields of study. In most Western nations, larger concentrations of foreign students are generally found at the major central institutions, with particular institutions claiming a disproportionate share. For example, the London School of Economics in Britain, the University of New South Wales in Australia, the University of Southern California, and a number of other institutions in the United States, all have high percentages of foreign students. These students tend to concentrate at the graduate level, and to choose fields like engineering, computer science, and management studies. The influence of these students on institutional culture and on other aspects of American higher education is significant.[371] A current issue in the United States, for example, is the problem of foreign teaching assistants in undergraduate education. On occasion, American students have complained about the facility in English of some foreign teaching assistants.[372]

There is no question that the curriculum in universities throughout the world is largely a Western curriculum. This is not surprising since the universal academic model is Western and the industrialized nations have for many years dominated research and scientific development. The use of English (and to some extent French) as the dominant international scientific language adds to this situation of inequality. Whether it is possible for alterations to be made in curricular orientations to meet the needs of students from the Third World is questionable in the broader sense. But it would be practical to introduce seminars, summer workshops, or other programs for foreign students to link their academic experiences more closely with the problems of their own countries and perhaps ease reentry when they do return home—and possibly even reduce the problem of nonreturn. The Institute of International Education implemented several programs in the 1990s to assist the transition of Asian students back to their home countries.

THE POLITICS AND POLICYMAKING OF FOREIGN STUDY

Decisions concerning foreign study are taken for many reasons by governments, academic institutions, and individuals. Although it has been argued that in many countries the situation is left to a series of ad hoc decisions at various levels, it is nonetheless helpful to study policymaking decisions and the means by which they are made.[373]

In many Third World nations, top governmental and educational policymakers are concerned with foreign study issues, in part because demands for access cannot be met at home. In some cases, local universities cannot provide specialized training in some fields. Approaches vary considerably, and a country may alter its basic policies from time to time. For example, China first sent large numbers of students to the Soviet Union, then kept students at home after the Sino-Soviet split, and, after the Cultural Revolution, has sent students overseas in large numbers, especially to Japan and the United States. Political, economic, and educational factors have all contributed to China's overseas student policy. For a time, China was attempting to modernize by simply copying Soviet models. China then turned inward in an effort to seek a new and revolutionary approach to industrialization. Later, after the Cultural Revolution was discredited, China embarked on a major effort to modernize, frequently using technology and models from abroad. After the Tienanmen Square repression in 1989, there was a slowing of the opening to the West. In China's example, overseas study policy was dictated by top government policy and the scope for individual or institutional decision making regarding overseas study was quite limited—policy has shifted on several occasions to conform to political as well as economic priorities.

Another large Third World nation, India, has also changed policy with regard to foreign students several times. After independence in 1947, India sent large numbers of students overseas with government scholarships and permitted many others to study abroad with their own resources. Students were sent to other countries to study in fields in which the Indian university system was weak, but self-sponsored students could study virtually any subject. This open policy proved expensive to implement, and it also resulted in a large number of nonreturning students. Indian authorities then adopted a more restrictive policy—selecting certain fields that were acceptable for overseas study and placing limitations on the number of students able to study abroad with their own resources by limiting the foreign exchange that could be taken out of the country. As India's own educational capacity grew, it was felt that overseas study was not necessary since students could obtain training in many fields within the country. Restrictions have remained on government scholarships for overseas study and to a limited extent on foreign exchange, but Indian students able to obtain scholarships from abroad are allowed to matriculate. Many of the most able graduates of Indian colleges—particularly of the prestigious institutes of technology—go abroad for graduate study and frequently do not return. In general, India has not been very successful in implementing controls on foreign study or in ensuring the return of graduates from overseas.

A frequently cited historical example of the successful use of overseas study to achieve modernization is Japan, which in the late nineteenth and early twentieth centuries had an active policy of sending students abroad to learn specific skills so that they could return home to implement innovations. This policy was extremely successful in terms of contributing to Japan's modernization, although there were complaints about foreign influences at the time.[374] In the postwar period, large numbers of Japanese students have gone abroad but usually for advanced, nondegree training, since degrees from foreign universities are only now gaining full acceptance. Government scholarships exist, particularly in fields in which the nation is concerned with international competition, such as computer technology and related areas. Many Japanese students go overseas with their own resources for study at both the undergraduate and graduate levels—the proportion of undergraduates going overseas is now more than 52 percent. In recent years, Japan has also been concerned about increasing the number of foreign students and scholars from other countries studying in Japan.

The Malaysian case has been mentioned earlier, since this country has been very active in sending students abroad to study. Malaysian policy is interesting in that it reflects many of the variations—and the contradictions—of Third World overseas student policy. Malaysia has expanded its educational system rapidly in the past three decades and has also enjoyed a high rate of economic growth. In common with many Third World nations and the NICs, it expanded its university system as well, and many now complain that a disproportionate amount is spent on higher education.[375] Yet the demand for higher education exceeds the availability of places in universities. Malaysia has an elaborate foreign scholarship program, which consistently sends 10,000 or more students abroad annually. But a total of more than 35,000 Malaysians are studying overseas, a majority of them privately sponsored. The government provides scholarships mainly for Malay students; students from the large Chinese minority are generally on their own. Traditionally, Malaysia sent students to Great Britain, but when the British government increased overseas student fees, the Malaysian government turned to the United States and Australia as the main foreign destinations for students: There are now 14,000 Malaysians in the United States—a number larger than those studying in the United Kingdom. Government policy has taken large numbers of Malay students, frequently from rural schools, and has sent them overseas for education. Adjustment and academic problems are common, and officials are now rethinking the overseas scholarship policy. Recent Malaysian government policy has stressed providing some postsecondary education at home before sending students overseas as part of "twinning" or other arrangements with foreign universities. These policies were aimed at reducing problems of adjustment for students and saving funds for the government.

Government policies of the host nations are a key ingredient in determining flows. The most dramatic and controversial example is Great Britain's 1980 decision to adopt a full-fee policy for overseas students, a policy that immediately raised tuition fees to as much as $13,000 per year and resulted in a decline in the number of foreign students. The Conservative government, faced with economic difficulties, had raised foreign student fees as an economic measure. But the ensuing debate about this policy included consideration of a much wider array of issues, including the value of an international element in British higher education, the research output of overseas students, access of British scholars to overseas institutions, the economic impact on the balance of payments, political factors—including the maintenance of goodwill toward Britain and providing training in democratic values—and, finally, British responsibilities to the Commonwealth. The policy has been somewhat modified but remains basically in force despite considerable criticism.

The British policy had wide repercussions on the attitudes of Third World nations regarding British education—Malaysia, in the most dramatic gesture, not only ordered its scholarship students to avoid Great Britain but also curtailed British imports. British policy, which was strongly opposed by the universities, reduced enrollments in some fields at a time when demographic pressures on enrollments were being felt. Other European nations have been reexamining foreign student policies and a few have started to limit enrollments in some fields. Germany, for example, has placed restrictions on the numbers of Third World students who study in some high-demand specialties.[376] Curiously, France, which has the highest proportion of foreign students in its universities (over 10 percent), has not altered its own quite liberal foreign student policy. There is, in Europe, a difference in policy for Third World students, for whom restrictions have increased, and for students from Western Europe, who are protected by EU agreements making it very easy to cross borders to study. Canada and Australia have also examined their traditional, relatively open policy toward foreign students and have dramatically increased the cost of study for overseas students.[377]

American policy, because of the decentralized nature of the educational system, has included many—frequently contradictory—elements. The federal government, through a variety of programs, sponsors foreign students. The U.S. Agency for International Development (AID) has brought thousands of foreign graduate students to study for advanced degrees in many fields. The Fulbright Program provides scholarships for students, professors, and others, usually for nondegree study. Both agencies have seen large budget reductions, and in consequence fewer students are being sponsored. Private foundations, especially Ford and Rockefeller, have sponsored many students from the Third World. Despite financial cutbacks in the 1980s, there remains strong national support for international education and foreign study. The states, which control basic higher education policy in the public sector, have by and large not developed consistent policies regarding foreign students, and frequently treat students from overseas in the same way they treat out-of-state American students. There has also been some questioning of the advisability of very high foreign student enrollments in some graduate fields, such as engineering. Some less selective private universities, faced with declining enrollments, have aggressively recruited foreign students. Their main concern has been to fill empty classrooms.

At the same time that the AID and other agencies were complaining about the numbers of foreign students remaining in the United States after finishing their studies, federal government immigration policy was providing opportunities for those with relevant skills to remain. Proposals to ensure that individuals who enter the United States to study return home after their degrees have been completed have been made and regulations have been tightened. Organizations like NAFSA and IIE have attempted to represent the international education community in the United States and to press government agencies at all levels and the universities themselves to take a more thoughtful and rational approach to foreign student policy. Efforts have been made, for example, to press universities to consider the curricular implications of large foreign student enrollments and to point out to government authorities that a comprehensive approach to foreign students would be advisable. A variety of interests, orientations, and institutional factors all contribute to a somewhat unstable and varied mix of policies at the institutional, state, and federal levels regarding foreign study. While Goodwin and Nacht's characterization of this situation as an "absence of decision" may be oversimplified, it is certainly the case that there is no consistent policy relating to foreign students.[378]

A range of issues impel governmental policy relating to foreign study. Budget shortages and a desire to ensure that foreign students pay their own way have played a key role in Great Britain, Australia, and Canada. In the United States, at the federal level, there is a desire to fit foreign student policy (and overseas aid in general) to the needs of foreign policy, as well as to the needs of the labor market.[379] Programs have fallen victim to federal budget cuts in the United States. In countries like Ethiopia and Nicaragua, political factors have meant changes in foreign student policy. In China, political, ideological, and economic priorities have influenced foreign study policy. In many Third World nations, pent-up demand for postsecondary education from the articulate middle classes tends to boost the numbers of students sent abroad, regardless of whether the economy needs the manpower to be trained overseas. Finally, in recent years there has been a rethinking of the early emphasis in many Third World nations on higher education as the main engine of development, and this may reduce the availability of scholarships for overseas study. The

Table 11.2.   Factors Affecting the Decision to Study Abroad by Third World Students

Home Country (Push Factors)	Host Country (Pull Factors)
1. Availability of scholarships for study abroad	1. Availability of scholarships to international students
2. Poor-quality educational facilities	2. Good-quality education
3. Lack of research facilities	3. Availability of advanced research facilities
4. Lack of appropriate educational facilities and/or failure to gain admission to local institution(s)	4. Availability of appropriate educational facilities with likely offer of admission
5. Politically uncongenial situation	5. Congenial political situation
6. Enhanced value (in the marketplace) of a foreign degree	6. Congenial socioeconomic and political environment
7. Discrimination against minorities	7. Opportunity for general international life experience
8. Recognition of inadequacy of existing forms of traditional education	

major aid agencies as well as the World Bank de-emphasized higher education in the 1980s and 1990s.[380] The factors that influence foreign student policy are complex. It is clear that political, ideological, economic, and sometimes educational issues are all mixed. This complexity makes the shaping of foreign student policy difficult. Table 11.2 provides insight into the "push" and "pull" factors relating to personal decision making concerning foreign study.

FOREIGN STUDY AND DEPENDENCY

Foreign study takes place in a context of global, economic, technological, and political inequality. The context of inequality is particularly dramatic precisely where the largest flow of students occurs—between Third World countries and the industrialized countries of the West and Japan. Analysis of the inequalities between countries and the influence of inequality on foreign study and international education has been rare. While it is clear that foreign study occurs in a situation of global inequality, most discussions are couched in terms of exchanges, mutual understanding, cooperation, and development.[381] It is not the purpose of this discussion to claim that all foreign study is necessarily detrimental to the Third World, but rather to point out the paradoxical character of foreign study from the perspective of the Third World—the principal generator of international student flows. International study for Third World nations represents a mixed blessing.[382]

The following aspects of foreign study relate to global inequalities and may, in some contexts, contribute to a continuation of inequality.

- Foreign students become acclimated to working in an international language—usually English or French—and often find it difficult to use an indigenous language for scientific work at home.[383]
- Foreign students become part of an international knowledge network of journals, books, associations, and informal relationships. This, of course, is an advantage in terms of keeping abreast of modern science, but it may have negative implications for the local scientific community and may hinder engaging in locally relevant research when the student returns home.
- Foreign students may absorb the culture of the host country as well as its technological knowledge, and this may engender unrealistic attitudes, orientations toward consumer goods, or working styles that make readjustment to their home countries difficult.[384] Returned foreign scholars may become consumers of Western products—both consumer goods and intellectual orientations.
- Foreign study frequently instills in the student the methodological norms, ideological approaches, and general scientific culture of the host nation. Such perspectives may be positive in some respects, but may also create a dependence of the local academic and research systems on foreign models.
- Foreign study bestows, in many nations, a certain prestige on the individual who has

been abroad. This prestige frequently leads to better job opportunities and access to power.

- The location of foreign study may make a difference not only in the outlook and attitudes of an individual but also in professional opportunities. Study in France, for example, frequently directs a foreign graduate toward the French academic network of journals, books, and scientific associations.
- Specific relationships between industrialized and Third World nations are key determinants of the nature of international student flows and of continuing intellectual and academic relationships among nations. Most important, of course, are the continuing links between France and Great Britain and their former colonial possessions. Traditionally, students from the colonies tended to go to the metropole. Linguistic factors, perceptions of educational quality and prestige, links between examination systems, an "old boy" network, and official policies of governments all contributed to this situation.

In general, foreign study tends to tie Third World nations more closely to the metropolitan centers to which they send their students. This is perhaps an inevitable result of the superior scientific and academic systems of the industrialized countries. In most cases, it is likely that the skills and knowledge obtained through foreign study outweigh the negative implications of this experience. It is also likely that careful planning can provide the means of alleviating some of the possibly negative impact of foreign study.

THE FUTURE OF FOREIGN STUDY

Foreign study is unquestionably a permanent phenomenon in higher education. Universities are, after all, international institutions that have traditionally drawn inspiration and innovation from all over the world. Academic models in the United States, and in most other parts of the world, are an amalgam of ideas and practices from other countries. Research and the curriculum know no international boundaries, and there is increasing recognition that an international orientation in higher education is a positive element. Foreign study has also become "big business" in many countries and an issue of considerable debate and controversy as well. It is very difficult to predict precise trends and flows, but several factors will help to determine patterns and policies of foreign study.

- The growth of indigenous academic systems in Third World nations will lessen the need for overseas study. Governments will cease to sponsor students for foreign study if places are available at home.
- Fiscal problems, currently endemic in a number of Third World nations, will continue to have a negative impact on the number of foreign students from that country. Countries with massive foreign debts, such as Brazil and Venezuela, or with overex-

tended development plans, like Nigeria, have already cut back on the numbers of foreign students. Mexico, which had large and well-funded overseas scholarship programs, has severely curtailed these efforts.

- As incomes rise in the Third World, there will be a tendency for families to sponsor foreign study privately. This is particularly true for minority groups or ethnic populations that feel themselves under actual or potential threat. An example here is the Chinese population in Southeast Asia, which sends its children overseas for study—thereby contributing to the brain drain, since many of these young people do not return to their countries of origin.
- Third World countries with foreign exchange problems may curtail foreign study opportunities, even those funded privately. This has already occurred in India, where foreign exchange is difficult to obtain and restrictions are placed on fields of study, approved institutions, and the like. This phenomenon is very evident in such NICs as Taiwan and Singapore.
- The balance between undergraduate and graduate students will continue to shift toward a preponderance of graduate students in foreign student populations, although this is not necessarily the case for industrialized countries.
- As some Third World nations, in their development plans, shift their emphasis from higher education to primary and secondary education, there will be less money available for overseas scholarship programs.

None of these factors necessarily presages a massive increase in the number of foreign students, and on balance, there is likely to be a reduction in rates of growth. As the statistics cited in this chapter show, there have been major swings in numbers of students going abroad from specific countries, although overall trends have been, and likely will continue to be, up. While some sending countries have encountered political and economic difficulties, there is a worldwide increase in demand for access to postsecondary education. Further, there is a trend toward encouraging cross-border education in the industrialized world, and especially in the EU nations.

Trends in the industrialized countries are somewhat difficult to discern. Great Britain's full-fee policy caught most analysts by surprise. There is a trend in Western Europe toward instituting restrictions on foreign students from Third World nations, while barriers to students from within Western Europe have been eliminated, contributing to a large increase in numbers. In the United States and Canada, there is increasing discussion of the perceived negative fiscal effects of foreign students, but at the same time a strong commitment to international education. In Canada, some restrictions have already been put in place, but in the United States, there have so far been no direct moves at the federal level against foreign students.

Those concerned with foreign study—policymakers in both Third World and industrialized nations, professionals who have responsibility for working with foreign students, academic administrators who determine institutional policy, and the students and their families—all seem to look at the issue with a growing sophistication. Cost-benefit analysis, accountability, and the relevance of foreign study for the job market are likely to be the elements of decision making in the coming period.

Nevertheless foreign study remains an important issue. Hundreds of thousands of students will make their way across international frontiers for study. Expenditures—by governments, foundations, families, and institutions—will continue in the millions of dollars annually. There will also be pressure on all concerned to develop innovative ways of dealing with an issue that has become both a challenge and a benefit in contemporary higher education.

IV

Peripheral Centers: The Newly Industrializing Countries

12

Higher Education, Democracy, and Development: Implications for Newly Industrializing Countries

Universities are central institutions in modern societies. They not only provide the education that is needed for technologically based economies but they are also the most important centers for research and innovation in many fields. They are essential parts of all modern societies. Universities are participants in the international knowledge system, ensuring that a society is aware of what is happening in the increasingly global world of science, scholarship, and research. Universities also play a key role in society by providing research on history and current societal development—essential for countries that have undergone great social and economic change. The academic community provides the largest and most talented group of scholars, researchers and intellectuals—people who constitute the knowledge base of the society and who, through their expertise, play a crucial role in society. Universities are also politically important, not only providing the elites with training but also educating the opposition. Universities are the source of ideas, and their very essence as knowledge-based institutions may have a profound impact on societies going through difficult periods of transformation—as is the case in the newly industrializing countries (NICs). In short, the university is, in many ways, the quintessential institution of the new knowledge-based society of the twenty-first century.

At the same time, universities can be controversial institutions, especially in transitional societies. They are often hotbeds of intellectual and sometimes political dissent. The professors, through their writings and teachings, may present alternative perspectives to established orthodoxy. Students may engage in political activism, even overthrowing governments.[385] The ideas, and sometimes the actions, emanating from campuses may cause difficulties for the authorities, but they are nonetheless valuable for society because these ideas are often the catalyst for innovation, modernization, and development. Universities and government authorities are frequently in conflict. Academic institutions, in most countries, are funded largely by the government.[386] As the research function of universities becomes more prominent, academic institutions are increasingly expensive to operate. Those who provide the bulk of the money for higher education naturally want a significant degree of control over the academic enterprise. In the NICs, additional problems arise because of the political and societal role of the universities. There are inevitable conflicts between the accountability that the government desires and the autonomy that is part of the academic tradition.

This chapter explores the role of the university at the turn of the century, focusing mainly on the rapidly growing NICs of the Pacific Rim. These nations—including the Republic of Korea, Taiwan, Singapore, and several others—have achieved impressive economic success and joined the ranks of the developed countries. In terms of per capita income, economic output, trade relations, literacy, and basic education, these countries are as modern as any in the world.[387] They are, in many respects, models for other Third World countries in terms of both economic progress and academic development.

HIGHER EDUCATION IN THE NICS

In all of the NICs, the economies are maturing, growing more complex and technology based, and are developing a larger service sector. As a result of these economic trends, universities become inevitably more central to economic development. It should be noted that research and high-tech industries did not play a major role in the initial economic success of the NICs. As was the case for Japan, development was based on relatively low-tech, low-wage industries able to compete internationally. For Korea, steel, shipbuilding, textiles, and relatively unsophisticated consumer products exemplified this stage of development. Where technological inputs were needed, they were purchased from abroad or were copied without regard to the legal niceties.[388] As the economies matured and as they faced growing competition from countries with lower wages and a desire to catch up, decisions were made to provide more high-tech and value-added products as a means of maintaining competitiveness in changing economic circumstances. Singapore was the first country to see the need for this model of development, and higher education, research, and training became a key part of Singapore's economic strategy.[389]

During the initial stages of development, universities were not seen as a major factor in the process. However, higher education did expand significantly as academic degrees became important for jobs in the growing civil service and in the expanding private sector. In the past decade, demands from the expanding middle class for access to postsecondary education caused students who experienced difficulty gaining access at home to go abroad to study in greater numbers. In Korea, as in Taiwan, much of this expansion was in the private sector; government involvement, while considerable, was nonetheless fairly circumscribed. In both Korea and Taiwan, private entrepreneurs have been active in establishing colleges and universities.[390] The universities were, almost without exception, oriented toward teaching; research was not emphasized. The development of the university as primarily a teaching institution and the traditions built up supporting this orientation have shaped academic structures in the NICs, making the emergence of research-oriented institutions difficult.

This is an ideal time to consider the expanding role of postsecondary education in the growing and increasingly sophisticated economies of the NICs. The traditional teaching function of the universities continues to be essential as many jobs in a modernizing economy require advanced education. Further, a differentiated economy needs many skills, which the universities are ideally suited to provide. Thus, the universities are now expected to offer a much wider range of programs, departments, and interdisciplinary centers in order to provide the education that the economy needs.[391]

Research and development (R and D) is becoming a more central part of the mission of the university. This means that there must be a basic change in patterns of funding higher education and in the ethos of the universities. It is not enough to have one high-quality institution—like the Korean Advanced Institute of Science and Technology, which in any case offers degrees only at the graduate level. The academic system as a whole must become more research oriented, although not every postsecondary institution needs to be heavily involved in research. The expansion of graduate education goes hand in hand with the development of research in the universities. There is not only a greater need for people with advanced degrees to work in industry as well as to teach in the higher education system, but also for graduate programs that are integrally related to the research enterprise.[392] While it has been common for the NICs to target the disciplines for research and graduate education carefully—an appropriate course given the limited resources—governments should also permit a fairly broad expansion of fields and disciplines since it is hard to predict what will be a priority field in the future.

Further, it is probably a mistake to rely on nonuniversity institutions for R and D. Although it may be more difficult to control the universities, in the long run the university environment seems the most appropriate one for a well-balanced research and training program.[393] While there has been great stress in recent years—both in the NICs and in industrialized countries—on applied research, universities have traditionally concentrated on basic research, where the results may not be of immediate usefulness. However, basic research lays the foundation for advanced training and is useful in terms of generating the theoretical knowledge required for subsequent applied research. Therefore, an appropriate balance between the "pure" and the "applied" research done in university settings must be reached.

Large, complex, and expensive higher education systems are a necessity in the NICs. The growing middle classes demand access to higher education for their children. The economy, at all levels, needs increasingly well-qualified workers. There is a shift from heavy, low-wage, low-tech industry to value-added, high-tech production, and the service sector. All of these require postsecondary training for the workforce. As the NICs become increasingly involved in the international knowledge system, the universities are the institutions that participate most directly in that system.

As in most of the rest of the world, expansion has been a key characteristic of higher education development in the NICs. The NICs are currently approaching an access rate for higher education that is similar to patterns in Western Europe—about one-quarter of the relevant age cohort. Indeed, it is likely that they will exceed this rate. Conflicts between expansion and an orientation toward research mark the development of universities in the Third World. With inadequate resources to expand higher education, maintain quality, and support research, much of the Third World has seen continuing rapid expansion of enrollments but also deterioration of academic standards.[394] The NICs, with more adequate financial resources and a growing base of highly educated personnel, do not necessarily face this common Third World dilemma to some extent.

THE DEVELOPMENT OF AN INDIGENOUS SCIENTIFIC SYSTEM

Traditionally, the NICs have been dependent on the industrialized nations for both basic and applied scientific research. They have been users rather than producers of science and technology. In the long run, the NICs cannot continue to rely on others to produce all of the research needed for emerging technologically based industries and academic institutions, but must develop their own scientific systems and academic institutions. There will always be a tension between research produced abroad and local needs and research productivity, but the development of a viable research base is important for several reasons. It is essential that some research be produced locally in response to the specific needs of local industry and development, not only in the sciences but also in the social sciences and humanities. A viable research base is also essential to analyze, interpret, and make use of advanced research and technology from abroad effectively. Academic institutions in the NICs are in the somewhat contradictory position of being both users and producers of advanced knowledge. The development of an extensive indigenous network of academic and research institutions is necessary for this purpose.

Although much of the attention has been on science and technology in terms of research development, the social sciences and humanities should not be neglected. As societies become more complex, there is a need to analyze social trends and emerging problems in order to deal with them effectively. Population trends, for example, have a profound impact on the labor market and the economy. Demographers and sociologists are required to interpret such developments. Scholars in the humanities contribute to an understanding of culture, literature, and history in societies undergoing rapid change. Understanding local social realities requires an active social science and humanities base in the universities. It is quite common to downplay or ignore these "soft" fields as academic systems expand. This is a mistake, since they can make significant contributions.

An adequate academic system is also necessary to provide indigenous training for the growing numbers of graduates required by the expanding and increasingly sophisticated economies of the NICs. At the present time, all of the NICs send a significant number of first-degree students overseas. For example, for a considerable period, more students from Hong Kong studied outside the territory than in it. This was probably a mistaken policy, as it is, in the long run, probably less costly to educate these students at home. Recent expansion has changed this situation. Further, a domestic education will yield positive results in terms of the appropriate socialization of the students. Significantly, Korea no longer offers government scholarships for study abroad at the undergraduate level, reflecting the country's increased emphasis on domestic universities. Naturally, significant numbers of students will go abroad for advanced degrees, although even at this level the NICs should be educating a larger proportion of their students at home. The link between graduate-level training and the production of basic and applied research in the universities is direct, and there are strong arguments for expanding graduate training despite the relatively high costs involved.

Building up the infrastructures of higher education is neither easy nor inexpensive, but it is vital. The transformation of academic institutions from mainly teaching institutions, in which the academic staff have heavy teaching responsibilities, to more research-oriented universities is a necessity. Facilities such as top-quality libraries and research laboratories are also required. Decisions concerning the use of these facilities must be made—few, if any of the universities in the NICs can aspire, as for example Harvard University does, to collect books and journals comprehensively in most fields of knowledge. Such comprehensiveness is probably beyond the fiscal capacities of institutions in most NICs. But it can be argued that there should be at least one academic institution that provides both wide and deep coverage of current scholarly materials from the major industrialized nations. In the NICs, this means collecting not only from the United States and Britain, but also from Japan, since Japanese science is developing rapidly and is relevant for the needs of the Asian NICs.[395]

Journals and books are integral to an indigenous academic and scientific system, and it is critical that means be available locally to disseminate knowledge. While science will be dominated by the major internationally circulated journals from the metropolitan countries, a local dissemination system is useful as well.[396] Some scholarly materials, in the social sciences and humanities as well as in the hard sciences, will not have international relevance but will nonetheless be of importance to the country in which they are produced. Local scholars must also have relatively easy access to sources of publication. It is interesting that several NICs have taken somewhat different approaches to journal development. In Korea, several indigenous-language journals in the sciences have been established along with a number of Korean-language publications in the social sciences, although these journals serve to some extent as vehicles for translations of articles written overseas. Taiwan, in contrast, has placed greater stress on local scholars publishing in international journals. Although the medium of instruction in Taiwan is Chinese, many of the journals in the sciences are in English in order to communicate Taiwanese science to an international audience and to ensure that Taiwanese scientists become part of the international knowledge system. Singapore, which uses English as the medium of instruction in higher education, has developed some scholarly journals in English but none in indigenous languages.[397] There are various approaches to creating an adequate scientific infrastructure, but it is crucial that careful attention be given to this aspect of the development of higher education.

The creation of an indigenous scientific system is a complex task. At its center is the academic profession itself, since the teachers and researchers are critical elements of the system. The other components of the scientific system cannot be ignored. The academic enterprise also depends on libraries, laboratories, journals, and the other elements of a modern academic and scientific system. Without the necessary array of institutions and structures, a fully effective scientific system is impossible.

HISTORICAL PATTERNS AND CONTEMPORARY VARIATIONS

Modern universities are Western institutions that have been transplanted all over the world.[398] The process of academic development in non-Western countries is not always an easy one, and care must be given to the implanting of academic institutions. In much of the Third World, the higher education model was imposed by the colonial power—and that basic institutional type has in all instances remained after independence.[399] For a few countries, such as Japan and Thailand, which have never undergone colonial rule, the choice of the academic model was without external coercion, but there, too, Western models were adopted. Korea is a rather unique case, since it adopted a generally American pattern on its own initiative in the nineteenth century, only to see the Japanese model imposed during the period of Japanese colonial rule between 1910 and 1945.[400] After independence was regained, the dominant external influence was again American. In all cases, a Western institutional model was adopted. In that sense, there is no "Third World" university, only Western transplants. Of course, there was a great deal of adaptation to suit local needs, and throughout much of the developing world, academic institutions have developed legitimacy.

The development of higher education was one of imposition and borrowing.[401] The process of entrenching the academic idea in its new environment was not always easy and was seldom complete. Academic institutions are fragile—after all, they developed in the West over a period of more than six centuries with many variations and much trial and error. To expect non-Western societies to immediately adopt all of the elements of the university without difficulties is unrealistic. Yet, for a university to fulfill its role completely and to aspire to the highest international standards, it must acquire most of the characteristics of the modern university—these include a considerable degree of academic freedom and autonomy, an appropriate level of support, high faculty morale, and the ability to set its own curriculum.[402]

History shows that it is not easy to build up a fully functioning academic ethos.[403] It takes strong leadership by academic institutions and a willingness by governments to permit the universities to develop autonomously. In many developing countries, academic institutions are unable to fulfill their potential because they have not been permitted sufficient autonomy. It is, of course, a challenge to governments—many of which are unfamiliar with the ethos of the university—to permit the emergence of an institution that may sometimes challenge the authority of the government and that, in any case, is using public funds.

There are several academic models to choose from in the modern world. The most influential at present is the American academic model.[404] For a number of reasons, this is the case. The American university idea—combining research, service to society, and access by a large and growing segment of the population—fits the needs of many developing countries. The United States has, through its assistance programs, fostered the American academic model in other countries.[405] American science is a powerful force worldwide, and this too has made the American academic model attractive. Finally, many of the leaders of Third World academic systems themselves graduated from American universities and, thus, naturally look to the American institutional model. Korea, both because of its historical and contemporary ties, has gravitated to the American model, probably without careful consideration of other available alternatives.[406] Yet, by readily adopting available foreign models, the relevance of the institution to its society may be diminished.

There are, of course, other patterns for university development. The British model remains a strong influence, especially in former British colonies, although it is fair to say that even in these countries, American influences are growing.[407] In former French colonies, the French academic model predominates. In Latin America, the original Spanish- and French-influenced academic models are being modified by American influences and by the rapid growth of private-sector higher education.[408]

In the NICs of Asia, it is possible to see a process of slow change and adaptation as academic systems grow and develop. The two academic systems patterned on the Japanese model—the Korean and Taiwanese—reacted somewhat differently to this model after the Japanese colonial period ended. Both Korea and Taiwan dropped the Japanese organizational pattern after 1945. In Korea, the Japanese model was replaced by an American oriented system. The American model familiar to the Koreans from the nineteenth century and was also strongly advocated by American aid officials, who were powerful in Korea in the aftermath of the Korean War. In

Taiwan, which became the Republic of China after the Nationalist defeat on the mainland and the migration of the Nationalist government to Taiwan, the mainland Chinese academic pattern, was put into place.[409] America's close ties with Taiwan and the fact that many Taiwanese students studied in the United States meant that the American academic model became influential in Taiwan as well. Singapore and Malaysia have retained the core of the British academic model but have adopted elements of the American system as well. Singapore is emphasizing research and graduate study as an increasingly integral part of the academic system, while Malaysia expanded higher education and shifted the language of instruction from English to Bahasa Malaysia.[410] These changes have been made to enable the academic system to respond to perceived needs. Two of the NICs, Korea and Taiwan, made a significant break from the immediate past in shaping their postwar higher education systems, but even in these cases the model adopted was not a new one. And the changes made in later years have been within the broad context of existing academic models.

While it is true that virtually all universities in the Third World were imported by colonial rulers or were chosen from external models, it is fair to say that academic institutions have been successfully integrated in most developing countries. While there is much criticism of the universities as "alien transplants," irrelevant to national needs, the fact is that academic institutions have flourished in this alien soil and have become central institutions in their societies.[411]

THE INTERNATIONAL CONTEXT OF INEQUALITY

It is not very difficult to create a modern university and ensure that it provides postsecondary education at the highest international levels to students. All that is required is money, good academic leadership, a long-term commitment to the institution, and the ability to select high-quality students. Academic institutions in all of the NICs have—through somewhat different strategies, orientations, and levels of quality—made efforts to build up world-class academic institutions. In Korea, Seoul National University and Yonsei University, among several others, provide "international-standard" higher education. In Taiwan, the National Taiwan University and several of the other national institutions fall into this category, as do the National University of Singapore and the University of Hong Kong. While these institutions may not match Harvard or Oxford in prestige, facilities, or in academic quality, they are quite competitive internationally. The academic institutions of the NICs not only form a "pecking order" within their countries, but they are also part of an international system of universities and will inevitably be ranked in this system.

These schools function in the international knowledge system, which places them at a disadvantage. It is virtually impossible for the universities of the NICs to achieve positions of full equality internationally. Language is one issue. English is the major language of scientific communication. Academic systems that do not function in English are at a disadvantage in this context. Publication is somewhat more difficult and it is harder to gain international scientific recognition. Even the Japanese universities, with strong traditions of scholarship, find themselves at a disadvantage in terms of communication and publication because of language. The United States, a few European countries, and Japan dominate R and D spending. It is extraordinarily difficult for newcomers to build up the scientific infrastructures or to spend the sums necessary to support basic scientific research in many fields. The patterns of R and D expenditures help to maintain the dominant positions of the major academic superpowers. Most of the world's more than 100,000 academic journals are edited and published in just a few countries, and the overwhelming proportion of key scientific journals are published in English.[412]

The very size of the academic systems in the major Western countries gives these universities significant advantages. In the United States, for example, there are more than 600,000 teachers in postsecondary education—perhaps 25 percent of the world's total academic profession. There are more than 3,000 institutions of higher education. American academic libraries are major purchasers of books and journals—indeed, they are the largest part of the market for scholarly materials in English. It is possible to provide one example of the advantage of size. Because scholars in the United States are the largest producers of science and also the largest consumers of scientific information through journals and books, they dominate the network of scientific communication. The research paradigms and concerns of American science naturally tend to dominate the networks.[413] Issues that may be important in smaller academic systems—especially those that are at the periphery in terms of language and contributions to basic science—will tend to be ignored in the international scientific marketplace.

It is clear that very significant inequalities exist in the international knowledge system— inequalities engendered by the nature, scope, and size of the system and not, generally, by deliberate policies of universities, governments, or publishers. However, those who dominate the system are not dissatisfied with it, and their policies and practices tend to work to perpetuate the status quo. The point of this discussion is that the nature of the international knowledge system and the world hierarchy of universities make it more difficult for the newly emerging universities of the NICs to gain positions of international prominence. Further, the relatively small scientific systems in the NICs will find it impossible to develop scientific equality in most fields. Careful choice of research specialization and investment in targeted areas may, however, permit the NICs to carve out areas of excellence and international prominence. It is, nonetheless, important to understand the nature of the international knowledge system and the place of the NICs within it. While the system is not unchangeable, it is nonetheless very strong and well entrenched.

KEY ELEMENTS OF HIGHER EDUCATION DEVELOPMENT

While higher education systems take into account international realities, the basic challenge is internal. The newly industrialized countries have the wealth, educational base, and societal need to build up "world-class" academic systems. Indeed, they have already made significant progress. Academic systems in the NICs—and in most other countries for that matter—must consider a number of issues when building and maintaining institutions of higher education.[414] Academic institutions, it must be remembered, are built up only with commitment and resources, but they are fragile institutions that require both support and the right policy environment if they are to flourish.

Autonomy and Accountability

Academic institutions are quite unusual in that they are, for the most part, funded by the state yet enjoy a significant amount of autonomy. The tension between accountability—state oversight and sometimes control over the finances and perhaps the activities of universities—and autonomy—the ability of academic institutions to make their own decisions concerning a wide range of matters—exists in every country.[415] In the industrialized nations, it has become a point of considerable controversy as the costs of higher education have risen at a time when public funds have declined. Indeed, the Thatcher government in Britain abolished the University Grants Committee, which provided government funds to the universities in a way that assured a maximum of autonomy, in favor of a new Universities Funding Council, which demands a much greater degree of accountability.[416] In the United States, autonomy has been increasingly limited by regulations of the federal government dealing with specific university policies—for example, with regard to access to information or aspects of the hiring of staff. It has also been limited by the states, which have been increasingly concerned about how funds are spent. It should be noted that in the United States, the private colleges and universities have more direct autonomy in terms of freedom from government control, but even they are not fully autonomous because if they accept any governmental financial aid, they are subject to some regulations.[417] Despite tensions, the consensus in the Western industrialized nations is that a significant amount of autonomy is needed for a university to function effectively.

Academic institutions need autonomy over their own governance and over the basic internal decision making in order to join the ranks of world-class institutions. It is, of course, possible to have functioning universities with a limited amount of autonomy, as was the case in the former Soviet Union. The best universities in the world are able to appoint and promote their own academic staff without interference from external authorities; admit students, establish the structure of degrees, and evaluate student performance; develop systems of internal governance that permit academic structures to operate within the universities free from external constraint or control; and, quite importantly, provide their staff members with a high degree of professional autonomy and with unfettered academic freedom. Not only is academic freedom protected in the public pronouncements of the universities, but policies and administrative structures have also been instituted to ensure that academic freedom is not violated. Academic freedom is generally seen as a key part of institutional autonomy and that of the individual professor.[418]

Issues of autonomy and accountability are particularly difficult in developing countries and in the NICs. Typically, Third World universities have had weaker traditions of autonomy, in large part because colonial authorities did not permit such traditions to develop. Further, after independence, Third World governments tried to harness universities to meet the goals of national development. They also feared that autonomous academic institutions might become centers of political opposition. Finally, the development of universities was a very expensive process, and governments naturally wanted maximum accountability and control over the goals and the operation of universities.[419]

There is a great need for an agreement concerning appropriate levels of autonomy and accountability in the NICs. The situation in Korea, for example, where 70 percent of academic institutions are private, is somewhat unusual because the government exerts considerable control over institutions in both the public and private sectors even though private institutions receive little if any funding from the government. While it is possible that institutional arrangements that work reasonably well in Western industrialized countries may need to be modified in the NICs, it is clear that an adequate level of autonomy is essential if universities are to develop to their full potential. Universities must have autonomy to participate in the international knowledge system and to gain the respect of the world academic community. In general, there is probably too much governmental control over universities in the NICs.

Academic Freedom

Related to autonomy but also distinct from it is the highly controversial issue of academic freedom. Developed first in the medieval universities of Europe and then expanded in the German universities in the nineteenth century, academic freedom was limited to the right to teach one's speciality in the classroom and to publish in one's field of expertise. Academic freedom did not extend outside the world of teaching and scholarship. In the United States, the concept of academic freedom was significantly expanded in the early twentieth century to include guarantees for the college and university teacher in the classroom, in publications, and in public life to express opinions not only in the area of scholarly expertise but also on other subjects, without threat from external authorities. In addition, academic freedom was linked to the tenure system, which guaranteed permanent appointments to academic staff after a lengthy probationary period and a careful evaluation of qualifications.[420] However, even in the United States, academic freedom has not always been fully protected—as, for example, during the "McCarthy Period" in the 1950s, when some professors were dismissed for political reasons and many others were intimidated.[421] Despite some lapses and variations among countries in the industrialized nations, academic freedom is recognized as a key policy for higher education, and guarantees are generally included both in the internal regulations of academic institutions and in the overall policy framework governing higher education.

The NICs face special problems, since academic freedom is not yet fully institutionalized there. In general, universities and individual academics have both more autonomy and more academic freedom than is the case for the rest of the population, but significant problems exist. Some NICs have inadequate legal and institutional protection for academic freedom. Others place limitations on topics for research and publication. Restrictions may be placed on publication or public statements by academics. Professors are sometimes dismissed from their jobs for ideological or political reasons. While the norms of academic freedom continue to be strengthened, both the concept and institutional norms need further development.

The Academic Profession

The heart of the contemporary university is the academic profession. No reform or institutional transformation is possible without the commitment of the professoriate. The professors do the teaching and conduct the research. They also play a primary role in university governance. Their attitudes and values have an impact on their students and on the ethos of the university.[422] Their influence, through their teaching and research, can be significant and extends beyond the classroom. In many countries, including the NICs, the professoriate plays an important societal role as well, influencing public opinion and contributing to public debate on many issues. The professoriate holds a respected position in society, and the views of academics are highly valued. Professors write for newspapers and appear on television. They sometimes serve in official governmental positions, even as ministers or senior advisers to key policymakers. Some academics may be active in oppositional organizations and as highly vocal critics of government policies.[423] In Korea, professors have frequently served in senior government positions, including the cabinet; currently, a number of academics from the top universities are serving in ministerial positions. The academic profession is a small but highly influential elite group in many societies. In countries that have restrictions on freedom of expression, a poorly developed mass media, or an emerging intellectual class, academics tend to be particularly powerful as opinion makers.

The professoriate is by no means a unified group. It is divided by discipline and speciality and composed of many different subcultures. Physicists think very differently from sociologists. Social scientists tend to be more to the left in their political attitudes than are engineers or those in the "hard" sciences. Further, professors in the elite universities are more likely to be interested in playing a societal role than are those in less prestigious institutions. It is also possible to divide the profession into "cosmopolitan professors"—who tend to be more oriented to their disciplines, to research, and to a national and international community of scholars—and those who are "locals"—who are oriented to their institutions and to teaching.[424] The cosmopolitan scholars are located in the more prestigious institutions and are better known not only among their colleagues but in the wider intellectual community as well. They are often involved in business enterprises and in government.

The academic profession is relatively underpaid when compared to individuals with similar qualifications, yet academics in most societies are solidly in the middle or upper-middle class. Where academics are underpaid, they will seek additional employment either by teaching at more than one university or by seeking consulting or other remunerative activities. Some of the most able will even take the opportunity to leave the country and take up positions where salaries and working conditions are better.[425] Thus, if academic institutions expect the full-time commitment of the professoriate, salaries must be appropriate.

It is also important to understand the social class backgrounds of the professoriate. Academics in most countries come from urban backgrounds and relatively privileged families. In some countries, particular groups in the population tend to choose academic careers. In Japan, Christians tend toward academic careers, as do Jews in the United States. They will tend to reflect the orientations and interests of their backgrounds. It is often difficult to convince the best professors to teach in universities located far from the major urban areas.

Academics often express liberal or even radical views on societal issues but are rather conservative on issues relating to the university. They generally oppose reforms that will alter established patterns of work and governance. Since the professoriate is the key force in academic governance, their attitudes toward change in higher education make change difficult. In Japan, for example, external events have been the main force for reform while the entrenched power of the academic profession has been a strong conservative element.[426]

The academic profession functions in an unusual institutional context. Professors, after all, are employees of large bureaucratic organizations and very often civil servants, although their working conditions provide a considerable measure of independence. At the same time, they have a great deal of institutional and personal autonomy. The ethos of the academic profession is one that stresses autonomy and academic freedom. Compared to others employed by large bureaucratic organizations, professors have an unusual degree of freedom. The self-image, working conditions, and ethos of the professoriate make it difficult to control and make change in the university problematical.

In the NICs, the transformation of the universities, and of the academic profession itself, from a teaching focus with a limited prestige and only a minor societal role to a greater emphasis on research and more prestige and power is not easy, but the NICs do have certain advantages. The academic profession is relatively young, and many of its members have been trained abroad, often in the best universities. These scholars have been trained abroad in a research tradition. Many NIC scholars have taken up professorships in the industrialized countries, contributing to the brain drain in their home countries. However, it may be possible to lure them back as local universities change their orientation and augment their academic and scientific facilities. The significantly increased levels of funding that are necessary for academic improvement are often available in the NICs. The conditions of work and facilities offered to the academic profession must be similar to the standard prevalent internationally. A common error in developing countries is to improve facilities yet at the same time retain quite heavy teaching loads. In the industrialized countries, professors at research-oriented universities generally teach approximately six classroom contact hours per week (or two courses per semester) in addition, of course, to advising graduate students. To expect a high level of research productivity under the duress of heavy teaching loads is impractical.

The academic profession is highly complex. Historical traditions, working conditions, relations with society, issues of autonomy and academic freedom, salaries, and diverse subcultures all affect the development and role of the profession. It is clear, however, that an academic institution cannot reach its potential without a productive academic profession that is committed to institutional goals.

Students

Students are also an important part of the higher education equation. Their choices regarding universities and major fields help to shape the higher education system. High student demand drives expansion of higher education. Students also constitute subcultures that have a large impact on the university and sometimes on society. Student subcultures are varied, ranging from social and athletic groups to political organizations.[427]

In the NICs, there has been much concern with student political activism and campus political subcultures. Students have been a potent political force in the NICs, as they have been in many Third World nations.[428] It is generally the case that where political regimes have widespread legitimacy in the country and where there is a considerable amount of freedom of expression, student movements will not have the potential to overthrow the regime. In the Western industrialized nations, even during times of major social unrest—such as in the United States during the Vietnam War and in the mid-1960s in Europe—student movements did not threaten the stability of the governments themselves. Students may point to severe societal problems or create the atmosphere for social change, but they do not have the potential to create significant instability.

In the NICs, which do not yet have fully institutionalized democratic regimes and where at least a segment of the population does not have faith in the existing political framework, there is potential for instability generated by student political activism. Once an array of functioning and legitimate political institutions and forms to express opinions and influence the political system—such as a free press, voluntary organizations, and political parties—are established, it is unlikely that student activism will play such an important role in society. Until these institutions are in place and functioning, however, students will continue to play a political role that could lead to societal instability.

While it is possible to use repression and intimidation to bring an end to a specific student political movement, it is not practical to combine permanent repression with the development of a high-quality academic system. A functioning academic system requires academic freedom, an atmosphere free of repression, and a significant amount of autonomy. Constant student disruption and the consequent involvement of the police or military on campus inevitably disrupt the institution and make normal academic life impossible.

It is necessary for both academic institutions and governments to understand the nature of student political involvement, the causes and possible consequences of activism, and the implications of repressive responses to activism. For their part, student movements seldom consider the likely results of their actions nor do they understand the potential or the limitations of activism. For NICs, student political activism is a matter of considerable importance, not only for the university but also for the political system and society.

The University and Democracy

The university is itself not a fully democratic institution. It is, rather, a semi-democracy of the faculty since the professors make most of the decisions; the majority—the students—has only a minor role in governance or decision making. The university is also a meritocracy, with faculty appointments going to the most able and students generally admitted on the basis of their qualifications. Yet, the university plays a very important role in a democratic society. It champions free and rational debate, not only on academic matters but also on issues of societal importance. In many countries, university faculty members are involved in shaping the national debate through their writings. Universities are among the few institutions in modern society that have the detachment and objectivity to pose alternatives and ask difficult questions. The academic community, almost by its very nature, is critical.

The university also provides training for future elites since in most societies virtually everyone who achieves political, cultural, or economic power is a graduate of a university. Thus, not only what is learned in the classroom but also the campus environment is of considerable importance to society. The open intellectual atmosphere and the spirit of inquiry found on campuses are key lessons for future elites. Further, the general attitude of the faculty also has an influence on students. The university, in some ways, is an institution that is profoundly subversive of intolerance, repression, and authoritarianism. Dictatorial rulers are correctly fearful of universities, and the most repressive regimes, such as in Burma or Nigeria, are in a sense right when they close the universities for extended periods.

In the NICs committed to the development of democratic institutions, universities play a vital role. The universities provide the ideas that are necessary for democracy, and they provide training for the future elites in an atmosphere of free inquiry and debate. They disseminate new ideas to the wider society and often interpret trends from abroad. Universities may also be very uncomfortable institutions from the perspective of the government. They are the source of debate and sometimes of unrest. They are the training ground not only of the establishment but also of the opposition. And they are funded by the very state authorities who are criticized on the campus. Nonetheless, academic institutions are of primary importance in building up democratic values and ideas.

CONCLUSION

This chapter has argued that universities are central institutions in the newly industrializing countries. They are central not only in educating people for increasingly complex and technologically oriented societies, but also in providing the research base that will permit these societies to create ideas and translate them into usable products. Academic institutions are also critical in analyzing and interpreting social trends and developments. They not only provide technological training but are also crucial for education for democracy. The NICs have begun the process of transforming academic institutions from their largely teaching functions to much more complex—and expensive—universities that focus on research and knowledge dissemination as well as teaching. While not simple, this transformation will help to shape the future of the NICs because without fully developed universities, these societies will be unable to compete internationally. Not only will there be a need for a large cohort of highly trained personnel, but the university's research and dissemination of knowledge are central to a technological economy. Universities are complex institutions that require freedom of inquiry if they are to develop fully. At the same time, universities are also central to a democratic society.

The university of the twenty-first century will not be radically different from contemporary academic institutions. After all, universities have a long historical tradition and are relatively slow to change. Yet, some international trends are evident that will affect academic institutions.

1. The great wave of expansion that characterized the post-World War II period in the industrialized nations seems to be coming to an end. While universities may expand to meet societal and demographic needs, growth will likely be slower. In the Third World, however, expansion will continue, although at a somewhat slower rate. The NICs are likely to see continued growth as well, as postsecondary education seeks to provide access as well as to provide advanced scientific research.

2. For the NICs, transforming higher education will require expanding the research role and improving academic quality, at least at the upper levels of the system. The accompanying changes in values, orientations, and facilities will constitute a significant challenge.

3. The university will play a more public and instrumental role in society. The emergence of "open universities" that provide wide access to higher education is an indication of this trend.

4. In the Western industrialized countries, lavish public financing of higher education is no more. A greater share of the burden of higher education is falling on individuals and families. Industries are funding an increasing proportion of research, although overall research expenditures are not expanding rapidly. This trend limits access to higher education for some groups in society and weakens the research base of the universities, particularly in basic research. The NICs—which are at a

different stage of academic development—will need to examine their own needs and aspirations carefully rather than simply following international trends.

5. As universities become more complex, sophisticated, and productive, they will also become increasingly vocal, and perhaps at times controversial. Academic institutions must be given a significant degree of autonomy and freedom if they are to become truly world class, even at the cost of occasional embarrassment to the authorities.

The university of the future will resemble the academic institution of the past and the present. However, new challenges and demands will necessitate change. The academic community as well as the society must be prepared for these changes.

13

Higher Education and Scientific Development in the NICs

Third World countries seeking to enter the mainstream of contemporary technology and commerce must include scientific development as a critical part of nation building. This chapter considers the many ramifications of the development of science in the Third World, looking at four key newly industrializing nations—Malaysia, Singapore, South Korea, and Taiwan—among the wealthiest and most successful of countries once considered to be in the Third World. All four countries have emphasized higher education, advanced technology, and scientific development. These nations deserve attention not only as part of Asia's growing economic force but also as the vanguard of Third World progress, whose experiences may be useful for other countries.

Our focus here is on the role of higher education in the process of scientific growth. This emphasis is especially relevant for Third World nations, where much of the scientific infrastructure is in the universities. Academic institutions not only are home to most of the scientific research that is conducted, but also employ the largest proportion of scientists. As in all countries, universities also provide training for scientists. Academic institutions stand at the center of the research network in all countries, particularly in the Third World.[429] Academic science relates to the wider world of industry, government, and the public. Professors frequently undertake applied research, often with funds from industry or government bodies. Some are also engaged in outside consulting.

Contemporary science is an international phenomenon, and Third World science is particularly dependent on the international knowledge network. One of the factors in scientific development is the perplexing issue of language. English, the current international scientific medium, is the language of choice for participating in the worldwide knowledge network. When an academic system functions in a language like Bahasa Malaysia or Korean, it faces special challenges in communicating internationally. Another aspect of the internationalization of science is what might be called the "scientific diaspora." Large groups of scientists from Third World countries work in the industrialized nations, while retaining close ties with their home countries. These scientists assist scientific development in their countries by serving as links.[430] Foreign scientific training also enters into the international equation. In the four newly industrializing nations under consideration here, the large majority of the top scientists were trained abroad. The outward flow of students continues, with a degree from a Western university still conferring a distinct advantage.

Malaysia, Singapore, South Korea, and Taiwan are among the most successful of the countries of the Third World. Education and technology have played a minor role, except for Malaysia, which has relied on export of natural resources and agricultural products. Economic growth in these countries has been built on relatively "low-tech" industrial development dependent on a cheap and efficient workforce. Singapore has also benefited from its position as the world's second-busiest port. However, all of this is changing as these four countries move to more sophisticated industries and develop independent scientific bases. Higher education and science are playing an ever greater role. With their efficient and increasingly well-educated labor forces and export-oriented industries, these countries will be powerful worldwide competitors for years to come. Their successes may also yield valuable lessons for other Third World nations in terms of development strategies. The example of the highly successful computer industry in Taiwan shows how technicians, highly educated workers, and the global economy can prove a powerful combination of forces.

THE INTERNATIONAL KNOWLEDGE SYSTEM

As frequently noted, Third World nations, however prosperous, are part of an international knowledge system that places them at a disadvantage in a system controlled in many respects by the advanced industrial nations. The major universities and research laboratories are located in such key countries as the United States, Britain, Germany, France, and, to a lesser extent, countries like Australia and Canada. These countries spend the bulk of the world's research and development funds, are the home base to the major publishers of scholarly books and scientific journals, and produce the largest number of patents. Their discoveries and innovations dominate world science and technology. The research agendas of these countries influence research. Many scientists and scholars from the Third World have been educated in the advanced industrialized nations and maintain ties with the metropolitan centers. These factors necessarily connect Third World nations the international knowledge system and make them largely dependent on "imported knowledge."

The international knowledge system affects all countries at the periphery of the system, including many of the smaller industrialized nations. The small scientific communities of these newly industrializing nations lack the personnel, equipment, and funds to maintain a world-class scientific infrastructure. In most fields, advanced training takes place in the metropolitan nations. There is pressure on scientists to publish their findings in international journals, which are seen to be more prestigious than local journals. Local scientists also desire access to a wider international audience for their work. Key research findings are almost always imported and the basic work is done elsewhere. Scientists look abroad for insights. There is a sense that the most important scientific research is being conducted elsewhere and this has negative implications for funding decisions and on the priority given to scientific development. A paradox is at work—attention is paid to the fostering of indigenous scientific institutions while at the same time foreign science is given the most prominence and the highest prestige. There are also practical implications of peripherality. Expensive scientific equipment must be imported. Researchers must often travel abroad to keep up with the latest work in their fields and to maintain contacts with the "invisible college" of researchers in their fields of study. The research orientation of Third World scientists is often undervalued in international circles. In sum, these scientific systems must constantly worry about keeping up with developments abroad—developments that inevitably place Third World science at a disadvantage.

Despite the basic structural disadvantages of peripherality, the countries with which we are concerned here show significant progress toward developing an indigenous scientific base and have made major financial and resource commitments to scientific development. Policymakers recognize that they will never be fully independent of the major centers. They are, nonetheless, convinced that local scientific development can contribute not only to a mature and productive academic system but also to scientific innovations that will be useful to domestic industry and technology. Indigenous development can also produce the personnel needed both for research and for high-tech industrial growth. In these countries, scientific development remains part of an international knowledge system but at the same time has increasingly strong local roots that have been nurtured by government and academic policies as well as funding for indigenous scientific development.[431]

THE LANGUAGE ISSUE

The four countries being considered in this chapter have different approaches to the complex issue of language policy and higher education. English is the main international language of science. All four countries are greatly influenced by English in terms of higher education and research, while having somewhat different language policies. Indeed, there is a kind of language-policy continuum evident among the countries.

In Singapore, all postsecondary education—and most education at the primary and secondary levels as well—is in English, and in some ways there is no "language issue" since English is the language of instruction and research. All scientific journals in Singapore are published in English. The Singapore government feels that the country must be fully involved in the international economy to survive and that English is a key ingredient for participation. In Singapore, English is the sole language of science and technology. The three other countries have a more mixed approach to language issues in education and science. In each, an indigenous language is the medium of instruction in education, including higher education. Efforts have been made to adapt indigenous languages to science and to ensure that vocabularies are appropriate for higher education and science. All four countries used foreign languages for higher education as well as governmental administration prior to independence. Their experiences may provide useful examples to other Third World nations faced with problems of linguistic adaptation.

English was the colonial language in both Malaysia and Singapore, and these two countries serve as intriguing examples of divergent language policies.[432] While Singapore retained English as the medium of education, government, and commerce, Malaysia slowly shifted to the national language, Bahasa Malaysia, for all purposes—changing the medium of instruction in the universities in the 1970s.[433] Malaysia has paid considerable attention to providing textbooks and other educational materials in Bahasa Malaysia. A few scholarly journals now appear in the language, and in a number of fields adequate materials exist for undergraduate instruction. For advanced learning and research, however, English remains a necessity in Malaysia. Moreover, Malaysian scholars fear that the standard of English has declined, jeopardizing graduate study and international collaboration. A government-funded agency, the Dewan Bahasa dan Pustaka (language and literature agency) has commissioned many textbooks at all levels of education and stimulated writing and publication in the national language in other ways. Several of Malaysia's universities have sponsored scholarly journals and published scholarly books in Bahasa Malaysia. The problems are serious and include high translation and publication costs for a small market—Malaysia's total population is under 15 million, with about 60,000 students and some 6,000 academic staff in the nation's tertiary institutions. There is also a shortage of translators and authors. Senior scholars continue to publish in English for international publications. Despite the problems, Malaysia has remained committed to developing Bahasa Malaysia as an adequate medium for education and research. It is, however, likely that scientific progress has been slowed because of the emphasis—and resources—placed on the development of the national language. In the 1990s, both the government and the academic community realized that reliance on the national language was having a detrimental effect on Malaysia's scientific and industrial development, and English was partially restored in the education system.

Taiwan and Korea share a similar colonial history. For more than half a century,

Japan was the colonial power and imposed Japanese as the sole medium of instruction in higher education. Japan was responsible for the establishment of modern universities in both countries; although during the colonial period access to these institutions for Taiwanese and Koreans was limited. Japanese colonial domination ended in 1945, after which the medium of instruction shifted to Chinese in Taiwan and Korean in Korea. The arrival of the Nationalist Government from mainland China in Taiwan, and later the impact of American involvement, meant that the Japanese influence was quickly diluted. For Korea, a particularly bitter colonial experience under the Japanese hastened the replacement of Japanese influence—again, the United States became the major model. In both countries, while indigenous languages became the media of instruction, English became the main language of contact with the outside world. While Korea established scholarly journals in Korean, Taiwan chose—at least in the sciences and technological fields—to publish academic journals in English so that they would have a significant international circulation. In both Taiwan and Korea, there is a range of postsecondary textbooks available at the undergraduate level. However, advanced training in the sciences requires knowledge of English, and many of the materials used, including graduate-level textbooks, are in English. In both countries, professors are expected to publish their research in English for promotion in the better universities. The situation in the humanities and social sciences differs in that a greater proportion of work is done in indigenous languages. Korea and Taiwan are interesting examples of Third World development, since they were the two major colonies of Japan. Their postindependence experiences have not been easy—both have been involved in conflicts with neighboring countries. The policy of using indigenous languages for higher education, combined with a reliance on English for more advanced work, has been successfully carried out. Korea, with a population more than twice that of Taiwan, has done more to entrench the local language as a scientific medium, complete with journals. Taiwan, on the other hand, has used English, even domestically, as the major language of advanced science and research.

Singapore's decision to use English as the only language of higher education and research, as well as commerce and government, was made because policymakers felt it important to tie the nation firmly to the international knowledge network and the international marketplace. It was also recognized that Singapore, as a small country with a Chinese majority in a region dominated by Malays, could best rely on English as its main means of communication. Singapore relies mostly on imported materials and therefore has had no problems with providing textbooks or other research materials for its university. Singaporean scholars write exclusively in English for publication—either in the small number of local scholarly journals or for international journals. The use of English in higher education has meant that expatriate teachers could be brought in—close to half the teaching staff at the National University of Singapore are expatriates. Policymakers have welcomed foreign academic staff, feeling that it is necessary in order to be in the mainstream of international ideas and that expatriates contribute to the country's cosmopolitanism.

These nations function in an international scientific system dominated by English, and all have made adjustments to this fact. Korea has the most successful scientific infrastructure that operates significantly in the indigenous language, including journals and other publications. Malaysia also has made great efforts at indigenization, but there are shortages of scientific materials of all kinds. In Taiwan, while teaching is done in Chinese, most advanced research materials, including textbooks, are in English. For a long period, Taiwan's flaunting of international copyright rules made the unauthorized reproduction of English-language books and journals inexpensive and easy.

All four countries rely on the international scientific community for validation of research excellence and productivity by academic scientists. Publication in international journals, mainly in English, is a key requirement for promotion in all countries although less stressed in Korea and Malaysia than in Singapore or Taiwan. The emphasis on international publication and international recognition of scientists in these countries helps to tie the local scientific communities not only to the English language as a means of communication but also to the norms and values of a broader scientific culture. This may have the advantage of linking the local community to the frontiers of science but may also separate science from local concerns and local technological problems.

THE SCIENTIFIC DIASPORA

An often ignored but crucially important phenomenon are the links to scientists and scholars who live and work in the United States or other metropolitan nations. For Taiwan and Korea, the numbers are quite large, and the Korean and Taiwanese overseas scientific communities are very important for research and technology and for the broader direction of academic life. For all four countries, the majority of doctoral degree holders have been trained overseas. A majority of the Taiwanese and Korean students who have gone overseas to study, mostly at the graduate level, have not returned home directly after completing their degrees. Many of these doctoral degree holders obtain good jobs in the United States or elsewhere and advance rapidly in their careers overseas. Some have been opposed to the political situation at home and have chosen to remain abroad. There are very likely more Korean and Taiwanese scientists and engineers working abroad than at home, although reliable statistics are lacking and there is a flow back and forth. Significantly fewer Singaporeans and Malaysians have remained abroad, although many Chinese Malaysians have emigrated in recent years, feeling that government policies favoring the indigenous *bumiputeras* (Malays) were harmful to their long-term prospects. Overall, both employment opportunities and living conditions have been more favorable in Singapore and Malaysia than in Taiwan and Korea.

There is no doubt that Korea and Taiwan have suffered an exodus of highly educated people during the past three decades. The literature relating to the migration of workers—skilled and unskilled—has recognized that in the contemporary world migration may not be an entirely negative phenomenon.[434] In the case of highly trained scientific personnel from the newly industrialized countries, the migration of talent is a complex matter. For the most part, scientists migrated for several reasons: working conditions were better abroad; it was possible to pursue scientific research in Western universities more easily than at home; and opportunities and salaries were better overseas. As Korea and Taiwan have expanded and improved their universities and research laboratories and as their industrial sectors have grown and become able to absorb more research personnel, opportunities and working conditions have improved, although jobs in academe remain difficult to obtain. In the absence of satisfactory prospects at home, it might be appropriate for skilled personnel to remain abroad.

Members of the Third World scientific diaspora often contribute to scientific development at home even while living abroad. Most scientists have family ties at home and return for visits. They may work with local researchers and enterprises, serving as paid consultants or sometimes as informal guides. They constitute vital links between the local and the international scientific communities. Speaking the local language and knowing the local conditions, they are able to make scientific innovations relevant to local conditions better than anyone else. In a real sense, they are bridges between cultures and technologies. Multinational firms often utilize the services of foreign-trained local personnel in their work in the Third World precisely because of their sensitivity to local conditions.

There is a two-way migration of talent. A large number of Asian scientists who have worked abroad are returning home to take positions in both academe and industry. In some cases, these individuals planned to remain abroad for only a few years for professional experience but, in some cases, improved opportunities and conditions at home have lured them back. It is possible that political liberalization in both Taiwan and Korea has contributed to this.

Scientists and researchers from Third World nations who choose to work outside of their borders are often not a complete loss to their countries of origin.[435] Many do not spend their entire careers abroad but rather return home permanently after a certain amount of time; others return from time to time. These peripatetic professionals are an increasingly important part of the international flow of knowledge. They are responding to "push" and "pull" factors involved in the decision to migrate—and later to return. Professional opportunities, family ties, the lure of high incomes, availability of scientific equipment and laboratories, political tensions, and immigration rules are factors in the decision making process. Some Third World countries have tried to keep their highly skilled personnel at home, while others have permitted easy migration. Industrialized nations also have differing policies concerning the immigration of highly trained personnel. In general, however, despite idealistic statements of leaders in the industrialized countries concerning the importance of Third World skills remaining at home, industrialized nations relax immigration restrictions when they need the skills offered by the immigrants. Some Third World countries seem to produce a large number of well-educated emigrants while others do not. Korea and Taiwan, as well as India, Pakistan, and the Philippines have traditionally had a large out-migration. Malaysia and Singapore have not. Countries like Indonesia and Thailand traditionally had relatively few highly skilled out-migrants, even when there were relatively few opportunities at home.

The migration of highly trained professionals is a matter of considerable complexity. A scientist from a Third World nation working abroad may in fact be participating in the scientific culture of his or her native country by maintaining contacts, working with local scientists, and reporting on the latest developments. Some send money home to help their families, and another group invests in the home economy, bringing needed capital and ideas about development. Many work in more than one country during their careers. Some contribute articles to local journals while working abroad. The scientific diaspora functions effectively as a means of communication and helps to ensure that countries like Taiwan and Korea have quick access to the latest developments in the metropole.

FOREIGN TRAINING

Asia is by far the largest exporter of foreign students to the industrialized nations, and the four countries discussed here contribute large numbers of foreign students.[436] Indeed, Taiwan, Korea, and Malaysia are all among the top 10 countries sending students to the United States—and the numbers are still increasing.[437] As noted, foreign-trained academics and scientists constitute a large proportion of the total numbers in these four countries—probably a majority. This is certainly the case in the upper ranks of the universities, among senior administrators and policymakers in higher education, and among the most productive researchers. Thus, those who are shaping both higher education and scientific development in the newly industrializing nations have been trained abroad.

Foreign training affects the academic and research systems of the newly industrialized nations in a number of ways. The reasons why these four nations—and most other Third World countries—have sent students and sometimes professionals abroad for higher education are straightforward. In almost all academic fields, the most advanced training facilities, the best libraries, and the most distinguished scholars are located in the major Western nations. Students go abroad to obtain this training because it is not available at home. In addition, foreign degrees have a certain prestige value. Foreign-degree holders generally acquire the needed expertise, and those who return home obtain places in industry or the academy.[438] Foreign training ties degree holders to an international scientific community, with both the positive and negative implications of those ties.

Foreign-trained scientists and academics sometimes have problems of readjustment to the norms and values of their societies and their home institutions. They may be impatient with the pace of change or with academic systems that have a great deal of respect for seniority. They may be reluctant to work on locally relevant research topics, since this research may not be at the cutting edge of international science and may not be publishable in internationally circulated journals. The training that they receive abroad may not be entirely relevant to domestic concerns and may be partly dysfunctional in some ways. As the four newly industrializing nations considered here move quickly to the international mainstream, readjustment problems become less serious. For most scientists, there seems to be a reasonable fit between an international scientific orientation and local issues and needs.[439]

Foreign training is a necessary element of the creation of a pool of scientific personnel in the Third World and will remain so for the foreseeable future. The cost of providing the laboratories and other facilities needed for advanced scientific training and research is beyond the resources of Third World nations. Further, given the small size of the academic communities in most of these countries, it would probably be unwise to make the investment even if resources were available. Indeed, the cost of building up a scientific infrastructure continues to increase, thus making it ever more difficult for Third World countries to catch up. For all of these reasons, foreign training, with its pluses and minuses, will remain an integral part of advanced training for these newly industrializing countries, as well as other Third World nations.

THE TRADITIONAL UNIVERSITIES

Universities in developing countries have been widely criticized for their lack of relevance, their high cost, and their elitism. Much of this criticism has come from those who do not comprehend the nature of the contemporary university. Further, despite any shortcomings, the universities are the core institutions for training scientific personnel and, in most countries, for conducting research. It is, therefore, essential to understand how academic institutions work. The university is a Western institution wherever it exists. With the exception of the Al-Azhar in Egypt, there is no functioning Third World academic model.[440] Universities that have grown in the sometimes not entirely hospitable soil of the Third World are transplanted institutions. They are meritocratic institutions in societies that sometimes have not completely accepted meritocracy. In many countries, they stem from a colonial past that has been rejected. They are seen as elitist institutions in Third World societies that have in many cases adopted the rhetoric of egalitarianism. Perhaps most important, they are highly developed, very complex institutions that are fragile. Universities change slowly, and forcing the pace of reform may damage the ethos that seems to be necessary for quality research and training.[441] There must be an informal agreement between the university and the state with regard to the goals of development and the appropriate role of higher education institutions in that process. In our four countries, some arrangements appear to have been made to ensure the independence of academic institutions while at the same time promoting the goals of development.[442] Debates concerning the traditional autonomy that universities need, on the one hand, and accountability to funding agencies for overall goals, and how the very substantial funds that government provides to universities are spent, continue. Academic institutions must be aware of the central and often quite sensitive role they play in their societies. On the other hand, governments have responsibility to recognize that in order for universities to function effectively, they need a sufficient degree of autonomy and freedom.

Universities, particularly in the Third World, are pulled in many different directions, creating tensions and demands that may be hard to meet. It must be kept in mind that very few of the world's universities are primarily research institutions. This distinction is held by only a small number of the most distinguished academic institutions and even these have major responsibilities for teaching as well as research. Third World universities were established primarily as teaching institutions by colonial authorities interested in training a loyal civil service and staffing an educational system.[443] Research was a secondary matter and was not encouraged. Further, Third World universities were not focused mainly on technology but rather on such professional fields as law and the traditional arts and sciences subjects. In terms of the patterns of enrollments, administrative structures, and facilities, most Third World universities resemble the middle-ranking public comprehensive universities in the United States or the newer "plateglass" universities in Britain, rather than elite institutions like Oxford or Harvard. Creating research-oriented institutions in the newly industrialized nations is, for these reasons among others, a difficult and time-consuming process.

Governments seek to have academic institutions conform to their wishes. Frequently, the universities are unable and sometimes unwilling to adjust to policy mandates. The governance processes of an academic institution are cumbersome, and the best universities are characterized by a great deal of autonomy for academic staff. Thus, rapid changes in policy and orientation are difficult. Universities are frequently hotbeds of political and social debate and dissent. They function best with academic freedom, and this often means toleration for a variety of opinions and sometimes dissent on campus. Many Third World countries, including at times the four newly industrializing nations under consideration here, are reluctant to permit a wide latitude of academic freedom on campus and tensions ensue. It is also likely, although there are no convincing data, that academic excellence and efficiency is diminished as academic freedom is violated. At a more mundane level, governments demand accountability for expenditures and seek to ensure that academic institutions provide the training and research programs that governments feel are needed. Sometimes, it is possible to meet to these demands—in other cases it is not. Third World universities are fairly new and do not have the entrenched power of tradition to fall back on in their relations with government. They are often less sure of their own goals and mission. Thus, they are in a less favorable position than universities in the West to resist pressures—and at the same time the pressures are often immense.[444]

In Singapore and Malaysia, the British established a university in 1949 that provided medical education and degrees in the social sciences and humanities—and very little else. This university was located in Singapore (a branch was later set up in Kuala

Lumpur) and served British possessions in Malaya. Not until well after independence and into the 1970s, did higher education expand dramatically in the two countries. The emphasis in both Malaysia and Singapore has been on science, technology, and fields like management training. Singapore has especially stressed science and technology. From the beginning, local universities were unable to serve the growing middle class demands for higher education and also the needs of rapidly expanding economies—although in Malaysia has seen more economic fluctuation and that has had some impact on the demand for first-degree graduates.

At the present time, Singapore has two universities and several polytechnic institutions. Tertiary education has an enrollment of over 60,000, with slightly less than half in the two universities. This academic system serves a city-state with a population of 2.6 million. The postsecondary sector is well funded and the government has made it clear that it expects the university to meet international standards. In part for this reason, it has recruited a large number of expatriate staff. Facilities, including the library and science laboratories, in the two universities are excellent. Fields emphasized by government planners, such as computer science and biotechnology, enjoy outstanding facilities and ample resources. In terms of its physical plant, both universities are world-class institutions. Research output and the productivity of its academic staff are also of a high standard, although it is unlikely that they can compete with the world's top-ranking institutions in these areas. Teaching loads for most academic staff are relatively high. Singaporean staff are relatively young and are drawn from a very small pool of talent. Despite high salaries and favorable living and working conditions, the university does not attract the most prominent expatriate professors. Singapore is somewhat out of the international academic mainstream, which is a disadvantage in attracting foreign staff. Further, few expatriates are given tenured appointments, and there is a sense of insecurity among them. In recent years, there have also been cases of nonrenewal of contracts of expatriate staff who have displeased government officials by their writings. On the other hand, Singapore's universities, because they use English as the sole language of research and teaching, have closer international ties than do most universities in the region. Higher education has placed its greatest stress in recent years on science and technology and the science and engineering faculties, along with management, have grown rapidly. Academe has also tried to build ties with local industry through the Singapore Science Council. The basic structure and focus of the universities, however, are quite traditional, and the pressure to increase enrollment, with the necessary added demands on teaching, has limited the amount of time and energy available for university-industry collaboration.

Malaysia's higher education system, more extensive than Singapore's, has more than 100,000 students, with another large number studying abroad. The science and engineering sectors have grown in the past few years and now produce at least one-quarter of the total graduates. In recent years the universities have confronted the need to increase enrollments in response to popular demand and government policy—overall growth in enrollments over a period of more than a decade has been 14 percent annually—expand the number of institutions, comply with laws to increase the number of indigenous (*bumiputera*) students in higher education, and change the medium of instruction from English to Bahasa Malaysia. These reforms have placed great strains on the universities and have probably been responsible for the relatively low rate of research productivity when compared to higher education institutions in the other three newly industrialized countries considered here. Nonetheless, Malaysian academics are involved in research, and promotion depends on research productivity and publication. The organization of the Malaysian universities was traditionally British, although in recent years there have been some moves to organize higher education in a more American direction. Malaysian universities remain predominantly teaching institutions, with relatively high teaching loads and continuing pressure to expand enrollment. While all of the five universities offer a full range of degree programs, the new institutions have specific concentrations—in science and technology, agriculture, and, in the case of the newest university, the Universiti Utara Malaysia, management studies. Malaysian authorities have been concerned about an overproduction of arts and social science first-degree graduates, and have attempted, not entirely successfully, to reduce enrollment in these fields. The shift in the medium of instruction placed great strain on the educational system, particularly on the universities. Instructors, many of whom were not very fluent in Bahasa Malaysia, had to prepare themselves to teach in the language, which had an inadequate vocabulary for academic purposes. Textbooks were unavailable and had to be prepared. Despite these difficulties, the Malaysian higher education system in general functions effectively and is moving in a more research-oriented direction. A number of academic journals in Bahasa Malaysia have been established.

Korean higher education stems from two rather different roots. American missionaries established academic institutions, including a medical school, in the late nineteenth century and higher education had a definite American orientation until the period of Japanese domination, between 1910 and 1945. The Japanese established their own university and at the same time hindered the operation of existing academic institutions. The Japanese Keijo Imperial University was closely modeled exactly on universities in Japan and, unlike the existing institutions that used Korean as the language of instruction, Japanese was the sole medium. Enrollment of Koreans was limited (the majority of students were Japanese). After World War II, American influence reasserted itself and after a period of reconstruction following the Korean War, higher education expanded rapidly, generally using the American model for the organization of higher education institutions. By 1986, there were 456 postsecondary institutions—including 111 universities—enrolling 1,250,000 students, with 34,000 faculty members. However, 70 percent of the institutions are private, and the large majority of these have little interest in research or publication. There are, in addition, 69,000 students working on advanced degrees in a number of graduate schools. Again, the majority (78 percent) of these students are in private institutions, which vary considerably in quality. Korean higher education has long had a science and engineering orientation, and currently more than 40 percent of the enrollments at the undergraduate level are in these areas. At the higher levels of the academic system, research and publication are emphasized, but most of the academic system—particularly in the low-status private universities and colleges—is very much oriented toward teaching. In this respect, the hierarchy of the Korean academic system is somewhat similar to that of the United States.

Korea has the largest academic system of the countries considered here—enrolling more than 31 percent of the relevant age cohort, compared to 54 percent for the United States, around 30 percent for Japan and Germany, 20 percent for Singapore, and 30 percent for Taiwan. It has moved from an "elite" system to a "mass" orientation to higher education. The establishment in 1971 of the Korean Advanced Institute of Science and Technology (KAIST) as a high-level training and research institution added a new dimension to Korean higher education. KAIST has more than 2,000 graduate students and an academic staff of over 150 and provides the best-quality training and research in the country. Korean higher education has always (except for the Japanese period) been conducted in Korean and there is an active scientific infrastructure, including journals and scholarly books, in Korean. Among the countries considered here, Korea has the most successful indigenous language publication system, although graduate students—and in some fields even undergraduates—must rely on texts and other materials in English. Korean professors, particularly in the sciences, publish some of their work in English for international journals, but a significant amount also appears in Korean. The Korean university system is similar to the American academic system in its diversity, organizational pattern, and variations in quality and orientation.

Taiwan shares with Korea a period of Japanese colonial domination, which ended in 1945. The Japanese established the first university in Taiwan. While it functioned in Japanese and a majority of its students were Japanese, it provided Taiwanese with their first opportunity for higher education and was for that reason welcomed. After World War II, the Nationalist (Kuomintang) government retreated from mainland China to Taiwan and brought with it higher education institutions and policies. A final and very important influence on Taiwan higher education came from the United States, where many students in Taiwan went to study and which provided much advice and assistance. Taiwan has more than 250,000 university students and well over 15,000 faculty members. The growth in both student enrollments and the number of institutions has been dramatic. The number of universities, for example, has grown from four in 1950 to 28 four decades later. Forty-five percent of students major in science or engineering fields. As in Korea, the majority of students attend private universities, where standards vary and there is little focus on research orientation. The public sector is the prestigious element of the higher education system. In the public universities, academic staff are expected to do research and to publish. In the sciences and engineering, most of this publication is in English so that an international audience can be reached. In these disciplines, journals published from Taiwan tend to be in English rather than in Chinese (the situation is different in the arts and social sciences, where local scholarly journals are generally in Chinese). Advanced-level students must read textbooks in English, although all teaching is done in Chinese throughout the academic system. Academics, mainly in the public institutions, find it fairly easy to obtain research funding from the National Science Council, although the grants tend to be small. The public universities are well equipped for research although they are not in general comparable to the best universities in the industrialized countries. Facilities are excellent in fields that have been stressed as national priorities, such as biotechnology and some fields of engineering and computer science. Taiwanese scholars tend to look to the United States for academic models and research norms.

Historical circumstances, cultural traditions, and language differences aside, these countries share some common elements. In all four, universities have been favored institutions. They have been provided, for the most part, with the needed resources. The professoriate is well paid, and university professor is a prestigious occupation. Foreign influences have helped shape higher education—and this remains true today. The colonial heritage is important—with the impact of British and Japanese antecedents still distinguishable in higher education. The more recent American influence is large in all four countries but is more pronounced in Taiwan and Korea. All four countries have expanded postsecondary education dramatically in the past decades and have increased resources to pay for this expansion. Nonetheless, the expansion has strained resources—particularly in terms of high teaching loads and insufficient numbers of well-trained faculty, especially at the senior levels. Universities have to be pressured to contribute to research and to concentrate on areas considered relevant to expanding and increasingly technologically based economies. Universities in all four countries have a higher proportion of their graduates in science and engineering fields than is the case in the United States or Britain. Government and university authorities have at times been at odds concerning the direction and speed of change and issues of autonomy and accountability. Through it all, universities have survived and government officials in general recognize that universities are not the same as other public agencies. Overall, these new academic systems have made very impressive progress and have succeeded in creating the basis for an academic ethic that values research. Teaching is of a high standard and the challenges have generally been handled creatively. In Korea and Taiwan, academic institutions vary in type, with the premier public universities most closely resembling metropolitan institutions. Malaysia and Singapore have more uniform standards in their academic institutions, perhaps reflecting their British backgrounds.

THE RESEARCH INFRASTRUCTURE

Progress has been made in developing research facilities in these four countries and substantial resources have been devoted by governments to building up research capacities. It is useful to point to several specific research trends in our four countries before generalizing about the development of scientific research in newly industrializing countries. Without question, the bulk of research done in each of the four countries takes place in the universities, although all four have also funded nonuniversity research as well. Much of the university-based research is not specifically funded by government or other sources but is rather undertaken as part of the regular responsibilities of academics.

In Singapore, the Science Council coordinates research, by working closely with government departments and with academic scientists. The government identified several areas for support and special funding—fields that are intended to contribute to Singapore's economic future. These include biotechnology, electrical engineering, and computer science. In addition, since Singapore sees itself as a major financial center, it has expanded management studies in the two universities to provide the needed personnel and expertise. Research initiatives have taken place either within the structure of the two universities or in institutions with strong university connections. For example, the Institute of Systems Science, located on the NUS campus, focuses on computer applications and related matters. Singapore has channeled considerable funding to research and development in the areas that have been identified as key priorities. Resources have gone to the university and in some instances to other agencies. The Singapore government has worked hard to ensure that the many high-tech multinational corporations that have manufacturing facilities in the country also set up research facilities there. These efforts have met with only limited success. Singapore has a tradition of centralized direction of effort in many spheres of the economy and society, and this has extended to coordination of research priorities and facilities. In 1984, the government established a science park to attract high-tech companies and to encourage research and development (R and D). Thirty-four organizations have settled in the park, more than 29 of which are from the private sector, while several are multinational corporations. The technologies represented in the park are mainly biotechnology and biomedical sciences, and computer software and hardware. These fields have seen tremendous growth in recent years. With more than 1,300 academic staff and advanced scientific facilities, the National Taiwan University is the largest scientific agency in the country. University-industry collaboration has been a priority for the university. It has engaged in a number of special manpower training programs with industry, as well as many research projects relating to local industrial needs. University academic staff frequently act as consultants, with the encouragement of university authorities.

Science and technology have traditionally been less of a priority for Malaysia than for Singapore, although Malaysia has recently placed stress on scientific development. Further, Malaysia has long had specialized research institutions related to the country's major agricultural products—especially rubber and palm oil. Well-funded, government-sponsored laboratories working on these products have operated for several decades. In the 1980s, Malaysia promulgated a science plan that stresses fostering high-tech industries as well as taking advantage of the country's rich natural resources as a base for further industrialization. While it has been recognized that university staff compose the largest number of scientific personnel in the country, there has been less emphasis placed on utilizing the university for applied scientific research. The universities have been busy expanding, changing the language of instruction, and in general working out the problems of rapid development. The situation is now changing, however, and attention is being directed toward higher education institutions as centers for research and development. The growth of the Science University in Penang has been important in this regard, as has been the establishment of an Institute for Advanced Study at the University of Malaya, the nation's premier academic institution. As Malaysia has now built up a technological base—the country is a major producer of relatively low-tech computer chips and related products and has developed a significant manufacturing sector—R and D will become more important.

Korea and Taiwan have developed impressive export-based industrial sectors since the 1970s. The base of their industrial strength has not been in high technology but rather in the efficient use of established processes combined with a skilled and relatively low-paid labor force. Now, as their economies mature, attention is being paid to the development of a scientific infrastructure that will permit these countries to compete technologically. There is a recognition that as wage rates rise, as competition from other Third World nations such as Bangladesh and Sri Lanka increases, and pressures from the global economy intensify, the economy must diversify to retain its competitive edge. Both countries have promulgated detailed science plans and have provided funding for their implementation. There are some important structural differences between Korea and Taiwan that have affected research and development. The existence in Korea of very large corporations—such as Daewoo, Hyundai, and Lucky-Gold Star—that have significant financial and technological resources, means that the private sector can make a significant contribution to research and development. Taiwan, in contrast, is characterized by a large number of relatively small firms that generally do not have the resources to invest in research and development. Therefore, the government has played a more important role.

Korea's interest in research and development dates back to the mid-1960s. The Ministry of Science and Technology, established in 1967, has established a number of research institutes in fields such as energy, metals, electronics, and telecommunications. The ministry has also helped to coordinate private-sector R and D and has worked to ensure that collaboration between industry and universities takes place. The Technology Development Promotion Law of 1972 has provided significant incentives for private-sector industry to invest in research and development. Unlike the other countries considered here, a high percentage (44 percent) of R and D personnel are located in private companies, while 38 percent are in universities and colleges. Further, only 15 percent of Korea's R and D personnel focus on basic science fields such as physics, biology, or chemistry. The large majority are in applied engineering. Private firms account for 65 percent of the R and D spending in Korea—a sharp contrast to the other three countries, where most R and D funding comes from public sources.

The top universities in the country, along with KAIST, also have an important role in the science infrastructure. They train most R and D personnel, and academic scientists conduct all of the basic science research. There have been efforts to link the universities with industrial research and development with some success. There has also been some criticism of academic scientists for their fairly low rate of publication in international journals. The Korean model of scientific development is rather different from the other countries considered here. Whether Korea will be successful in the long run relying mainly on the private sector for the development of its scientific research capability remains to be seen.

Taiwan has focused on the development of a strong research infrastructure. The National Science Council (NSC), established in 1959, is the main funding and coordinating body. A series of national science and technology conferences have been held to coordinate activities and ensure momentum. Two main agencies are involved in scientific research—the universities and the Academia Sinica (AS), a body similar to the Academy of Sciences in the former Soviet Union. The AS operates some 30 research institutes, most located on its campus in Taipei. Much of the work of the AS institutes is basic, but there is some collaboration with industry and research on applied topics. The universities also engage in research as well, both applied and basic. Research is limited mainly to the major public universities in Taipei and its vicinity and is unusual in the private institutions, which are mainly devoted to undergraduate teaching. The NSC provides research grants to scientists in all fields—including the social sciences and humanities—on a competitive basis and has sufficient funds so that assistance is not too difficult to obtain. However, the grants tend to be fairly small, and thus large-scale research efforts are unusual with NSC assistance. There is also relatively little collaboration between the institutes of the AS and the universities. Taiwan has also stressed the development of research capability and the establishment of a scientific infrastructure. The Science-Based Industrial Park, which is located close to several key public universities in the suburbs of Taipei, involves academic researchers with the expansion of private high-tech industry. The bulk of funding for R and D has come from government sources. Private industry has been slow to invest in research, in part because most companies are small and cannot afford such expenditure. The government has been willing to provide funding, particularly in high-tech areas such as biotechnology, computers, and several engineering fields where it feels there will be a significant payoff in terms of export-linked industrial development.

All four countries have placed emphasis on the development of scientific infrastructures. Their approaches are related, but there are some variations. Malaysia and Korea have come later to a recognition of the importance of scientific research for development. Korea has relied more on private-sector industry to fund and conduct research than the other countries. All of the countries, however, have placed considerable stress on the involvement of universities in the enterprise, and recognize that academic institutions are the key training grounds for scientific personnel. Since the 1970s, they have invested funds and energy to ensure that there is an adequate base for R and D. They have tried to coordinate activities and all have developed national science plans to help guide developments.

RESEARCH IN SMALL SCIENTIFIC COMMUNITIES

Some of the problems of research in these four countries are common to research systems in any small country, regardless of level of economic development. The scientific and academic communities in these countries are small, and the institutional and resource base for research is similarly limited. These scientific communities will inevitably be dependent on larger scientific communities in other countries, particularly in the metropolitan centers. In Korea, the largest of the countries considered here, there are fewer than 36,000 academics in all of the country's universities and research institutes with 10,300 in the public institutions, where most of the research is done. In Taiwan, the total number of academics is 8,300, with 5,200 in the research-oriented public institutions. Malaysia has fewer than 6,000 academics and Singapore boasts a bit more than 1,500. When divided into the various academic disciplines, the communities of academics are quite small.[445]

Fully self-sufficient research communities are not possible in such small academic environments. This is particularly the case when there is only a limited amount of scientific literature available in the language used in the country. In Bahasa Malaysia, for example, there is virtually no basic scientific literature—the current generation of Malaysian academics (along with the very limited research community in Indonesia) is basically creating a new literature in the national language. The Korean academic community, despite its fairly successful efforts to develop a viable scientific communications network in the Korean language, relies for the most part on foreign publications for new knowledge. In the long run, it is possible that a fully autonomous research network in Chinese may emerge as the People's Republic of China develops its research institutions. However, this is a long way off, and it is significant that Taiwan has chosen to use English as the main means of scientific communication rather than to pioneer a network in Chinese.

It is necessary for small research communities to forge relationships with other research groups to form a viable network for communications and expertise. In general, the relationships are between the various peripheries and a metropolitan center. All four countries considered here look to the industrialized world for scientific sustenance, and largely to the United States. While there is some collaboration between Singapore and Malaysia, reflecting traditional ties, and Taiwan now looks to Japan for some research guidance, regional collaboration is virtually nonexistent. This is typical of Third World scientific communities. Where regional cooperation has been tried, as in the University of East Africa experiment in the 1960s, it has in general been unsuccessful. However, there are also some uniting elements. The use of English as a major scientific language in all four countries is a major advantage. The various programs of the Association of Southeast Asian Nations (ASEAN) might be expanded, at least in concept, to include other Asian countries. The four countries have some common problems, including the need to share scientific information. It might well be that regional cooperation could build a stronger consciousness of scientific independence in a world dominated by the metropolitan centers. It might be possible to establish scientific journals throughout Asia that could have an international standard of excellence, thus building confidence and providing an outlet for research and communication.

The challenges facing small scientific communities are, however, daunting and are by no means limited to Third World or newly industrializing nations. Scientific communities in countries like Canada, Sweden, and Belgium tend to rely on their larger neighbors for basic scientific direction and for innovations in most scientific fields. They increasingly use one of the metropolitan languages (English or French) for scientific communication and publication. The experiences of these countries indicate that it is possible to have a strong and active scientific community in a small country but that autonomy is problematic and the scientific agenda tends to be set from the outside, even where local scientific traditions are centuries old.

THE ROLE OF SCIENTIFIC RESEARCH IN NEWLY INDUSTRIALIZED NATIONS

How is science used in these four countries? Does it play a role in development and in the expanding economies? Three of these nations—Taiwan, Korea, and Singapore—take scientific research very seriously and see it as an important contributor to future development. However, there is relatively little evidence to date that indicates that indigenous scientific research has contributed to the impressive progress made. It would seem that development has been based on established industrial processes, imported technologies, or, as in the case of Malaysia, the export of natural resources.

Because of continuing economic growth and the sophistication of these countries, expansion in higher education has been rapid. The example of Japan may be relevant. Japan moved from a relatively low-wage, low-tech economy in the 1960s and developed a major R and D infrastructure—in industry as well as in the universities—to assist the nation's economic development. Japanese R and D now ranks among the world's best and many Japanese innovations, both basic and applied, have resulted in new patents and products. Japan is now a major scientific power in its own right. These four countries are, in different ways and to different degrees, emulating the Japanese example.

These four countries have a long way to go to catch up to Japan—and as noted earlier, their small size is a serious disadvantage. However, all of them are taking R and D more seriously. All except Malaysia have paid careful attention to planning for science and identified key targets for scientific R and D. These countries are now experiencing rising wages, and their products will inevitably become more expensive on world markets. They also see nations with even lower wages—like Thailand, Indonesia, and Bangladesh—becoming industrialized. Singapore made a conscious decision to increase the wages and also the overall skill levels of its workers so that the labor force could play a key role in an international service economy and in highly skilled manufacturing. Research in fields like computer engineering and biotechnology has been emphasized as part of this thrust. So far, research initiatives have come from government rather than from industrial firms. The Singapore government, however, has encouraged multinational firms to locate research facilities in Singapore and has offered incentives for this purpose. It is not clear what the results will be.

Korea and Taiwan face some difficult decisions if they wish to strengthen high-tech industries and have indigenous research contribute to this development. While there has been a recognition that research is an important element in future economic development, there has been little movement by the traditional industries to build R and D capability themselves or to contribute to other efforts for research development. Korea is a partial exception, but even in Korea the contributions of industry have been modest. These four countries stand at a crossroads in terms of the use of research for development and economic growth. Even at this early stage, there are some interesting differences among the four countries, indicating that there is more than one approach.

THE ROLE OF THE UNIVERSITY

Universities inevitably play a key role in scientific research in any country, and it is likely that they will play an even more crucial role in these four nations. They are, first and foremost, existing institutions with libraries, laboratories, and highly skilled personnel.[446] They have a research tradition and orientation. In these four countries, the universities have not only stressed research and publication as a means of recognition and promotion through the academic ranks, but have also emphasized key areas of science and technology. Particularly in the elite sectors, the universities in these four countries are more oriented toward science and technology than universities in Western countries. Contrary to the colonial models from which they emerged, these academic institutions have become very much oriented toward technological development, due largely to patterns of resource allocation in the past two decades.[447]

Universities are the key source of training for technologically skilled manpower. As industry becomes more sophisticated, it needs a larger supply of well-educated personnel. The universities provide this personnel. New specializations in such fields as management, computer technology, economics, and others have contributed the skills needed for development. The universities are therefore providing the rank-and-file personnel for sophisticated economic development. They are also educating small numbers of research workers with a higher level of skills that can serve the universities as teachers and researchers (frequently after advanced education overseas) or go into government or industry in positions of considerable authority.

Because universities have the basic infrastructures for research, they can be a source of R and D assistance. Scholars in the biological sciences can work on biotechnology issues, for example. New facilities can be built and incentives offered to scholars to work on interdisciplinary subjects. In Singapore, new research facilities have been located on the campus of the National University. In Taiwan, the location of the Science-Based Industrial Park is near two of the nation's best technologically oriented universities and helps to foster close relations. It is generally easier to utilize university staff and facilities in the development of new research initiatives than to build entirely new facilities. It is often the case that the universities have the only qualified staff in many scientific fields and it would be difficult to obtain the necessary expertise without academic cooperation.

Academic institutions also have some disadvantages from the viewpoint of applied R and D. Academic scientists are often more interested in "basic science" and in the issues that have a broader theoretical relevance to the international scientific community than to the applied concerns that are directly relevant to industrial development. They may sometimes be reluctant to shift their research focus. The academic freedom to engage in research is a strength for the long-term development of the university and the best researchers, but it is a potential problem when seeking to harness academic talent for applied research. Universities tend to value research that has theoretical importance. Highly applied work is sometimes held in low esteem. Universities are also teaching institutions—the emphasis on teaching is greater in developing countries than in the industrialized nations—and the heavy teaching loads of academic staff may interfere with concentration on research. Academic structures may inhibit interdisciplinary initiatives or work with private-sector firms or even government agencies. The very independence of the university, which is one of its most strongly held values, makes it difficult to move quickly in applied directions.

Despite these drawbacks, universities are the most important sources of scientific research in these four countries, and they are likely to remain so. There are increasingly close links to government and industry in terms of research, and the incentives provided by government to ensure the cooperation of the universities have generally been successful. Universities offer unparalleled flexibility so that academic personnel may vary their responsibilities among teaching and research functions. Graduate students may be used as research workers at relatively low salaries. University staff have international contacts so that they can keep in touch with scientific developments in the larger international centers. Universities, in short, offer the resource base, flexibility, and orientation that serves research well.

However, if universities are to serve their full potential, governments must recognize both their strengths and weaknesses. This understanding between the universities and government must evolve so that academic institutions will have appropriate autonomy while at the same time universities will accept the responsibility to participate fully in the process of development. Universities in these four countries have done a very effective job of balancing the often quite severe pressures of external authorities for expansion—in some instances political conformity—and an orientation toward the sciences with a commitment to academic values.

ACKNOWLEDGMENT

I am indebted to William Cummings, Thomas Eisemon, and Sungho Lee for their comments on an earlier version. This chapter is based on "Higher Education and Scientific Development: the Promise of Newly Industrialized Countries," in *Scientific Development and Higher Education: The Case of Newly Industrializing Countries*, ed., Philip G. Altbach et al. (New York: Praeger, 1989), 3–30.

Notes

1 For a historical perspective, see Charles Haskins, *The Rise of Universities* (Ithaca, N.Y.: Cornell University Press, 1957).

2 Philip G. Altbach, *The Knowledge Context: Comparative Perspectives on the Distribution of Knowledge* (Albany: State University of New York Press, 1987).

3 For further discussion of this point, see A. B. Cobban, *The Medieval Universities: Their Development and Organization* (London: Methuen, 1975).

4 The history of British higher education expansion in India and Africa is described in Eric Ashby, *Universities: British, Indian, African* (Cambridge: Harvard University Press, 1966).

5 See Philip G. Altbach and Viswanathan Selvaratnam, eds., *From Dependence to Autonomy: The Development of Asian Universities* (Dordrecht, Netherlands: Kluwer, 1989).

6 Irene Gilbert, "The Indian Academic Profession: The Origins of a Tradition of Subordination," *Minerva* 10 (July 1972): 384–411.

7 For a broader consideration of these themes, see Lawrence Stone, ed., *The University in Society*, 2 vols. (Princeton, N.J.: Princeton University Press, 1974).

8 Joseph Ben-David, *Centers of Learning: Britain, France, Germany, the United States* (New York: McGraw-Hill, 1977), 16–17.

9 Friedrich Lilge, *The Abuse of Learning: The Failure of the German University* (New York: Macmillan, 1948).

10 Charles E. McClelland, *State, Society and University in Germany, 1700–1914* (Cambridge: Cambridge University Press, 1980). See also J. Ben-David and A. Zloczower, "Universities and Academic Systems in Modern Societies," *European Journal of Sociology* 3, no. 1 (1962): 45–84.

11 In the German-originated chair system, a single full professor was appointed in each discipline. All other academic staff served under the direction of the chair holder, who held a permanent appointment to the position. Many other countries, including Japan, Russia, and most of Eastern Europe, adopted this system. In time, it was criticized as too rigid and hierarchical.

12 Laurence Veysey, *The Emergence of the American University* (Chicago: University of Chicago Press, 1965). For a somewhat different analysis, see E. T. Silva and S. A. Slaughter, *Serving Power: The Making of the Academic Social Science Expert* (Westport, Conn.:

Greenwood, 1984).

[13] In Egypt, the Al-Azhar University still offers Islamic higher education in the traditional manner. There are virtually no other universities that fundamentally diverge from the Western model. For a discussion of the contemporary Islamic university, see H. H. Bilgrami and S. A. Ashraf, *The Concept of an Islamic University* (London: Hodder and Stoughton, 1985).

[14] Philip G. Altbach, "The American Academic Model in Comparative Perspective," in this volume, chapter 4.

[15] For a case study of British higher education policy in India, see David Lelyveld, *Aligarh's First Generation: Muslim Solidarity in British India* (Princeton, N.J.: Princeton University Press, 1978).

[16] Michio Nagai, *Higher Education in Japan: Its Take-off and Crash* (Tokyo: University of Tokyo Press, 1971).

[17] See Altbach and Selvaratnam, *From Dependence to Autonomy* for case studies of a variety of Asian universities.

[18] See Philip G. Altbach, David Kelly, and Y. Lulat, *Research on Foreign Students and International Study: Bibliography and Analysis* (New York: Praeger, 1985), for a full discussion of the issues relating to foreign study.

[19] Hyaeweol Choi, *An International Scientific Community: Asian Scholars in the United States* (Westport, Conn.: Praeger Publishers, 1995).

[20] A telling example in this respect is that the number of American students going abroad is only a small proportion of the number of foreigners coming to the United States—and the large majority of Americans who do study in other countries go to Canada and Western Europe and not to the Third World. See also Robert Arnove, "Foundations and the Transfer of Knowledge," in *Philanthropy and Cultural Imperialism*, ed. Robert Arnove (Boston: G. K. Hall, 1980), 305–330.

[21] For a discussion of higher education development in the NICs, see Philip G. Altbach, et al., *Scientific Development and Higher Education: The Case of Newly Industrializing Countries* (New York: Praeger, 1989).

[22] Martin Trow, "Problems in the Transition from Elite to Mass Higher Education" (paper prepared for a conference on mass higher education held by the Organization for Economic Cooperation and Development, Paris, 1975).

[23] For documentation concerning African higher education, see World Bank, *Education in Sub-Saharan Africa: Policies for Adjustment, Revitalization and Expansion* (Washington, D.C.: World Bank, 1988), particularly chap. 6.

[24] Altbach, et al., *Scientific Development and Higher Education.*

[25] Max A. Eckstein and Harold J. Noah, "Forms and Functions of Secondary School Leaving Examinations," *Comparative Education Review* 33 (August 1989): 295–316.

[26] It is also the case that academic institutions serve as important "sorting" institutions in modern society, sometimes diverting students from highly competitive fields. See, for example, Steven Brint and Jerome Karabel, *The Diverted Dream: Community Colleges and the Promise of Educational Opportunity in America, 1900–1985* (New York: Oxford University Press, 1989).

[27] Roger L. Geiger, *Private Sectors in Higher Education: Structure, Function and Change in Eight Countries* (Ann Arbor: University of Michigan Press, 1986). For a focus on Latin America, see Daniel C. Levy, *Higher Education and the State in Latin America: Private Challenges to Public Dominance* (Chicago: University of Chicago Press, 1986).

28 It is significant that private higher education institutions are being established in Vietnam and in China. At the same time, Malaysia has rejected proposals for the establishment of private universities.

29 D. Bruce Johnstone, *Sharing the Costs of Higher Education: Student Financial Assistance in the United Kingdom, the Federal Republic of Germany, France, Sweden and the United States* (Washington, D.C.: The College Board, 1986).

30 It is worth noting that agencies such as the World Bank have strongly argued against continued expansion of higher education, feeling that scarce educational expenditures could be much more effectively spent on primary and secondary education. See *Education in Sub-Saharan Africa: Policies for Adjustment, Revitalization and Expansion* (Washington, D.C.: World Bank 1988).

31 Trow, "Problems in the Transition from Elite to Mass Higher Education."

32 See Ladislav Cerych and Paul Sabatier, *Great Expectations and Mixed Performance: The Implementation of Higher Education Reforms in Europe* (Trentham, England: Trentham Books, 1986), part 2, for a consideration of access to higher education in Western Europe.

33 Jasbir Sarjit Singh, "Malaysia," in *International Higher Education: An Encyclopedia*, ed. Philip G. Altbach (New York: Garland, 1991), 511–524.

34 There are also some significant national variations. For example, Britain under Margaret Thatcher's leadership consistently reduced expenditures for postsecondary education, with significant negative consequences for higher education. Tony Blair's Labour government of the 1990s seems unlikely to provide major new resources for the universities. See, for example, Sir Claus Moser, "The Robbins Report 25 Years After: And the Future of the Universities," *Oxford Journal of Education* 14, no. 1 (1988): 5–20.

35 For broader considerations of the reforms of the 1960s, see Cerych and Sabatier, *Great Expectations*; Ulrich Teichler, *Changing Patterns of the Higher Education System* (London: J. Kingsley, 1989); and Philip G. Altbach, ed., *University Reform: Comparative Perspectives for the Seventies* (Cambridge, Mass.: Schenkman, 1974).

36 For an example of an influential student proposal for higher education reform, see Wolfgang Nitsch, et al., *Hochschule in der Demokratie* (Berlin: Luchterhand, 1965).

37 Jan Erik Lane and Mac Murray, "The Significance of Decentralization in Swedish Education," *European Journal of Education* 20, nos. 2–3, (1985): 163–172.

38 See Alexander Astin, et al., *The Power of Protest* (San Francisco: Jossey-Bass, 1975), for an overview of the results of the ferment of the 1960s on American higher education.

39 "The Legacy of Robbins," *European Journal of Education* 14, no. 1 (1988): 3–112.

40 For a critical viewpoint, see Hans Daalder and Edward Shils, eds., *Universities, Politicians and Bureaucrats: Europe and the United States* (Cambridge: Cambridge University Press, 1982).

41 See, for example, "Universities and Industry," *European Journal of Education* 20, no. 1 (1985): 5–66.

42 Of course, this is not a new concern for higher education. See Thorstein Veblen, *The Higher Learning in America: A Memorandum on the Conduct of Universities by Business Men* (New York: Viking Press, 1918).

43 See Klaus Hufner, "Accountability," in *International Higher Education: An Encyclopedia*, ed. Philip G. Altbach (New York: Garland, 1991), 47–58.

44 Philip G. Altbach, "Academic Freedom in Asia: Learning the Limitations," *Far Eastern Economic Review*, June 16, 1988, 24–25.

45 Edward Shils, *The Academic Ethic* (Chicago: University of Chicago Press, 1983).

46 A classic discussion of the development of the modern university is Joseph Ben-David and Awraham Zloczower, "Universities and Academic Systems in Modern Societies," *European Journal of Sociology* 3, no. 1 (1962): 45–84.

47 See, for example, Robert Nisbet, *The Degradation of the Academic Dogma: The University in America, 1945–1970* (New York: Basic Books, 1971). Allan Bloom, in his *The Closing of the American Mind* (New York: Simon & Schuster, 1987), echoes many of Nisbet's sentiments.

48 It is significant to note that in those countries that have located much of their research in nonuniversity institutions, such as the academies of sciences in Russia and some Central and Eastern European nations, there has been some rethinking of this organizational model, a sense that universities may be more effective locations for the major research enterprise. Since the collapse of the Soviet Union, there have been some moves to abolish the "academy" model entirely. See Alexander Vucinich, *Empire of Knowledge: The Academic Sciences of the USSR (1917–1970)*.

49 See Thomas W. Shaughnessy, et al., "Scholarly Communication: The Need for an Agenda for Action–A Symposium," *Journal of Academic Librarianship* 15, no. 2 (1989): 68–78. See *also Scholarly Communication: The Report of the National Commission* (Baltimore, Md.: Johns Hopkins University Press, 1979).

50 These issues are discussed in Altbach, *Knowledge Context*. See Irving Louis Horowitz, *Communicating Ideas: The Crisis of Publishing in a Post-Industrial Society* (New York: Oxford University Press, 1986), for a different perspective.

51 For an American perspective, see Howard Bowen and Jack Schuster, *American Professors: A National Resource Imperiled* (New York: Oxford University Press, 1986).

52 Levy, *Higher Education and the State in Latin America*. See also Geiger, *Private Sectors in Higher Education.*

53 Gail P. Kelly, "Women in Higher Education," in *International Higher Education: An Encyclopedia*, ed. Philip G. Altbach (New York: Garland Publishers, 1991): 297–327.

54 Possible exceptions to this situation are the universities in Britain, where a decade of financial cuts by the Thatcher government sapped the morale of the universities and made it difficult for even such distinguished institutions as Oxford and Cambridge to continue top-quality research. See Geoffrey Walford, "The Privatization of British Higher Education," *European Journal of Education* 23, nos. 1 and 2 (1988): 47–64.

55 World Bank, *Education in Sub-Saharan Africa*, 68–81.

56 For a survey of student movements, see Philip G. Altbach, ed., *Student Political Activism: An International Reference Handbook* (Westport, Conn.: Greenwood Press, 1989).

57 I am indebted to the late Gail P. Kelly for her comments on an earlier draft of this paper. Some of these themes are elaborated in Philip G. Altbach and Gail P. Kelly, eds., *Education and the Colonial Experience* (New Brunswick, N.J.: Transaction Publishers, 1984).

58 Johann Galtung, "A Structural Theory of Imperialism," *African Affairs* 1 (1972): 93–138; and Edward Shils, *Center and Periphery: Essays on Macrosociology* (Chicago: University of Chicago Press, 1975). For a perspective that relates directly to universities, see Joseph Ben-David, *Centers of Learning: Britain, France, United States* (New York: McGraw-Hill, 1977), 1–7. See also Edward Silva, "Cultural Autonomy and Ideas in Transit: Notes from the Canadian Case," *Comparative Education Review* 24 (1980): 63–72.

59 Philip G. Altbach, "Servitude of the Mind? Education, Dependence, and Neocolonialism," *Teachers College Record* 79, no. 2 (December 1977): 187–204. See also Robert Arnove, "Comparative Education and World Systems Analysis," *Comparative*

Education Review 24 (1980): 48–62.

60 Galtung, "Structural Theory of Imperialism."

61 V. I. Lenin, *Imperialism: The Highest Stage of Capitalism* (Moscow: Foreign Languages Publishing House, n.d.); and James Cockcroft, Andre Gunder Frank, and D. Johnson, eds., *Dependence and Underdevelopment: Latin America's Political Economy* (Garden City, N.Y.: Anchor Books, 1972).

62 Edward Shils, "Metropolis and Province in the Intellectual Community," in *The Intellectuals and the Powers and Other Essays*, ed. Edward Shils (Chicago: University of Chicago Press, 1972), 355–371.

63 Altbach, "Servitude of the Mind?" See also Tibor Mende, *From Aid to Recolonization: Lessons of a Failure* (New York: Pantheon, 1973).

64 David Riesman, "The Academic Procession," in *Constraint and Variety in American Education*, ed. David Riesman (Garden City, N.Y.: Anchor Books, 1958), 25–65.

65 In countries like Indonesia, Thailand, and Ghana, the fact that some of the most able academics serve government has been an impediment to the emergence of scholarly excellence, since the numbers of highly trained academics are limited.

66 One of the most influential modern critiques is Ivan Illich's *Deschooling Society* (New York: Harper & Row, 1970). See also Julius Nyerere, *Freedom and Socialism* (Dar es Salaam: Oxford University Press, 1968).

67 Joseph Ben-David and A. Zloczower, "Universities and Academic Systems in Modern Societies," *European Journal of Sociology* 3 (1962): 45–84.

68 See Robert F. Arnove, ed., *Philanthropy and Cultural Imperialism: The Foundations at Home and Abroad* (Boston: G. K. Hall, 1980).

69 Gail P. Kelly, "Colonial Schools in Vietnam: Policy and Practice," in Altbach and Kelly, *Education and Colonialism*, 96–121.

70 Douglas Foley, "Colonialism and Schooling in the Philippines from 1898 to 1970," in Altbach and Kelly, *Education and Colonialism*, 69–95. See also Renato Constantino, *Neocolonial Identity and Counter Consciousness: Essays on Cultural Decolonization* (White Plains, N.Y.: M. E. Sharpe, 1978).

71 Eric Ashby has written persuasively about the transfer of institutions. See especially Eric Ashby, *Universities: British, Indian, African* (Cambridge: Harvard University Press, 1966) and Eric Ashby, *African Universities and Western Tradition* (Cambridge: Harvard University Press, 1964).

72 The situation in Latin America, of course, is different (except in countries such as Peru with large non-Spanish speaking Indian populations) since Spanish (or Portuguese) is the mother tongue of the majority of the population.

73 For a discussion of the complexity of language issues, see "Languages," in *Towards a Cultural Policy*, ed. Satish Saberwal (Delhi: Vikas, 1975), 97–134.

74 See Thomas Owen Eisemon, "African Scientists: A Study of Scientists at the University of Ibadan and Nairobi," *Annals of the American Academy of Political and Social Science* 448 (1980): 139–150.

75 The question of knowledge networks and their control by the West been discussed elsewhere. See Keith Smith, "Who Controls Book Publishing in Anglophone Middle Africa," *Annals of the American Academy of Political and Social Science* 42 (1975): 140–150; and Philip G. Altbach, "Literary Colonialism: Books in the Third World," *Harvard Educational Review* 45 (1975): 226–236.

76 For a summary of literature on foreign study, see Seth Spaulding et al., *The World's*

Students in the United States (New York: Praeger, 1976).

[77] For an elaboration of some of these themes, see Philip G. Altbach, *Publishing in India: An Analysis* (Delhi and New York: Oxford University Press, 1975).

[78] Armand Mattelart, "The New Multinational Educators," (paper delivered to the 1976 IAMCR Conference, session on the structures and context of media production). See also Herbert Schiller, *Communication and Cultural Domination* (White Plains, N.Y.: International Arts and Sciences Press, 1976).

[79] Philip Coombs, *The Fourth Dimension of Foreign Policy: Education and Cultural Affairs* (New York: Harper & Row, 1964).

[80] Maurice Line and Stephen Roberts, "The Size, Growth, and Composition of Social Science Literature," *International Social Science Journal* 28 (1976): 133.

[81] Alvin Gouldner, "Cosmopolitans and Locals: Toward an Analysis of Latent Social Roles, I and II," *Administrative Science Quarterly* 2 (1957 and 1958): 281–303, 444–467.

[82] Edward H. Berman, "The Foundations' Role in American Foreign Policy: The Case of Africa, Post-1945," *Harvard Educational Review* 45 (May 1979): 145–180.

[83] See Suma Chitnis and Philip G. Altbach, eds., *Higher Education Reform in India: Experience and Perspectives* (New Delhi: Sage, 1993).

[84] For a general discussion of current developments in higher education, see Amrik Singh and Philip G. Altbach, eds. *The Higher Learning in India* (Delhi: Vikas, 1974).

[85] Philip G. Altbach, "Gigantic Peripheries: India and China in the World Knowledge System," in this volume, chapter 9.

[86] Hasan Ali Al-Ebraheem and Richard P. Stevens, "Organization, Management, and Academic Problems in the Arab University: The Kuwait University Experience," *Higher Education* 9 (1980): 203–218.

[87] Ben Russak, "Scholarly Publishing in Western Europe and Great Britain: A Survey and Analysis," *Annals of the American Academy of Political and Social Science* 42 (1975): 106–117.

[88] Philip G. Altbach and Lionel S. Lewis, "The Academic Profession in International Perspective," in *The International Academic Profession,* ed. Philip G. Altbach (Princeton, N.J.: Carnegie Foundation for the Advancement of Teaching, 1996), 3–50.

[89] See Laurence Veysey, *The Emergence of the American University* (Chicago: University of Chicago Press, 1965), for a discussion of how American higher education emerged from its "semicolonial" status.

[90] For an elaboration of these points, see Ben-David and Zloczower, "Universities and Academic Systems."

[91] Ikuo Amano, "Continuity and Change in the Structure of Japanese Higher Education," in *Changes in the Japanese University,* ed. William Cummings et al. (New York: Praeger, 1979), 10–39.

[92] See, for example, Teresa Hayter, *Aid as Imperialism* (Harmondsworth, England: Penguin, 1971); and Mende, *From Aid to Recolonization.*

[93] See Hyaeweol Choi, *An International Scientific Community: Asian Scholars in the United States* (New York: Praeger, 1995).

[94] Eric Ashby, *Universities: British, Indian, African* (Cambridge: Harvard University Press, 1966). See also Eric Ashby, *African Universities and Western Tradition* (Cambridge: Harvard University Press, 1964).

[95] Michio Nagai, *Higher Education in Japan: Its Take-Off and Crash* (Tokyo: University of Tokyo Press, 1971).

96 Ruth Hayhoe and Marianne Bastid, eds., *China's Education and the Industrialized World: Studies in Cultural Transfer* (Armonk, N.Y.: M. E. Sharpe, 1987).

97 "English: Out to Conquer the World," *U.S. News and World Report* (February 18, 1985): 49–57.

98 See Philip G. Altbach, ed., *The Relevance of American Higher Education to Southeast Asia* (Singapore: Regional Institute of Higher Education and Development, 1985).

99 For further discussion of this theme, see Philip G. Altbach, *The Knowledge Context: Comparative Perspectives on the Distribution of Knowledge* (Albany: State University of New York Press, 1987).

100 The Philippines is attempting to move gradually toward the use of Pilipino as a medium of instruction in higher education. Numerous obstacles have been encountered—among them a lack of textbooks and the reluctance of academic staff to teach in the language.

101 Julia Kwong, *Cultural Revolution in China's Schools, May 1966–April 1969* (Stanford, Calif.: Hoover Institution Press, 1988).

102 E. Garfield, "Mapping Science in the Third World," *Science and Public Policy* (June 1983): 112–126. See also E. Garfield, "Science in the Third World," *Science Age* (October/November 1983): 59–65.

103 Lawrence B. Krause, Koh Ai Tee, and Lee Tsao Yuan, *The Singapore Economy Reconsidered* (Singapore: Institute of Southeast Asian Studies, 1987). See also Chng Meng Kng, Linda Low, Tay Boon Nga, and Amina Tyabji, *Technology and Skills in Singapore* (Singapore: Institute of Southeast Asian Studies, 1986).

104 William Cummings, et al., eds., *Educational Policies in Crisis: Japanese and American Perspectives* (New York: Praeger, 1986).

105 Ashby, *Universities: British, Indian, African.*

106 Joseph Ben-David, *Centers of Learning: Britain, France, Germany, United States* (New York: McGraw-Hill, 1977), 93–126.

107 Laurence R. Veysey, *The Emergence of the American University* (Chicago: University of Chicago Press, 1965).

108 E. Patricia Tsurumi, *Japanese Colonial Education in Taiwan, 1895–1945* (Cambridge: Harvard University Press, 1977).

109 George Makdisi, *The Rise of Colleges: Institutions of Learning in Islam and the West* (Edinburgh, Scotland: Edinburgh University Press, 1981).

110 See Philip G. Altbach and Gail P. Kelly, eds., *Education and the Colonial Experience* (New Brunswick, N.J.: Transaction, 1984).

111 Ronald Dore, *Taking Japan Seriously: A Confucian Perspective on Leading Economic Issues* (Stanford, Calif.: Stanford University Press, 1988).

112 Philip G. Altbach, "Knowledge Networks in the Modern World," in *The Knowledge Context,* 169–186.

113 For example, see Ali Marzui, "The African University as a Multinational Corporation: Problems of Penetration and Dependency," *Harvard Educational Review* 45 (May 1975): 191–210; and Keith Smith, "Who Controls Book Publishing in Anglophone Middle Africa?" *Annals of the American Academy of Political and Social Science* 421 (September 1975): 140–150.

114 R. M. Thomas, *A Chronicle of Indonesian Higher Education* (Singapore: Chopmen, 1973).

115 Aparna Basu, *The Growth of Education and Political Development in India, 1898–1920* (Delhi: Oxford University Press, 1974).

[116] Ashby, *Universities: British, Indian, African.*

[117] Basu, *Growth of Education.*

[118] Irene Gilbert, "The Indian Academic Profession: The Origins of a Tradition of Subordination," *Minerva* 10 (July 1972): 384–411.

[119] Nagai, *Higher Education in Japan.*

[120] Philip West, *Yenching University and Sino-Western Relations, 1916–1952.* (Cambridge: Harvard University Press, 1976).

[121] Hayhoe and Bastid, eds., *China's Education.* See also Merle Goldman, *China's Intellectuals: Advise and Dissent* (Cambridge.: Harvard University Press, 1981).

[122] See Ruth Hayhoe, *China's Universities, 1895-1995: A Century of Cultural Conflict* (New York: Garland Publishing, 1996).

[123] T. H. Silcock, *Southeast Asian University: A Comparative Account of Some Development Problems* (Durham, N.C.: Duke University Press, 1964).

[124] David Wyatt, *The Politics of Reform in Thailand: Education in the Reign of King Chulalongkorn* (New Haven, Conn.: Yale University Press, 1964).

[125] For a broader perspective, see Philip G. Altbach, *Higher Education in the Third World: Themes and Variations* (New York: Advent, 1987).

[126] For a consideration of foreign student issues in Asia, see William Cummings and Wing Cheung So, "The Preference of Asian Overseas Students for the United States: An Examination of the Context," *Higher Education* 14 (August 1985): 403–424.

[127] See Philip G. Altbach, David Kelly, and Y. Lulat, *Research on Foreign Students and International Study* (New York: Praeger, 1985) for a consideration of issues related to foreign study.

[128] See Hans Weiler, "The Political Dilemmas of Foreign Study" in *Bridges to Knowledge,* ed. E. Barber et al. (Chicago: University of Chicago Press, 1984), 184–195.

[129] Philip G. Altbach and S. Gopinathan, "Textbooks and Third World Higher Education," in *Textbooks in the Third World,* ed. Philip G. Altbach and Gail P. Kelly (New York: Garland, 1988), 51–73.

[130] Roland Pucetti, "Authoritarian Government and Academic Subservience: The University of Singapore," *Minerva* 10 (April 1972): 223–241.

[131] Philip G. Altbach, "The American Academic Model in Comparative Perspective," in this volume, chapter 5.

[132] See, for example, John W. Hanson, *Education, Nsukka: A Study of Institution Building Among the Modern Ibo* (East Lansing: Michigan State University, 1968).

[133] Y. Raghaviah, ed., *Third World Education and Postwar American Influences* (Hyderabad, India: Osmania University, 1982).

[134] Wichit Srisa-an, *Innovations in Higher Education for Development in Thailand* (Singapore: Maruzen, 1982).

[135] Banphot Virasai, ed., *Higher Education in Southeast Asia in the Next Decade* (Singapore: Regional Institute for Higher Education and Development, 1977). See also Altbach, *Higher Education in the Third World.*

[136] David Lelyveld, *Aligarh's First Generation: Muslim Solidarity in British India* (Princeton, N.J.: Princeton University Press, 1978).

[137] Amrik Singh, *Redeeming Higher Education* (Delhi: Ajanta Books, 1985).

[138] V. Selvaratnam, "The Higher Education System in Malaysia: Metropolitan, Cross-National, Peripheral or National?" *Higher Education* 14 (October 1985): 477–496.

[139] Edward Shils, *The Academic Ethos* (Chicago: University of Chicago Press, 1983).

[140] In Singapore, however, expatriate academics feel that contract renewals may be jeopardized by publications considered critical.

[141] S. Gopinathan, "Intellectual Dependence and Indigenization Response: Singapore and Malaysia." (Ph.D. diss., State University of New York at Buffalo, 1984).

[142] For an overview of the contemporary situation, see Philip G. Altbach, Robert O. Berdahl, and Patricia J. Gumport, eds., *American Higher Education in the 21st Century: Social, Political and Economic Challenges* (Baltimore, Md.: Johns Hopkins University Press, 1998, in press).

[143] Martin Trow, "The Expansion and Transformation of American Higher Education," *International Review of Education* 18, no. 1, (1972): 61–82. See also Martin Trow, "Problems in the Transition from Elite to Mass Higher Education" (paper presented to a conference of the Organisation for Economic Cooperation and Development, 1973).

[144] See *A Classification of Institutions of Higher Education, 1994 Edition* (Princeton, N.J.: Carnegie Foundation for the Advancement of Teaching, 1994), for a description of the levels of the American academic system.

[145] Michael D. Cohen and James G. March, *Leadership and Ambiguity* (Boston: Harvard Business School Press, 1984), 2nd edition.

[146] Jack Embling, *A Fresh Look at Higher Education: European Implications of the Carnegie Commission Reports* (Amsterdam: Elsevier, 1974).

[147] See Philip G. Altbach and Gail P. Kelly, eds., *Education and the Colonial Experience* (New Brunswick, N.J.: Transaction, 1984).

[148] David Wyatt, *The Politics of Reform in Thailand: Education in the Reign of King Chulalongkor* (New Haven: Yale University Press, 1969) and Michio Nagai, *Higher Education in Japan: Its Take Off and Crash* (Tokyo: Tokyo University Press, 1971).

[149] Irene Gilbert, "The Indian Academic Profession: The Origins of a Tradition of Subordination," *Minerva* 10 (July 1972): 384–411.

[150] A classic statement on the development of the Western academic system is Joseph Ben-David and Awarham Zloczower, "Universities and Academic Systems in Modern Societies," *European Journal of Sociology* 3 (1962): 45-84.

[151] Philip G. Altbach, "The University as Center and Periphery," in this volume, chapter 2.

[152] Robert Arnove, "Comparative Education and World Systems Analysis," *Comparative Education Review* 24 (February 1980): 45–62.

[153] Laurence Veysey, *The Emergence of the American University* (Chicago: University of Chicago Press, 1965). See also Joseph Ben-David, *American Higher Education: Directions Old and New* (New York: McGraw-Hill, 1972) and Richard J. Storr, *The Beginnings of the Future: A Historical Approach to Graduate Education in the Arts and Sciences* (New York: McGraw-Hill, 1973).

[154] For an overview of the early development of universities, see Charles H. Haskins, *The Rise of Universities* (Ithaca, N.Y.: Cornell University Press, 1957).

[155] While indigenous academic traditions persist in a few institutions such as the Al-Azhar in Cairo, which remains an important center of Islamic learning, Third World universities are in all basic respects Western institutions transplanted to developing countries.

[156] Julie A. Reuben, *The Making of the Modern University: Intellectual Transformation and the Marginalization of Morality* (Chicago: University of Chicago Press, 1996).

[157] Christopher Jencks and David Riesman, *The Academic Revolution* (Chicago: University of Chicago Press, 1977): 1–28, 155–198.

[158] Hugh Hawkins, *Between Harvard and America: The Educational Leadership of*

Charles W. Eliot (New York: Oxford University Press, 1972).

159 For a wide-ranging discussion of the community college, see Arthur M. Cohen and Florence Brawer, *The American Community College* (San Francisco: Jossey-Bass, 1982).

160 See David Riesman, "The Academic Profession," in *Constraint and Variety in American Education* , David Riesman (Garden City, N.Y.: Doubleday, 1958): 25–65.

161 Clark Kerr, *The Uses of the University* (Cambridge: Harvard University Press, 1995).

162 Alexander W. Astin and Calvin B. T. Lee, *The Invisible College: A Profile of Small Private Colleges with Limited Resources* (New York: McGraw-Hill, 1972). For a survey of the impact of college on students, see Alexander M. Astin, *Four Critical Years* (San Francisco: Jossey-Bass, 1977).

163 For a classic statement of the role and function of the community college, see Burton Clark, *The Open Door College* (New York: McGraw-Hill, 1960).

164 Arthur W. Chickering, ed., *The Modern American College: Responding to the New Realities of Diverse Students and a Changing Society* (San Francisco: Jossey-Bass, 1981).

165 Eric Ashby, *Any Person, Any Study: An Essay on Higher Education in the United States* (New York: McGraw-Hill, 1971).

166 Neil J. Smelser and Gabriel Almond, eds., *Public Higher Education in California* (Berkeley: University of California Press, 1974).

167 Dean McHenry, ed., *Academic Departments* (San Francisco: Jossey-Bass, 1977).

168 Recently, however, American universities have been concerned about a concentration of staff at the full professor level and with some having most or all of their staff on permanent appointments because of the fact that in many fields few junior staff have been hired in recent years due to fiscal and enrollment problems.

169 Paul Dressel and Lewis Mayhew, *Higher Education as a Field of Study* (San Francisco: Jossey-Bass, 1974).

170 It should be noted that the American Council on Education, the Council of Graduate Schools and other organizations sponsor seminars and short training courses for senior administrators in order to provide these neophytes with introduction to their new positions.

171 Generally recognized as the main research journals serving the field of higher education are *The Review of Higher Education, The Journal of Higher Education, Research in Higher Education,* and *Higher Education.* The Association for the Study of Higher Education is the professional organization serving the higher education research community.

172 For an interesting study of how the scope of higher education in America expanded to meet national needs, see Carol S. Gruber, *Mars and Minerva: World War I and the Uses of the Higher Learning in America* (Baton Rouge: Louisiana State University Press, 1975).

173 Robert Nisbet, *The Degradation of the Academic Dogma: The University in America, 1945–70.* (New Brunswick, N.J., 1997). See also Edward Shils, *The American Ethic* (Chicago: University of Chicago Press, 1984).

174 Kerr, *Uses of the University.*

175 For an international perspective, see Joseph Ben-David, *Fundamental Research and the Universities: Some Comments on International Differences* (Paris: Organisation for Economic Cooperation and Development, 1968) and Burton R. Clark, *The Higher Education System* (Berkeley: University of California Press, 1983), 11–26.

176 It has been noted, for example, that the majority of American academics produce no publications beyond their doctoral thesis, perhaps an article or two based on it. See Lionel S. Lewis, *Scaling the Ivory Tower: Merit and Its Limits in Academic Careers* (Baltimore, Md.: Johns Hopkins University Press, 1975).

[177] See J. Eugene Haas, "The American Academic Profession," in *The International Academic Profession: Portraits of Fourteen Countries*, ed. Philip G. Altbach. (Princeton, N.J.: Carnegie Foundation for the Advancement of Teaching, 1996), 343–390.

[178] Alvin W. Gouldner, "Cosmopolitans and Locals: Toward An Analysis of Latent Social Roles," *Administrative Science Quarterly* 2 (December 1957): 281–303.

[179] Berdahl, "Autonomy and Accountability in Higher Education." See also Robert O. Berdahl and T. R. McConnell, "Autonomy and Accountability: Who Controls Academe?" in *American Higher Education in the 21st Century: Social, Political and Economic Challenges*.

[180] Patricia H. Crosson, *Public Service in Higher Education: Practices and Priorities* (Washington, D.C.: Association for the Study of Higher Education, 1983).

[181] See Sheila Slaughter and Larry L. Leslie, *Academic Capitalism: Policies, Policies, and the Entrepreneurial University* (Baltimore, Md.: Johns Hopkins University Press, 1997).

[182] For a discussion of curriculum reform, see Arthur Levine, *Handbook of Undergraduate Curriculum* (San Francisco: Jossey-Bass, 1978).

[183] Sandra Kanter, Zelda Gamson and Howard London, *General Education in a Time of Scarcity* (Boston: Allyn and Bacon, 1997).

[184] Kenneth P. Mortimer and Michael L. Tierney, *The Three R's of the Eighties: Reduction, Reallocation and Retrenchment* (Washington, D.C.: American Association for Higher Education, 1979). See also James R. Mingle, ed. *Challenges of Retrenchment* (San Francisco: Jossey-Bass, 1981).

[185] Ann F. Austin and Zelda F. Gamson, *Academic Workplace: New Demands, Heightened Tensions* (Washington, D.C.: Association for the Study of Higher Education, 1983). See also Winfred A. Melendez and Rafael de Guzman, *Burnout: The New Academic Disease* (Washington, D.C.: Association for the Study of Higher Education, 1983).

[186] Arthur Levine, *Why Innovation Fails: The Institutionalism and Termination of Innovation in Higher Education* (Albany: State University of New York Press, 1980).

[187] For a broad overview, see Frederick Rudolph, *Curriculum: A History of the American Undergraduate Course of Study since 1636* (San Francisco: Jossey-Bass, 1977).

[188] For a discussion of the indigenization of curriculum in Southeast Asia, see S. Gopinathan, "Intellectual Dependency and the Indigenization Response: Case Studies of Three Disciplines in Two Third World Universities" (unpublished Ph.D. diss., State University of New York at Buffalo, 1984).

[189] Joseph Ben-David and Awraham Zloczower, "Universities and Academic Systems in Modern Societies," *European Journal of Sociology* 3, no. 1 (1962), 45–84.

[190] Burton R. Clark, *The Academic Life: Small Worlds, Different Worlds* (Princeton, N.J.: Carnegie Foundation for the Advancement of Teaching, 1987).

[191] Edward Shils, *The Academic Ethic* (Chicago: University of Chicago Press, 1983). See also Edward Shils, *The Order of Learning and the Crisis of the University* (edited and with an introduction by Philip G. Altbach) (New Brunswick, N.J.: Transaction, 1997).

[192] Material in this article is cited mainly from two volumes related to the Carnegie Foundation international survey of the academic profession. These are Philip G. Altbach, ed., *The International Academic Profession: Portraits of Fourteen Countries* (Princeton, N.J.: Carnegie Foundation for the Advancement of Teaching, 1996), and Ernest L. Boyer, Philip G. Altbach, and Mary Jean Whitelaw, *The Academic Profession: An International Perspective* (Princeton, N.J.: Carnegie Foundation for the Advancement of Teaching, 1994). Additional material is cited from tables prepared by the Carnegie Foundation from the survey. The countries included are the United States, England, Germany, the Netherlands, Russia, and Sweden

in Europe; Hong Kong, Japan and Korea in Asia; Brazil, Chile, and Mexico in Latin America; Israel in the Middle East; and Australia. A common questionnaire of more than 200 items was developed, and a common methodology for the selection of institutions and individuals was used. For a discussion of the research design of this study, see Mary Jean Whitelaw, "The International Survey of the Academic Profession, 1991–1993: Methodological Notes," in *The International Academic Profession: Portraits of Fourteen Countries*. 669–678.

[193] Results taken from Tables 63 and 66 of Boyer, Altbach, and Whitelaw, *Academic Profession*.

[194] Alvin Gouldner, "Cosmopolitans and Locals: Toward an Analysis of Latent Social Roles," *Administrative Science Quarterly* 2 (December 1957), 281–303.

[195] Hyaeweol Choi, *An International Scientific Community: Asian Scholars in the United States* (Westport, Conn.: Praeger, 1995).

[196] Todd M. Davis, ed., *Open Doors, 1995/96: Report on International Educational Exchange* (New York: Institute of International Education, 1996).

[197] J. Eugene Haas, "The American Academic Profession," in *International Academic Profession*, 355–356.

[198] *A Classification of Institutions of Higher Education, 1994 Edition* (Princeton, N.J.: Carnegie Foundation for the Advancement of Teaching, 1994).

[199] Haas, "The American Academic Profession," 363.

[200] See, for example, Philip G. Altbach, "Gigantic Peripheries: India and China in the World Knowledge System," in this volume, chapter 9.

[201] See Harriet Zuckerman, *Scientific Elite: Nobel Laureates in the United States* (New Brunswick, N.J.: Transaction, 1996), for a discussion of how the elite scientific system works.

[202] Judith M. Gappa and David W. Leslie, *The Invisible Faculty: Improving the Status of Part-Timers in Higher Education* (San Francisco: Jossey-Bass, 1993).

[203] William K. Cummings, *The Changing Academic Marketplace and University Reform in Japan* (New York: Garland Publishing, 1990).

[204] Jürgen Enders, *Die wissenschaftlichen Mitarbeiter: Ausbildung, Beschäftigung, und Karriere der Nachwuchswissenschaftler und Mittelbau-angehörigen an den Universitäten* (Frankfurt am Main: Campus Verlag, 1996).

[205] Jürgen Enders and Ulrich Teichler, "The Academic Profession in Germany," in *International Academic Profession*, 437–490.

[206] Philip G. Altbach, "The Pros and Cons of Hiring 'Taxicab' Professors," *Chronicle of Higher Education*, (January 6, 1995), B3.

[207] See Richard P. Chait, "The Future of Academic Tenure," *Priorities* 3 (Spring, 1995), 1–12. *Priorities* is a publication of the Association of Governing Boards. See also Cathy A. Trower, *Tenure Snapshot* (Washington, D.C.: New Pathways: Faculty Careers and Employment for the 21st Century: A Project of the American Association for Higher Education, 1996), working paper.

[208] See Charles J. Sykes, *ProfScam: Professors and the Demise of Higher Education* (Washington, D.C.: Regnery, 1988) and Martin Anderson, *Impostors in the Temple* (New York: Simon and Schuster, 1992).

[209] Matthew W. Finken, ed., *The Case for Tenure* (Ithaca, N.Y.: Cornell University Press, 1996). See also Richard P. Chait, "The Future of Academic Tenure," in *Revitalizing Higher Education*, eds. William F. Massy and Joel W. Meyerson (Princeton, N.J.: Peterson's, 1995), 19–36.

[210] See Maurice Kogan, Ingrid Moses, and Elaine El-Khawas, *Staffing Higher Education: Meeting New Challenges* (London: Jessica Kingsley, 1994).

[211] Rob Cuthbert, ed., *Working in Higher Education* (Buckingham, England: Open University Press, 1996).

[212] Suma Chitnis and Philip G. Altbach, eds. *The Indian Academic Profession* (Delhi: Macmillan, 1979).

[213] Edward Shils, "Academic Freedom," in *International Higher Education: An Encyclopedia* ed. P. G. Altbach (New York: Garland, 1991), 1–22.

[214] Tables 54 and 57 of *Academic Profession: An International Perspective.*

[215] Table 37 of *Academic Profession: An International Perspective.*

[216] Ernest L. Boyer, *Scholarship Reconsidered: Priorities of the Professoriate* (Princeton, N.J.: Carnegie Foundation for the Advancement of Teaching, 1990).

[217] Table 17 of *Academic Profession: An International Perspective.*

[218] Tables 18, 21, and 23 of *Academic Profession: An International Perspective*

[219] Ernest L. Boyer, et al., *Scholarship Assessed* (San Francisco: Jossey-Bass, 1997).

[220] See Roger Ellis, ed., *Quality Assurance for University Teaching* (Buckingham, England: Open University Press, 1993) and Angela Brew, ed., *Directions in Staff Development* (Buckingham, England: Open University Press, 1995).

[221] The material in this section is based on the results of the Carnegie Study of the International Academic Profession. See *The Academic Profession: An International Perspective.* See also Haas, "The American Academic Profession," in *International Academic Profession: Portraits of Fourteen Countries.*

[222] Denise K. Magner, "Increases in Faculty Salaries Fail to Keep Pace with Inflation," *Chronicle of Higher Education* (July 3, 1997), A8.

[223] Haas, "American Academic Profession," in *International Academic Profession,* 347–348.

[224] For opposite sides of this debate, see John K. Wilson, *The Myth of Political Correctness: The Conservative Attack on Higher Education* (Durham, N.C.: Duke University Press, 1995), and George Roche, *The Fall of the Ivory Tower: Government, Corruption and the Bankrupting of American Higher Education* (Washington, D.C.: Regnery, 1994).

[225] Lionel S. Lewis and Philip G. Altbach, "Faculty Versus Administration: A Universal Problem," *Higher Education Policy* 9, no. 3 (1996), 255–258.

[226] William G. Tierney and Estela Mara Bensimon, *Promotion and Tenure: Community and Socialization in Academe* (Albany, N.Y.: State University of New York Press, 1996).

[227] Oliver Fulton, "The Academic Profession in England on the Eve of Structural Change," in *International Academic Profession,* 389–436.

[228] Clark Kerr, *The Uses of the University* (Cambridge: Harvard University Press, 1995).

[229] Philip G. Altbach, ed., *Student Political Activism: An International Reference Handbook* (Westport, Conn.: Greenwood, 1989).

[230] Todd Gitlin, *The Sixties: Years of Struggle, Days of Rage* (New York: Bantam, 1988). For a different perspective, see Roger Rosenblatt, *Coming Apart: A Memoir of the Harvard Wars of 1969.* (Boston: Little, Brown, 1997).

[231] Louis Menand, ed., *The Future of Academic Freedom* (Chicago: University of Chicago Press, 1996).

[232] Charles Haskins, *The Rise of Universities* (Ithaca, N.Y.: Cornell University Press, 1965), 27–58.

[233] Joseph Ben-David and A. Zloczower, "Universities and Academic Systems in Modern Societies," *European Journal of Sociology* 3 (1962): 47–61.

[234] Shigeru Nakayama, "Independence and Choice: Western Impacts on Japanese Higher

Education," in *From Dependence to Autonomy: The Development of Asian Universities*, ed. Philip G. Altbach and Viswanathan Selvaratnam (Dordrecht, Netherlands: Kluwer, 1989), 97–116.

235 Merle Curti and V. Carstensen, *The University of Wisconsin: A History, 1848–1925* (Madison: University of Wisconsin Press, 1949).

236 Laurence Veysey, *The Emergence of the American University* (Chicago: University of Chicago Press, 1965).

237 Edward Silva and Sheila Slaughter, *Serving Power: The Making of the Academic Social Science Expert* (Westport, Conn.: Greenwood, 1984).

238 Edward Shils, *The Intellectuals and the Powers and Other Essays* (Chicago: University of Chicago Press, 1972).

239 Everett Carll Ladd, Jr. and Seymour Martin Lipset, *The Divided Academy: Professors and Politics* (New York: McGraw-Hill, 1975).

240 Asoke Basu, *Culture, Politics and Critical Academics* (Meerut, India: Archana, 1981).

241 Louis Namier, *1848: The Revolution of the Intellectuals* (New York, 1964).

242 Suma Chitnis and Philip G. Altbach, eds., *The Indian Academic Profession* (New Delhi: Macmillan, 1979).

243 Wilhelm Hennis, "Germany: Legislators and the Universities," in *Universities, Politicians and Bureaucrats: Europe and the United States*, ed. Hans Daalder and Edward Shils (Cambridge: Cambridge University Press, 1982) 1–30.

244 Paul Berman, ed., *Debating P.C.: The Controversy over Political Correctness on College Campuses*. (New York: Dell, 1992).

245 Philip G. Altbach, "The Academic Profession," in *International Higher Education: An Encyclopedia*, ed. Philip G. Altbach (New York: Garland, 1991), 23–46.

246 Alvin Goulder, "Cosmopolitans and Locals–I," *Administrative Science Quarterly* 2 (1957): 281–306.

247 In India, professorial trade unions are widespread, and are often involved in political activism in the universities and in society, occasionally linking with student activist organizations.

248 Edith H. Altbach, "Vanguard of Revolt: Students and Politics in Central Europe, 1815–1848," in *Students in Revolt*, ed. S. M. Lipset and P. G. Altbach (Boston: Beacon, 1969), 451–474.

249 Michael S. Steinberg, *Sabers and Brown Shirts: The German Students' Path to National Socialism, 1918-1935* (Chicago: University of Chicago Press, 1977). See also Geoffrey Giles, *Students and National Socialism in Germany* (Princeton, N.J.: Princeton University Press, 1985).

250 See S. M. Lipset, "University Students and Politics in Underdeveloped Nations," *Comparative Education Review* 10 (June 1966): 132–62.

251 Stephen A. Douglas and Harsja Bachtiar, "Indonesian Students: The Generation of 1966," in *The Student Revolution*, ed. P. G. Altbach (Bombay: Lalvani, 1970), 156–160.

252 Chow Tse-tung, *The May Fourth Movement* (Cambridge: Harvard University Press, 1960). See also John Israel, *Student Nationalism in China, 1927–1937* (Stanford, Calif.: Stanford University Press, 1966).

253 For a historical overview of the Asian case, see Philip G. Altbach, "Student Movements in Historical Perspective: The Asian Case," *Youth and Society* 1 (March 1970): 333–357.

254 Richard J. Walter, *Student Politics in Argentina: The University Reform and Its Effects, 1918–1964* (New York: Basic Books, 1966).

[255] See Robert Cohen, *When the Old Left Was Young: Student Radicals and America's First Mass Student Movement, 1929–1941* (New York: Oxford University Press, 1993).

[256] Helen Lefkowitz Horowitz, *Campus Life: Undergraduate Cultures from the End of the Eighteenth Century to the Present* (Chicago: University of Chicago Press, 1988).

[257] Japan, which has had a strong tradition of student political activism, is a partial exception to this generalization. Japanese higher education at the undergraduate level is not very competitive, and there is little pressure to pass difficult examinations. This is in sharp contrast to the highly competitive situation in secondary education.

[258] In postindependence India, much student activism has been confined to campus-based issues, such as the improvement of student living conditions, and the impact of such "indiscipline," as it is called in India, seldom extends beyond the university. See S. H. Rudolph and L. I. Rudolph, *Education and Politics in India: Studies in Organization, Society and Politics* (Cambridge: Harvard University Press, 1972).

[259] Todd Gitlin, *The Whole World Is Watching: Mass Media in the Making and Unmaking of the New Left* (Berkeley: University of California Press, 1980).

[260] See Ronald Fraser, *1968: A Student Generation in Revolt* (New York: Pantheon, 1988).

[261] Donald K. Emmerson, ed., *Students and Politics in Developing Nations* (New York: Praeger, 1968).

[262] Fraser, *1968*, 203–230, 261–280.

[263] James A. Michener, *Kent State: What Happened and Why* (New York: Random House, 1971).

[264] Wolfgang Nitch, et al., *Hochschule in der Demokratie* (Berlin: Luchterhand, 1965).

[265] Alexander W. Astin, et al., *The Power of Protest* (San Francisco: Jossey-Bass, 1975).

[266] Philip G. Altbach, ed., *Turmoil and Transition: Higher Education and Student Politics in India* (New York: Basic Books, 1968).

[267] For the United States, see James L. Wood, *The Sources of American Student Activism* (Lexington, Mass.: Lexington Books, 1974), for an overview of research on the sociological and psychological origins of activists. For India, see Jacob Aikara, *Ideological Orientation of Student Activism* (Poona: Dastane Ramchandra, 1977). See also Ross Prizzia and Narong Sinsawasdi, *Thailand: Student Activism and Political Change* (Bangkok: D. K. Book House, 1974) and Arthur Liebman, Kenneth N. Walker, and Myron Glazer, *Latin American University Students: A Six Nation Study* (Cambridge: Harvard University Press, 1972).

[268] S. M. Lipset and P. G. Altbach, "Student Politics and Higher Education in the United States," *Comparative Education Review* 10 (June 1966): 320–349.

[269] See Kenneth Keniston, *Young Radicals: Notes on Committed Youth* (New York: Harcourt Brace & World, 1968) and Kenneth Keniston, *Youth and Dissent* (New York: Harcourt Brace Jovanovich, 1971) for an elaboration of this point of view.

[270] Robert Liebert, *Radical and Militant Youth: A Psychoanalytic Inquiry* (New York: Praeger, 1971).

[271] Stanley Rothman and S. Robert Lichter, *Roots of Radicalism: Jews, Christians and the New Left* (New York: Oxford University Press, 1982).

[272] Lewis Feuer, *The Conflict of Generation: The Character and Significance of Student Movements* (New York: Basic Books, 1969).

[273] See Edward Shils, "Dreams of Plenitude, Nightmares of Scarcity," in *Students in Revolt*, ed. S.M. Lipset and P.G. Altbach (Boston: Beacon Press, 1969), 1–33.

[274] Keniston, *Young Radicals*.

[275] Otto Klineberg, Marisa Zavalloni, Christaine Louis-Guerin, and Jeanne Ben-Brika,

Students, Values and Politics: A Cross-Cultural Comparison (New York: Free Press, 1979).

[276] Cohen, "Revolt of the Depression Generation." See also Philip G. Altbach, *Student Politics in America* (New Brunswick, N. J.: Transaction, 1997).

[277] James Miller, *Democracy Is in the Streets: From Port Huron to the Siege of Chicago* (New York: Simon & Schuster, 1987). See also Maurice Isserman, *If I Had a Hammer... the Death of the Old Left and the Birth of the New Left* (New York: Basic Books, 1987).

[278] Fraser, *1968.*

[279] B. Lintner, "Burma: The Wrath of the Children," *Far Eastern Economic Review* (July 21, 1988): 18–19.

[280] Alain Schnapp and Pierre Vidal-Naquet, *The French Student Uprising: An Analytical Documentary* (Boston: Beacon Press, 1971).

[281] Gitlin, *Whole World Is Watching.*

[282] See Philip G. Altbach and Kofi Lomotey, eds., *The Racial Crisis in American Higher Education* (Albany: State University of New York Press, 1991).

[283] Sara Evans, *Personal Politics* (New York: Knopf, 1979).

[284] Students contributed to significant political upheaval in the following countries, among others: Argentina, Uruguay, Peru, Bolivia, Thailand, South Korea, Iran, Bangladesh, Indonesia, Burma, Turkey, Nigeria, Liberia, Ghana, and Nicaragua. Students did not necessarily topple regimes in these countries, but their actions had significant political results.

[285] N. Jayaram, "Sadhus No Longer: Recent Trends in Indian Student Activism," *Higher Education* 8 (November 1979): 683–700.

[286] Joel Barkan, *An African Dilemma: University Students, Development, and Politics in Ghana, Tanzania and Uganda* (Nairobi: Oxford University Press, 1975).

[287] This chapter reflects almost three decades of observation of student political activism. See Philip G. Altbach, *Student Politics in Bombay* (Bombay: Asia Publishing House, 1968); Philip G. Altbach, ed., *Turmoil and Transition: Student Politics and Higher Education in India* (New York: Basic Books, 1968); Philip G. Altbach, *Student Politics in America* (New York: McGraw-Hill, 1974); Philip G. Altbach, ed., *Student Politics: Perspectives for the Eighties* (Metuchen, N.J.: Scarecrow, 1981); Seymour Martin Lipset and Philip G. Altbach, eds., *Students in Revolt* (Boston: Beacon, 1970); and Philip G. Altbach, ed., *Student Political Activism: An International Reference Handbook* (New York: Greenwood Press, 1989).

[288] For two opposing theoretical perspectives, see Lewis Feuer, *The Conflict of Generations* (New York: Basic Books, 1969) and Michael Miles, *The Radical Probe: The Logic of Student Rebellion* (New York: Athenaeum, 1971). Both of these volumes, by Western social scientists, relate mainly to the industrialized nations.

[289] W. J. Hanna and J. L. Hanna, "Students as Elites," in *University Students and African Politics*, ed. W. J. Hanna and J. L. Hanna (New York: Africana, 1975).

[290] K. Keniston, *Youth and Dissent* (New York: Harcourt Brace Jovanovich, 1971); O. Klineberg, *Students, Values and Politics: A Cross-Cultural Comparison* (New York: Free Press, 1979).

[291] R. O. Berdahl and T. R. McConnell, "Autonomy and Accountability: Who Controls Academe?," in *American Higher Education in the 21st Century: Social. Political and Economic Challenges*, eds. Philip G. Altbach, Robert Berdahl, and Patricia Gumport (Baltimore, Md.: Johns Hopkins University Press, 1998, in press).

[292] R. Walter, *Student Politics in Argentina* (New York: Basic, 1968); J. Maier and R. Weatherhead, eds., *The Latin American University* (Albuquerque.: University of New Mexico Press, 1979).

293 P. Van der Berghe, *Power and Privilege in an African University* (London: Routledge and Kegan Paul, 1973); Philip G. Altbach, *The University in Transition: An Indian Case Study* (Cambridge, MA: Schenkman).

294 Edward Shils, *The Intellectuals and the Powers and Other Essays* (Chicago: University of Chicago Press, 1972).

295 There are, of course, exceptions to this generalization. Recent increased interest in Islamic values among Malay students in Malaysia, for example, has tended to separate ethnic groups on campus.

296 A. Basu, *Culture and Politics and Critical Academics* (Meerut, India: Archana, 1981). See also chapters 5 and 6 in this book.

297 N. Jayaram, "Sadhus No Longer: Recent Trends in Indian Student Activism," *Higher Education* 8 (1979): 683–700; Altbach, *Student Politics in Bombay*; Altbach, *Turmoil and Transition*.

298 Philip G. Altbach, "Student Movements in Historical Perspective: The Asian Case," in *Higher Education in the Third World: Themes and Variations*, ed. Philip G. Altbach (Singapore: Maruzen, 1982).

299 Daniel C. Levy, "The Decline of Latin American Student Activism," *Higher Education* 22 (September, 1991): 129–145.

300 A. Liebman, et al., *Latin American University Students: A Six Nation Study* (Cambridge: Harvard University Press, 1972).

301 D. Lelyveld, *Aligarh's First Generation* (Princeton, N.J.: Princeton University Press, 1978).

302 T. Chow, *The May Fourth Movement* (Cambridge: Harvard University Press, 1960).

303 J. Silverstein, "Burmese Student Politics in a Changing Society," *Daedalus* 97 (1968): 274–292.

304 The history of the influence of international events and of international organizations on students has yet to be written. There is evidence, for example, that Asian students studying in Japan during the early twentieth century had a good deal of contact with nationalist ideas. Similarly, students from the various British colonies studying in England were in close touch, and several organizations emerged to serve their interests. Ho Chi Minh and Chou Enlai were in contact with colonial students studying in France in the 1920s, while Sukarno was engaged in nationalist politics as a student in the Netherlands. A generation of post-Independence leaders of formerly British colonies were educated at the London School of Economics and influenced by their experiences there.

305 Lipset and Altbach, *Students in Revolt*; E. Bakke and M. Bakke, *Campus Challenge* (Hamden, Conn.: Archon, 1971).

306 Seymour Martin Lipset, *Rebellion in the University* (Chicago: University of Chicago Press, 1976).

307 E. Shils, "Dreams of Plenitude, Nightmares of Scarcity," in *Students in Revolt*, ed. Lipset and Altbach.

308 M. Steinberg, *Sabers and Brown Shirts: The German Students' Path to National Socialism, 1918–1935* (Chicago: University of Chicago Press, 1977).

309 D. Levy, "Student Politics in Contemporary Latin America," in *Student Politics*, ed. Philip G. Altbach (Metuchen, N.J.: Scarecrow, 1981), 186–213.

310 John Nkinyangi, "Student Protests in Sub-Saharan Africa," *Higher Education* 22 (September, 1991): 145–157.

311 S. Douglas, *Political Socialization and Student Activism in Indonesia* (Urbana:

University of Illinois Press, 1970).

[312] Erik W. Thulstrup, *Improving the Quality of Research in Developing Country Universities* (Washington, D.C.: Education and Employment Division, Population and Human Resources Department, World Bank, 1992).

[313] There are a few non-Western academic institutions remaining, such as the Al-Azhar in Egypt, but these do not play a key role in modern scientific development.

[314] See Philip G. Altbach, et al., *Scientific Development and Higher Education: The Case of Newly Industrializing Nations* (New York: Praeger, 1989).

[315] For a complete discussion of the knowledge system, see Philip G. Altbach, *The Knowledge Context: Comparative Perspectives on the Distribution of Knowledge* (Albany: State University of New York Press, 1987).

[316] Lewis Coser, "Publishers as Gatekeepers of Ideas," *Annals of the American Academy of Political and Social Sciences* 421 (September 1975): 14–22.

[317] See Diana Crane, *Invisible Colleges: Diffusion of Knowledge in Scientific Communities* (Chicago: University of Chicago Press, 1972).

[318] For current analysis of Indian higher education, see Suma Chitnis and Philip G. Altbach, eds. *Higher Education Reform in India: Experience and Perspectives* (New Delhi: Sage Publications, 1993) and Moonis Raza, *Higher Education in India: Retrospect and Prospect* (New Delhi: Association of Indian Universities, 1991).

[319] For a discussion of current developments in Chinese higher education, see Hubert O. Brown, "People's Republic of China," in *International Higher Education: An Encyclopedia*, ed. P. G. Altbach (New York: Garland Press, 1991), 451–466.

[320] Eugene Garfield, "Science in the Third World," *Science Age* (October-November 1983): 59–65.

[321] See Ruth Hayhoe, *China's Universities, 1895–1995: A Century of Cultural Conflict* (New York: Garland, 1996).

[322] Philip G. Altbach, "The Dilemma of Change in Indian Higher Education," *Higher Education* 26 (1993): 3–20.

[323] Marianne Bastid, "Servitude or Liberation? The Introduction of Foreign Educational Practices and Systems to China from 1840 to the Present," in *China's Education and the Industrialized World*, ed. R. Hayhoe and M. Bastid (Armonk, N.Y.: M. E. Sharpe, 1987): 3–20.

[324] Ronald F. Price, "Convergence or Copying: China and the Soviet Union," in *China's Education and the Industrialized World*, 158–183 and Leo A. Orleans, "Soviet Influence on China's Higher Education," in *China's Education and the Industrialized World*, 184–198.

[325] Jurgen Henze, "Educational Modernization as a Search for Higher Efficiency," in *China's Education and the Industrialized World*, 252–270.

[326] Eric Ashby, *Universities: British, Indian, African* (Cambridge: Harvard University Press, 1966). See also Aparna Basu, *The Growth of Education and Political Development in India, 1898–1920* (Delhi: Oxford University Press, 1974).

[327] For a detailed discussion of the nuances of foreign contacts and foreign study in the Chinese context, see Ruth Hayhoe, *China's Universities and the Open Door* (Armonk, N.Y.: M. E. Sharpe, 1989).

[328] For an interesting general discussion of this theme, see Joel Kotkin, *Tribes: How Race, Religion and Identity Determine Success in the New Global Economy* (New York: Random House, 1993).

[329] Hyaeweol Choi, *An International Scientific Community: Asian Scholars in the United States* (Westport, Conn.: Praeger, 1995).

[330] Bind Khadria, "Migration of Human Capital to the United States," *Economic and Political Weekly*, August 11, 1990, 1784–1794.

[331] Ali N. Alghafis, *Universities in Saudi Arabia: Their Role in Science, Technology and Development* (Lanham, Md: University Press of America, 1992). See also H. A. Al-Ebraheem and R. P. Stevens, "Organization, Management and Academic Problems in the Arab University: The Kuwait University Experience," *Higher Education* 9 (1980): 203–221.

[332] Not surprisingly, there is little discussion of military-related research in either China or India because of the national security implications involved. These comments are, therefore, based on general observation.

[333] H. Steve Hsieh, "University Education and Research in Taiwan," in *Scientific Development and Higher Education*, 177–213.

[334] P. G. Altbach, *The Knowledge Context: Comparative Perspectives on the Distribution of Knowledge* (Albany: State University of New York Press, 1987).

[335] The statistical information in this chapter is taken from Todd Davis, *Open Doors, 1995–1996* (New York: Institute of International Education, 1996).

[336] Hyaeweol Choi, *An International Academic Community: Asian Scholars in the United States* (Westport, Conn.: Praeger, 1995).

[337] This is changing as some countries implement curricula and programs designed specifically for international students and often presented in an international language. For example, many Dutch universities have started programs in English for Dutch and international students. Japan and Germany also have a limited number of such programs.

[338] P. Williams, ed., "Britain's Full-Cost Policy For Overseas Students," *Comparative Education Review* 28 (May 1984): 258–278.

[339] Britain, as well as the rest of the European Union, may not charge higher fees for EU students than are charged for domestic students. This does not apply, of course, to students from outside of the EU.

[340] R. Myers, *Education and Emigration* (New York: McKay, 1972).

[341] M. A. Hood and K. Shieffer, eds., *Professional Integration: A Guide for Students from the Developing World* (Washington, D.C.: National Association for Foreign Student Affairs, 1984).

[342] S. Gopinathan, *Academic Publishing in ASEAN: Problems and Prospects* (Singapore: Festival of Books Singapore, 1986).

[343] Philip G. Altbach and Y. G. M. Lulat, "International Students in Comparative Perspective: Towards a Political Economy of International Study," in *Research on Foreign Students and International Study: An Overview and Bibliography*, eds. P. G. Altbach, D. Kelly, and Y. G. M. Lulat (New York: Praeger, 1985), 1–52.

[344] Williams, "Britain's Full-Cost Policy."

[345] S. E. Fraser, "Overseas Students in Australia: Governmental Policies and Institutional Programs," *Comparative Education Review* 28 (May 1984): 279–299.

[346] P. Williams, ed., *The Overseas Student Question: Studies for a Policy* (London: Heinemann, 1981).

[347] J. E. Hicks, "Foreign Student Policy in Japan: Getting Ready for the 21st Century," *Daigaku Ronsho* 14 (1985): 189–208.

[348] M. Zikopoulos and E. G. Barber, *Profiles: Detailed Analyses of the Foreign Student Population* (New York: Institute of International Education, 1985).

[349] J. P. Jarousse, A. Smith, and C. Woesler, *Les Etudiants Etrangers: Comparison Internationale Desflux et des Politiques* (Paris: European Institute of Education, 1982).

350 W. K. Cummings, "Going Overseas for Higher Education: The Asian Experience," *Comparative Education Review* 28 (May 1984): 241–257.

351 A. Sims and M. Stelcner, *The Costs and Benefits of Foreign Students in Canada: A Methodology* (Ottawa: Canadian Bureau for International Education, 1981).

352 L. C. Solmon and B. J. Young, *The Foreign Student Factor* (New York: Institute of International Education, 1987).

353 S. P. Dresch, *The Economics of Foreign Students* (New York: Institute of International Education, 1987).

354 J. T. Gullahorn and J. E. Gullahorn, "An Extension of the U-Curve Hypothesis," *Journal of Social Issues* 19 (1963): 33–47.

355 K. Kitamura, *The Internationalization of Japanese Higher Education* (Tamagawa: Tamagawa University Press, 1986), in Japanese.

356 H. Jenkins, ed., *Foreign Student Recruitment: Realities and Recommendations* (New York: College Entrance Examination Board, 1980).

357 R. B. Kaplan, "English as a Second Language: An Overview of the Literature," in *Bridges to Knowledge*, ed. E. Barber, P. Altbach, and R. G. Myers (Chicago: University of Chicago Press, 1984), 247–258.

358 For a broader overview of issues related to foreign student policy, see Committee on Foreign Students and Institutional Policy, *Foreign Students and Institutional Policy: Toward an Agenda for Action* (Washington, D.C.: American Council on Education, 1982).

359 See Philip G. Altbach and Y. G. M. Lulat, "International Students in Comparative Perspective: Toward a Political Economy of International Study," in *Foreign Students and International Study*, ed. P. G. Altbach, D. H. Kelly, and Y. C. M. Lulat (New York: Praeger, 1985), 1–64.

360 C. D. Goodwin and M. Nacht, *Absence of Decision: Foreign Students in American Colleges and Universities* (New York: Institute of International Education, 1983).

361 For statistical trends, see Institute of International Education, *Open Doors 1983–1984: Report on International Educational Exchange* (New York: Institute of International Education, 1984).

362 K. H. Lee and J. P. Tan, "The International Flow of Third Level Lesser Developed Country Students to Developed Countries: Determinants and Implications," *Higher Education* 13(1984): 687–708.

363 Jean Pierre Jarousse et al., *Les étudiants étrangers: comparison internationale des flux et des politiques, 1960–1980* (Paris: Institute European d'Educacion et de Politique Sociale, 1982).

364 "Exodus West," *Asiaweek* 11 (March 1985): 21–30.

365 William Cummings and Wing-Cheung So, "The Preference of Asian Overseas Students for the United States: An Examination of the Context," *Higher Education* 14 (1985): 403–424.

366 Alan Smith, "Foreign Study in Western Europe: Policy Trends and Issues," in *Bridges to Knowledge: Foreign Students in Comparative Perspective*, ed., Elinor Barber, Philip G. Altbach, and Robert Myers (Chicago: University of Chicago Press, 1984), 115–129.

367 David Lansdale, "Institutional Culture and Third World Student Needs at American Universities," in *Bridges to Knowledge*, 196–206.

368 See Sheldon Schaeffer and John Nkinyangi, eds., *Educational Research Environments in the Developing World* (Ottawa: International Development Research Centre, 1983).

369 John N. Hawkins, "Educational Exchanges and the Transformation of Higher

Education in the People's Republic of China," in *Bridges to Knowledge*, 19–31.

[370] V. F. Stanis, *University of Friendship* (Moscow: Progress Publishers, 1980).

[371] Y. G. M. Lulat, "The Academic Impact of Foreign Graduate Students: Perceptions of Faculty," (Unpublished Ph.D. Diss., State University of New York at Buffalo, 1993).

[372] K. M. Bailey, F. Pialorsi, and J. Zukowski-Faust, eds., *Foreign Teaching Assistants in U.S. Universities* (Washington, D.C.: National Association for Foreign Student Affairs, 1984).

[373] Goodwin and Nacht, *Absence of Decision*; see also Peter Williams, *A Policy for Overseas Students: Analysis, Options, Proposals* (London: Overseas Students Trust, 1982).

[374] A. W. Burks, ed., *The Modernizers: Overseas Students, Foreign Employees and Meiji Japan* (Boulder, Col.: Westview, 1985).

[375] Sharom Ahmat, "The Relevance of the American Higher Education Model for Malaysia," in *An ASEAN-American Dialogue*, ed. Philip G. Altbach (Singapore: Regional Institute for Higher Education and Development, 1985), 111–121.

[376] Smith, *"Foreign Study."*

[377] Stewart Fraser, "Overseas Students in Australia: Governmental Policies and Institutional Programs," in *Bridges to Knowledge*, 94–114.

[378] Goodwin and Nacht.

[379] The classic statement of these goals is Philip Coombs, *The Fourth Dimension of Foreign Policy: Education and Cultural Affairs* (New York: Harper & Row, 1964).

[380] Philip Coombs, *The World Crisis in Education* (New York: Oxford University Press, 1985).

[381] Hans N. Weiler, "The Political Dilemmas of Foreign Study," in *Bridges to Knowledge*, 184–195.

[382] Philip G. Altbach, "The University as Center and Periphery," in this volume, chapter 2.

[383] Ali A. Mazrui, *The Political Sociology of the English Language* (The Hague: Mouton, 1975).

[384] S. Bochner, "Cultural Diversity: Implications for Modernization and International Education," in *Bonds without Bondage*, ed. K. Kumar (Honolulu: University Press of Hawaii, 1979), 231–256.

[385] See Philip G. Altbach, ed., *Student Political Activism: An International Reference Handbook* (Westport, Conn.: Greenwood, 1980), for a perspective on student political involvement worldwide. For analysis concerning Korea, see Shinil Kim, "South Korea" in *Student Political Activism*, 173–182.

[386] Korea shows a significant variation from the norm because the very large majority of Korean students study in private institutions, and only one of the country's top five universities, Seoul National University, is a public institution. Government financial involvement will inevitably increase as research becomes more important. The Korean government, despite its relatively modest investment in higher education, nonetheless seeks to maintain political and other controls over the academic system. Thus, financial involvement and governmental restrictions are not necessarily linked. Further, the government has sought to control enrollments in the private universities. The Ministry of Education holds considerable power throughout the higher education sector.

[387] For a consideration of the role of higher education in the newly industrialized countries, see Philip G. Altbach, Charles H. Davis, Thomas O. Eisemon, S. Gopinathan, H. S. Hsieh, Sungho Lee, Pang Eng Fong, and Jasbir Sarjit Singh, *Scientific Development and Higher Education: The Case of Newly Industrializing Nations* (New York: Praeger, 1989).

[388] In the Korean case, there were widespread violations of copyright, patents, and other

legal controls concerning intellectual property. This situation has significantly improved with the adherence of Korea to copyright in 1987. It should also be noted that Taiwan and Singapore were also violators of copyright, trademark, and patent regulations—and China still is.

[389] See Kernial Singh Sandhu and Paul Wheatley, eds., *Management of Success: The Moulding of Modern Singapore* (Boulder, Colo.: Westview Press, 1989). See especially Pang Eng Fong, Tan Chwee Huat, and Cheng Soo May, "The Management of People," in *Management of Success*, 128–143, "The Restructuring of the Economy," in *Management of Success*, 201–453. See also H. E. Wilson, *Social Engineering in Singapore* (Singapore: Singapore University Press, 1978).

[390] In Korea, a number of private universities were established after a land reform act in 1948. By establishing educational institutions, large landowners could retain much of their land. See Kwangho Lee, "A Study of the Systematic Characteristics of the Korean Educational System in the Reorganization Era, 1945–1955" (Unpublished Ph.D. diss., Yonsei University, 1991), 66.

[391] It should be noted here that higher education in Russia tends to be specialized, still following the old Soviet model with only modest modification, thus making it somewhat difficult for graduates to shift rapidly from one position to another.

[392] Joseph Ben-David, *Fundamental Research and the Universities: Some Comments on International Differences* (Paris: Organization for Economic Cooperation and Development, 1969).

[393] For a perspective on the not completely successful Soviet efforts to develop research separately from the universities, see Alexander Vucinich, *Empire of Knowledge: The Academic of Sciences of the USSR (1917–1970)* (Berkeley: University of California Press, 1984).

[394] India is a good example of these conflicts and the associated fiscal dilemmas. See Andre Beteille, "A Career in a Declining Profession," *Minerva* 28 (Spring 1990): 1–20.

[395] Decisions concerning which languages to use for library collections are quite serious. In practical terms, the only solution is to collect materials mainly in English, since English is not only the second language of most academics in the NICs but also the primary language of scientific publication. Keeping abreast of journals and books in Japanese is also advisable. This means that little will be collected in other Third World languages—for example, libraries in Taiwan will not collect materials in Korean although there might be some useful publications in that language. Other important Western languages, such as French and German, will also be largely ignored.

[396] S. Gopinathan, "Academic Journal Publishing in the Context of the Crisis of Third World Publishing" in *Publishing and Development in the Third World*, ed. Philip G. Altbach (Oxford, England: Hans Zell Publishers, 1992), 287–306.

[397] Thomas O. Eisemon and Charles H. Davis, "Publication Strategies of Scientists in Four Peripheral Asian Scientific Communities: Some Issues in the Measurement and Interpretation of Non-Mainstream Science," in *Scientific Development and Higher Education*, 325–376.

[398] Eric Ashby, *Universities: British, Indian, African* (Cambridge.: Harvard University Press, 1966).

[399] See Philip G. Altbach and V. Selvaratnam, eds., *From Dependence to Autonomy: The Development of Asian Universities* (Dordrecht, Netherlands: Kluwer, 1989).

[400] Sungho Lee, "The Emergence of the Modern University in Korea" in *From Dependence to Autonomy*, 227–256.

[401] The Chinese case is a very interesting one from this perspective. See Ruth Hayhoe,

China's Universities and the Open Door (Armonk, N.Y.: M. E. Sharpe, 1989).

402 Edward Shils, *The Academic Ethic* (Chicago: University of Chicago Press, 1983).

403 Irene Gilbert, "The Indian Academic Profession: The Origins of a Transition of Subordination," *Minerva* 10 (July 1972): 384–411.

404 Philip G. Altbach, "The American Academic Model in Comparative Perspective," in this volume, chapter 4.

405 See Robert F. Arnove, ed., *Philanthropy and Cultural Imperialism: The Foundations at Home and Abroad* (Boston: G. K. Hall, 1980).

406 Americans had a profound impact on the early development of higher education in Korea in the late nineteenth century. See Sungho Lee, "Emergence of the Modern University in Korea," in *From Dependence to Autonomy,*, 227–256.

407 John Hanson, *Education Nsukka: A Study of Institution Building among the Modern Ibo* (East Lansing: Michigan State University, 1968).

408 Daniel C. Levy, *Higher Education and the State in Latin America: Private Challenges to Public Dominance* (Chicago: University of Chicago Press, 1986).

409 E. Patricia Tsurumi, *Japanese Colonial Education in Taiwan, 1895–1945* (Cambridge: Harvard University Press, 1977), 177–206.

410 S. Gopinathan, "University Education in Singapore: the Making of a National University," in *From Dependence to Autonomy*, 207–225 and V. Selvaratnam, "Change Amidst Continuity: University Development in Malaysia," in *From Dependence to Autonomy*, 187–206.

411 See, for example, J. N. Kaul, ed., *Higher Education, Social Change and National Development* (Simla, India: Indian Institute of Advanced Study, 1975) for a discussion of the contemporary Indian university situation.

412 It is significant that the Institute of Scientific Information (ISI), headquartered in Philadelphia, uses only about 7,000 journals for its influential citation indices. These indices track the influence of published material and are considered the standard measures for scientific impact. It is also noteworthy that the ISI drastically underrepresents journals that are not published in English.

413 Some of these issues are discussed in Philip G. Altbach, *The Knowledge Context: Comparative Perspectives on the Distribution of Knowledge* (Albany: State University of New York Press, 1988).

414 For a perspective concerning Africa, see Thomas O. Eisemon and Charles H. Davis, "Can the Quality of Scientific Training and Research in Africa be Improved by Training?" *Minerva* 29 (Spring 1991): 1–26.

415 For a discussion of these issues, see Edward Shils, "Academic Freedom," in *International Higher Education: An Encyclopedia*, ed. Philip G Altbach (New York: Garland, 1991), 1–22; and Klaus Hufner, "Accountability," in *International Higher Education*, 47–58.

416 For a discussion of the development of the UGC, see Christine Helen Shinn, *Paying the Piper: The Development of University Grants Committee, 1919-1946* (London: Falmer, 1986).

417 For a discussion of these issues in the American context, see Robert O. Berdahl and T. R. McConnell, "Autonomy and Accountability: Who Controls Academe?" in *American Higher Education in the 21st Century*, ed. Philip G. Altbach, R. O. Berdahl, and Patricia Gumport (Baltimore, Md.: Johns Hopkins University Press, forthcoming 1998). See also Roger Geiger, "Ten Generations of American Higher Education," in *American Higher Education in the 21st Century*.

[418] Philip G. Altbach, "Academic Freedom in Asia," *Far Eastern Economic Review* (June 16, 1988): 24–25.

[419] These themes are developed further in Ashby, *Universities: British, Indian, African.*

[420] Edmund L. Pincoffs, *The Concept of Academic Freedom* (Austin: University of Texas Press, 1976) and Louis Joughin, ed., *Academic Freedom and Tenure: A Handbook of the American Association of University Professors* (Madison: University of Wisconsin Press, 1969).

[421] Ellen W. Schrecker, *No Ivory Tower: McCarthyism and the Universities* (New York: Oxford University Press, 1986) and Lionel Lewis, *Cold War on Campus* (New Brunswick, N.J.: Transaction, 1988).

[422] See Burton Clark, *The Academic Life: Small Worlds, Different Worlds* (Princeton, N.J.: Carnegie Foundation for the Advancement of Teaching, 1987) and Burton Clark, *The Academic Profession: National, Disciplinary and Institutional Settings* (Berkeley: University of California Press, 1987) for broader perspectives on the role of the professoriate.

[423] Philip G. Altbach, "Professors and Politics: An International Perspective," in this volume, chapter 6.

[424] Alvin W. Gouldner, "Cosmopolitans and Locals: Toward an Analysis of Latent Social Roles-I," *Administrative Science Quarterly* 2 (December 1957): 281–303.

[425] A brain drain of some of the top academics from Britain to the United States has characterized the 1980s as British salaries have lagged behind and the university budgets have been cut by the conservative Thatcher government. Some of the most prominent professors have responded by taking more remunerative positions in the United States and Canada.

[426] Kazayuki Kitamura and William K. Cummings, "The 'Big Bang' Theory and Japanese University reform," *Comparative Education Review* 16 (June 1972): 303–24.

[427] For an interesting American analysis, see Michael Moffett, *Coming of Age in New Jersey: College and American Culture* (New Brunswick, N.J.: Rutgers University Press, 1989). A classic discussion of this topic is Helen Lefkowitz Horowitz, *Campus Life: Undergraduate Cultures from the End of the Eighteenth Century to the Present* (Chicago: University of Chicago Press, 1987). Unfortunately, the literature concerning student cultures for other countries is very limited.

[428] Philip G. Altbach, "Student Political Activism," in this volume, chapter 7.

[429] Joseph Ben-David, *Fundamental Research and the Universities* (Paris: Organization for Economic Cooperation and Development, 1968).

[430] Hyaeweol Choi, *An International Scientific Community: Asia Scholars in the United States* (Westport, Conn.: Praeger, 1995).

[431] Michael Moravcsik, *Science Development: The Building of Science in Less Developed Countries* (Bloomington, Ind.: International Development Research Center, 1973).

[432] S. Gopinathan, "Higher Education and the Indigenization Response: The Cases of Singapore and Malaysia" (unpublished Ph.D. diss. State University of New York, Buffalo, 1986).

[433] Singapore is an interesting case study. It has four official languages for its population of 2.5 million—English, Chinese, Malay, and Tamil. Although Bahasa Malay has been designated as the "national language," English is used for all postsecondary education (and the bulk of primary and secondary schooling), for all governmental business, commerce, and the legal system.

[434] "Voluntary Servitude: Asian Migrant Workers," *Economist,* September 10, 1988, 21–24.

[435] Some Third World nations export professionals to other developing countries. There

are, for example, large numbers of Indian teachers, scientists, and engineers working in Africa, the Middle East, and other parts of Asia, either under specific contract or as migrants. Palestinian professionals are important in the Arabian Gulf states.

[436] William K. Cummings, "Going Overseas for Higher Education: The Asian Experience," *Comparative Education Review* 28 (May 1984): 241–257. See also William K. Cummings and W. C. So, "The Preference of Asian Overseas Students for the United States: An Examination of Context," *Higher Education* 14 (August 1985): 403–423.

[437] For an extensive analysis of foreign student issues see Elinor Barber, Philip G. Altbach, and Robert Myers, eds., *Bridges to Knowledge: Foreign Students in Comparative Perspective* (Chicago: University of Chicago Press, 1984). See also Philip G. Altbach, "The New Internationalism: Foreign Students and Scholars," in this volume, chapter 10.

[438] At the present time, none of the four countries has any problem in absorbing into the economy advanced degree holders trained abroad, although there is some unemployment of first-degree holders in Malaysia. This was not always the case as both Korea and Taiwan had problems in employing all graduates, and this contributed to the brain drain. Many other Third World nations have serious problems of unemployment of advanced degree holders and while foreign-trained individuals often have an advantage, there are difficulties.

[439] These countries have less serious problems than many other Third World nations because their academic and research systems more closely resemble those of the metropolitan centers and research issues are often related to those which are current in the international scientific community.

[440] For further discussion of these issues, see other chapters in this volume.

[441] Edward Shils, *The Academic Ethic* (Chicago: University of Chicago Press, 1982).

[442] Philip G. Altbach, "Academic Freedom in Asia: Learning the Limitations," *Far Eastern Economic Review,* June 16, 1988, 24–25.

[443] For a perspective on the British experience, see Eric Ashby, *Universities: British, Indian, African* (Cambridge: Harvard University Press, 1968).

[444] Western academic institutions have not always been able to resist societal pressures. The German universities did not put up strong resistance to the demands of the Nazi authorities in the 1930s—and in part as a result have never regained their academic preeminence. In the United States, many universities did not strongly defend academic freedom during the McCarthy period in the 1950s, although the most prestigious institutions were generally more vigorous than smaller and less affluent campuses.

[445] Except for Korea, these statistics are based on 1986 information and have expanded significantly since then.

[446] Ben-David, *Fundamental Research in the Universities.*

[447] For perspectives from Latin America on the role of higher education in research, see Hebe M. C. Vessuri, "The Universities, Scientific Research and the National Interest in Latin America," *Minerva* 24 (Spring 1986): 1–38 and Osvaldo Sunkel, "Underdevelopment, the Transfer of Science and Technology and the Latin American University," *Human Relations* 24, No. 1 (1970): 1–18.

Author Index